The Austro-Hungarian Dual Monarchy
(1867–1918)

The Austro-Hungarian Dual Monarchy (1867–1918)

NEW HOLLAND

Published in 2008 by New Holland Publishers (UK)
Ltd
London • Cape Town • Sydney • Auckland
www.newhollandpublishers.com
Garfield House, 86–88 Edgware Road, London W2
2EA, United Kingdom
80 McKenzie Street, Cape Town 8001, South Africa
Unit 1, 66 Gibbes Street, Chatswood, NSW 2067,
Australia
218 Lake Road, Northcote, Auckland, New Zealand

10 9 8 7 6 5 4 3 2 1

ISBN 978 1 84773 007 7

Publishing Director: Rosemary Wilkinson
Publisher: Aruna Vasudevan
Editors: Kate Parker, Julia Shone
Consultant historian: Paul Hanebrink
Translation: © Adrian Hart, Krisztina Sarkady-Hart
Production: Melanie Dowland
DTP: Peter Gwyer
Reproduction by GMN Repro Studio Hungary
Printed and bound in Hungary by Dürer Nyomda,
Gyula

Originally published in Hungary in 2008 as
Egy közép-európai birodalom
Az Osztrák - Magyar Monarchia (1867–1918)
Edited by © Zsuzsa Gáspár
Consultant historian: András Gerő
Text © László Csorba, John Swanson, Péter Hanák,
Csaba Fazekas, Paul A.Hanebrink, András Gerő
Designed by © Johanna Bárd
Picture editor: Zsuzsa Gáspár
Assistance: József Demmel, Csilla Kiss and
Éva Résch

Cover painting entitled The Coronation of Eduard
von Engerth
Cover photograph © József Hapák

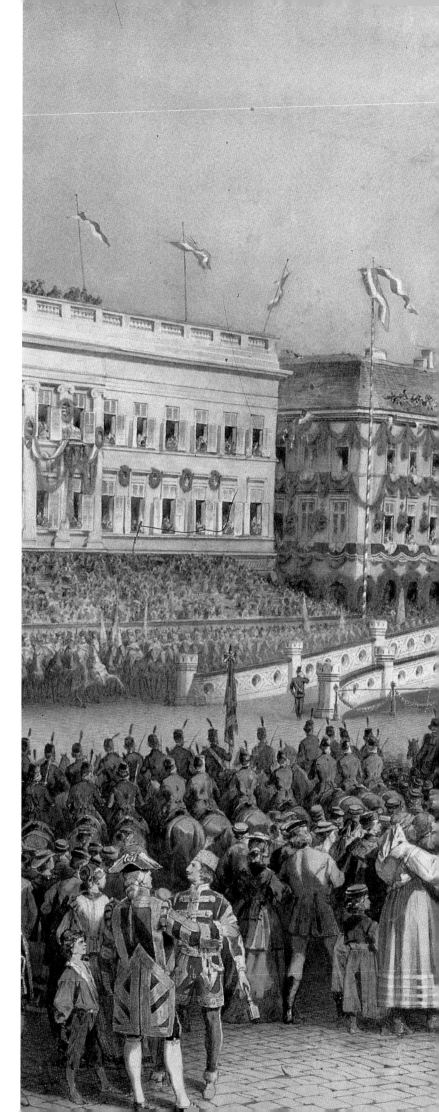

CONTENTS

András Gerő

Foreword

The Austro-Hungarian Monarchy was the last form of the Habsburg Empire. It disappeared from the map of Europe in 1918 as a consequence of World War I (1914–1918), known at the time as the Great War. It was replaced by small states, many of which no longer exist today.

The exact time of the Monarchy's death is therefore not in question. Theoretically, the point in time when it began is known: the Austro-Hungarian Monarchy came into being in 1867 along with the Austro-Hungarian Compromise. However, the Habsburg Empire was able to look back upon a past stretching back centuries before the Compromise. Therefore, the imperial and royal, *kaiserlich und königlich*, i.e. k. und k. state can truly be called the last form of an ensemble of countries which had a great past and which operated within a changing territorial framework.

This book aspires to present the k. und k. world in all its diversity. Of course it also touches upon the early antecedents: the rise of the Habsburg family and the story of how they began their ascendancy in the Middle Ages and went on to make their mark throughout almost all of European history, and how under the leadership of the Habsburg dynasty the history of the state, often coined by posterity as the Danubian Monarchy, emerged, changed and assumed different shapes. However, the book fundamentally focuses on the Austro-Hungarian Monarchy, the final form of the Habsburg Empire. To some extent the life of the Empire can be compared to the life of a human being. One can consider its body, its spirit and soul, everyday life, celebrations and illnesses; preferences for various kinds of food and drink and what beliefs are adhered to. This is no easy matter since the Monarchy was made up of many different peoples and cultures and thus the same emphasis must be placed – figuratively speaking – on the Czech knedlík, the Wiener Schnitzel and the Hungarian gulyás, as well as on schnaps, borovička, tzuika and pálinka.

However, this book is not – again, figuratively speaking – just about a dead empire, or about an empire that once existed. On the one hand, it is true that the imperial and royal monarchy passed away in 1918. On the other hand, it left in its wake a truly diverse legacy, like a person who passes on a spiritual and material imprint of himself to his successors. Of course to some extent I have to contradict myself here since the concept of historical death is different to biological death. In the latter case the individual ceases to exist in this world, and his heirs – if there are any – share his material and spiritual legacy. However, historical death simply means that a body, a political system or entity fades away but the people who made it function live on and continue their lives in a new context. Consequently, death and the end of something in history mean continuation just like the cessation of the same continuity. Expressed more precisely: the process of continuity manifesting itself at various levels and relations can always be detected behind the often spectacular cessation of continuity.

Thus, it follows that although it is possible to write the date of the Monarchy's death on its headstone, we must bear in mind that the only thing we can be certain of is that the state passed away. Yet everything that it contained is still with us and in us in changed and new proportions, and what has passed on is not the past but a process. Complete and perfect biological death exists; complete and perfect historical death does not.

I believe that it is perhaps for this very reason that the Austro-Hungarian Monarchy is a fascinating subject: one can learn a great deal about what characterised and characterises its diverse cultures and peoples. And now that the majority of the peoples of the former Monarchy are part of a new kind of empire, the European Union, perhaps this makes it possible to analyse our shared past not just nationally but along the lines of integration. Because what once caused division in the past – now paradoxically – was also a bond. That same bond holds us together now and will do so for a long time to come.

László Csorba

Emperors and Kings – Antecedents of the Dual Monarchy

The Habsburg family: From Habichtsburg to a World Empire

At the foothills of the Jura Mountain Range in Aargau Canton, near the charming Schinznach Baths stands an old castle keep by the forest above Aare River. It was once called Hawk Castle, or Habichtsburg, and gave its name in an abridged form to the family who owned it. A charter dating to as early as 1090 mentions a Habsburg count, a certain rich, Swabian nobleman called Ottocar, who named himself Count of Habsburg after the castle. One of his offspring, called Ratbod, furthered his ambitions through a providential union of marriage to the daughter of the Duke of Lotharingia. The coming generations of the family continuously increased their wealth in the service of the imperial dynasty of the Hohenstaufen and they could be equally relied upon to render their loyal services in the second half of the 12th century to Frederick Barbarossa and in the 13th century to Frederick II. Their loyal help and bravery was amply awarded, thus at this point the Habsburg family found themselves in possession of so much land that they were able to aspire to the highest class of landowners. The eldest son, Albert, was given the Alsatian and northern Swiss estates, while his younger brother inherited the central Swiss domains. Albert's branch of the family survived and prospered for more than 20 generations over 600 years and played a key role in the modern history of Central Europe and indeed of the whole continent.

Emperor Frederick II died in 1250 and the most powerful provincial rulers did not elect a king for decades, therefore the pope was unable to crown a new Holy Roman Emperor. It was only 23 years later that the right circumstances were in place for the empire to be ruled by one monarch. By joining their forces, the princes and prelates successfully defeated the strongest self-appointed candidate, Bohemian King Přemysl Ottocar II, and finally elected Count Rudolph of Habsburg of Upper-Lotharingia, as the emperor, who ascended to on the throne on 1 October 1273, at the age of 55, and began a radically new policy. Having recognised that the imperial title only enabled him to increase the family estates, Rudolph began the work of organising his Austrian inheritance in the eastern edge of the empire, during which he again came into conflict with his rival, the Bohemian King Ottocar II.

Emperor Frederich I had raised the status of the 'eastern empire' to an independent princedom, and bestowed it upon the Babenberg family. After this family died out, the

Above: *The coat-of-arms of the Habsburg counts.*

Opposite: *The castle of Habichtsburg in a 16th-century picture.*

Below: *The meeting of Rudolf I and László (Kun) IV on the field of battle at Morvamező. According to Hungarian tradition, László had a key role in the defeat of Ottocar II, the king of Bohemia, who fell in the battle. Mór Than's work, painted in 1872 in the historicising style, despicts the scene.*

ALBERTVS CÆSAR XXXI REX HVNG

Above: *Albert I, the first Habsburg to ascend to the Hungarian throne.*

princedom was occupied by Ottocar, who was defeated by Emperor Rudolph in the Battle of Morvamező in 1278, assisted by the troops of King László (Ladislaus) IV of Hungary, said troops – at least according to Hungarian tradition – playing a decisive role in the defeat of the Bohemian army in a battle in which Ottocar himself fell.

In 1282, Rudolph bestowed Lower and Upper Austria, Styria, Carinthia and Craina, upon his sons. One year later, a family settlement modified this: the entire overlordship was inherited by just one of Rudolph's sons, Albert – the same Albert who had also become heir apparent to the Tyrolian marquisate through his wife. Thus, an enormous area of territory stretching from the Danube to the Adriatic fell into the hands of the Swabian counts.

In the following decades the Habsburgs continued to consolidate their power in the Austrian territories. In the middle of the 14th century they expanded towards the Adriatic and managed to gain possession of Tyrol. At the same time another Rudolph, the son-in-law of Emperor Charles IV of Luxemburg, did his utmost to have his father-in-law recognise charters granting greater independence to the Austrian princedom than ever before in its history. In the generations that succeeded Rudolph, Albert II married the daughter of Sigismund of Luxembourg and became part of the imperial family. Since Sigismund was also the king of Hungary, after his death Albert inherited the Hungarian Kingdom and thus became the first Habsburg to sit on the Hungarian throne.

In 1440 Albert II died unexpectedly and some months later his son, László, was born (the future László V). Albert's widow did not trust the Hungarian lords: she took the child out of Hungary, seeking the protection of her husband's half-cousin Frederick of Habsburg, the prince of Styria. She also arranged for the Hungarian crown to be stolen from Visegrád Castle in order to ensure a valid coronation for the child. Frederick became the child's guardian and, in 1440, took the title of emperor as Frederick III. László died at a young age, without an heir, so the Hungarians elected Mátyás Hunyadi as their king, and George Podjebrad became the king of Bohemia. Mátyás conquered Moravia and Silesia after 1470 and the Austrian princedom in 1485, after which he was happy to take up residence in Vienna. However, his rival Frederick fought against him and outlived him. Frederick tried, but failed, to occupy Hungary in 1490.

By the 15th century the countries along the Swiss mountain straits and those located in the areas along the Rhein and to the west of it – Burgundy, Lotharingia and the Dutch provinces – constituted one of the continent's most dynamically developing and wealthy zones at the forefront of urbanisation and a developing manufacturing industry. When Archduke Maximilian of Austria, the son of the emperor Frederick III, married Mary of Burgundy, the daughter of Charles the Bold (Duke of Burgundy), he spent most of his time in Flanders, where he became the most erudite ruler of this time. In 1496, Maximilian arranged two marriages: his son, Philip the Handsome, married Joanna of Castile, the youngest daughter of the Spanish ruling couple, Ferdinand of Aragon and Isabella of Castile, while Margaret (Philip's younger sister) was married to Juan, Prince of Asturias, the heir apparent to the Spanish throne. After a series of unexpected deaths, Joanna and Philip became the heirs apparent to the Spanish throne. This was the Spain unified through the marriage in 1469 of royal cousins Isabella of Castille (1451–1504) and Ferdinand of Aragon (1452–1516). It had become one of the most powerful countries in Europe and controlled Naples and Sicily.

Maximilian continued his lucrative policy of arranging marriages, when in 1515 he concluded a mutual, bilateral family contract with the Jagiellons who controlled Hungary. Accordingly Ferdinand, his youngest grandson, would marry Anna, the older sister of Louis Jagiellon (the king of Hungary and Bohemia), while his other grandchild, Mary, would be married to the nine-year-old Louis (who, a year later, would occupy the throne). Through these marriages the two great houses mutually ensured the succession to the throne. It was a question of luck which dynasty would remain in control – and 11 years later it was the Habsburgs upon whom luck again smiled.

Charles, the first son of Philip the Handsome, was born in the Flemish city of Ghent. In 1515, at the age of 15, he was inaugurated as the ruler of the Seventeen Provinces in the Low Countries. A year later he was crowned King of Spain and, in June 1519, the electing ruling princes of Germany unanimously elected him as their emperor. The new ruler convoked an Imperial Diet in 1521 in Worms. Since during this period,

later known as the Reformation, one of the most contentious issues of the time was the 'renewal of faith', he summoned Martin Luther (1483–1546), a former Augustine monk, to the assembly to recant his views. Luther refused to do this and sought protection from the prince-elector of Saxony. In the following decades participating in the Reformation was one of the most important forms of resistance demonstrated by the German orders

Above: This painting (1870) by Bertalan Székely depicts an anecdote passed down to us by the chronicler whereby the young László V is distracted from his state duties by the court entertainment arranged by his uncle, Ulrik Cillei.

Above: *Charles V was attributed with the saying 'the sun never sets on my empire', in which he made reference to his American colonies too. Van Orley's picture (above) is now preserved in the Budapest Museum of Fine Arts.*

Below: *Ferdinand, the younger grandson of Emperor Maximilian, married Anna, the elder sister of Louis Jagiellon (later king of Hungary and Bohemia), while the Emperor's other grandchild, Mary, married the 9-year-old Louis. These marital contracts enabled Ferdinand to acquire the Hungarian throne in 1526. The stove tiles depicting Ferdinand and Anna Jagiellon (below) were made in the early 16th century.*

in the face the emperor's aspirations to centralise power. Emperor Charles also dealt with family matters in Worms, handing over the Austrian princedom to his younger brother, Ferdinand. Charles V is attributed with coining the phrase 'an empire on which the sun never sets', alluding to his colonies in America.

Where else would the French and the Germans wage war for hegemony in Europe than in Italy and for Italy? In 1525 at the battle of Pavia the emperor won a major victory over the French King, Francis I, whose ally Pope Clement (Medici) VII was forced to make peace with Charles and crown him Holy Roman Emperor. (This was the last time that the pope would crown an emperor. The rest of the Habsburg emperors had themselves crowned in Frankfurt on German soil.) In the meantime the tugs-of-war between the emperor and the orders became completely enmeshed in the religious conflict arising from the Reformation. The famous conclusion of these struggles was the decree known as the Peace of Augsburg (1555), which stipulated *cuius regio, eius religio*, meaning the one that owns the land owns the religion, i.e. subjects were obliged to take up their feudal lord's religion. Then, in 1555, Charles V split his empire into two: he handed over the Low Countries, Spain and Naples to his son, Philip, and imperial rule to Ferdinand. Charles' death brought an entire chapter in the history of the Habsburgs to a close. He had come to realise that a world empire could not be directed by just one hand.

In Philip's time Spain was the most important power in Europe. However, towards the end of his life, escalating conflict occured. Philip aspired to control the world but his ambitions were thwarted by an England in the ascendancy. Philip established the largest fleet of the era, the Armada, in order to break his enemy but in 1588 a storm scattered his fleet and it was defeated by the English. Philip met with failure of similar historical proportions in the Low Countries, where the stubborn resistance of the rebellious factions finally led to the complete independence of the northern provinces (Holland came into being with the Union of Utrecht in 1579), while in the south (the Spanish Netherlands – Belgium) the majority of feudal rights remained. During Philip's reign that expansion of the Ottoman Empire was brought to a halt in the Mediterranean Basin. He entrusted his half-brother, Don Juan, with a battle fleet, established in a close alliance with Venice, Geneva and his Austrian Habsburg relatives, and dispatched his fleet to reoccupy Cyprus. On 7 October 1571, the allies came upon the Turkish fleet moored in the

Above: *János Corvinus, the illegitimate son of Mátyás Hunyadi, on the ornamented initial of the* Philostratus codex
of the Corvina library. The volume was made in Florence after the occupation of Vienna (1485).

Corinthian Gulf near Lepanto. After a battle lasting several hours they almost entirely destroyed it thus dealing a lethal blow to the naval power of the Ottoman Empire.

In the meantime, the younger branch of the Austrian Habsburgs were successful in their politics in Central Europe. Ferdinand, the Spanish-born younger brother of Charles, soon became accustomed to the German world; furthermore, he realised an old dream: the acquisition of the Hungarian crown. When Louis Jagiellon was drowned in the rapid flow of the Csele River at the Battle at Mohács (29 August 1526), after fleeing from the victorious Turks, the Bohemian and Hungarian thrones became bereft of a king at one stroke. The Bohemians did not raise an objection to the solution offered and accepted Ferdinand as their king in 1526 in exchange for a consolidation of their privileges. However, only some of the Hungarian orders went over to the Habsburg side, while the others cast their votes in favour of the wealthiest Hungarian landowner, János Szapolyai. Sultan Suleiman (ruler of the Ottoman Empire, 1520–1566) intervened in the dispute on the side of Szapolyai and by 1529 his cannons were thundering below the walls of Vienna. However, Vienna was too far from Constantinople (modern-day Istanbul) and by the time the Turkish army had organised itself and penetrated as far as Vienna, the season for military campaigning was almost over. Instead, the sultan waited for Szapolyai's death and only then, in 1541, occupied Buda and Hungary's central territory. Ferdinand took possession of the

Above: *The cumbersome galleys of the invincible Armada are defeated in the stormy waters of the English Channel by the more modern English ships.*

northern and western territories of the country, which were defended against possible Turkish attacks by a chain of fortresses financed from aid provided by the empire.

On 23 May 1618, infuriated Bohemian nobles literally threw two high-ranking officials representing the emperor out of the windows of the Hradčany Prague Castle. After this spectacular demonstration of their split with the Habsburg ruler who had tried to restrict their feudal rights, the Bohemians called on Frederick, the Protestant prince-elector of Pfalz, who had been supported by the Transylvanian prince Gábor Bethlen in his military campaign against Vienna, to the throne. Ferdinand II, the new emperor, smashed the Bohemian forces at a battle fought at Fehérhegy on 8 November 1620.

It is difficult to overestimate the importance of this victory in regard to the development of power in the region since as a result of the ruthless practices of the Counter Reformation the positions of authority held by feudal orders were virtually eliminated. In the years that followed, Ferdinand II, a stubborn character, eliminated positions of authority held by the Austrian, Styrian and Corinthian orders and instituted his unfettered rule in the family provinces.

Ferdinand II's last will and testament (dated 1621) was the first document to stipulate in no uncertain terms that the central objective of the Habsburg family strategy was for the Central European provinces to be inherited in one undivided unit. From this time onwards the expression 'hereditary provinces' (owned through inheritance) was used as a generally recognised and employed name for every part of the territories that belonged to the Hungarian crown. Since Ferdinand II was not successful in dealing with the Hungarian orders, the Hungarian Diet and the feudal organisations retained the right to have a say in the running of the country. In the meantime, the war that started between the empire and the Bohemians carried on and eventually lasted for 30 years. The empire's Danish, Swedish and French neighbours also joined the series of conflicts, which were partly religious and partly related to power politics. The peace treaty was finally signed in 1648, after 3 years of negotiations, in the small towns in Wesphalia, by the new ruler Ferdinand III, who had ascended to the throne in 1637.

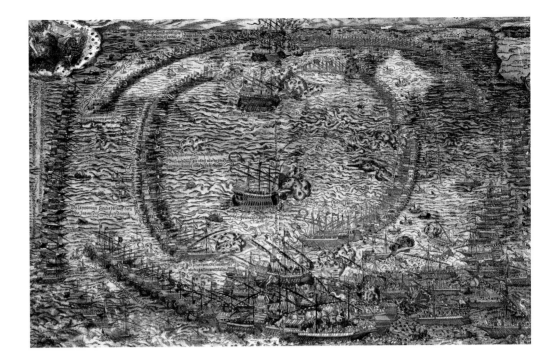

Above: *The victory won at the Battle of Lepanto (1571) saved Europe from rule by the Ottoman Turks. They tried to break through by sea to the heart of Europe from the south by sea, after being stopped by the Hungarian system of fortresses.*

Ferdinand III was succeeded by his son Leopold in 1657, who was elected emperor in 1658. He dealt with state affairs but as he was an excellent composer, he also spent time writing several hundred musical pieces, most of which were sacred in theme. In 1683, he was forced to flee when the Turks pushed westward with a ferocity not seen for more than 100 years, and were again at the walls of Vienna. The counterattack launched against the Turkish troops not only brought liberation to the imperial city but started the process of re-occupying Hungary. After a long siege the troops of the Holy League drove out the Turks from Buda Castle on 2 September 1686 and this liberation was celebrated by Europe as a victory for Christianity. After this, the struggle against the Turks continued

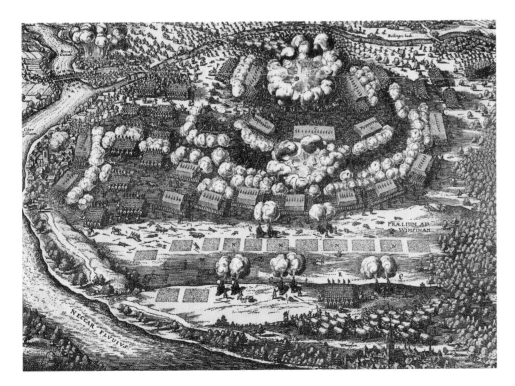

Left: *A battle scene from the Thirty Years' War (1618–1648). Print by Matthäus Merian The Elder (1593–1650).*

with mixed success until Prince Eugène of Savoy (1663–1736) won a victorious battle at Zenta in 1697, which decided the final outcome of the war. Following the Peace of Karlóca, (named after the village in Vojvodina, Serbia, where the negotiations took place, also known as Sremski Karlovci in Serbian) in 1699, the Ottomans were forced to withdraw from almost all of Hungary's territory for the first time in 150 years.

With the reoccupation of Hungary, the territory of the Habsburg family suddenly increased dramatically in Central Europe. Transylvania, which until this point had been independent, also fell into their hands and although it was not added to the Hungarian State administratively, Leopold did take the title of Grand Archduke of Transylvania.

After the death of Charles II (1661–1700), the last monarch of the Spanish Habsburg dynasty, the Spanish government was dominated by a French orientation. The king's last will and testament bequeathed the country to Philippe of Anjou (1683–1746, Philip V of Spain), the youngest grandson of the Sun King, Louis XIV. In response to this the Viennese court began the War of the Spanish Succession (1701–1713) but then another enemy emerged: the Hungarian orders took up arms in order to bring the policy the Viennese court had initiated after the expulsion of the Turks to a halt. The Hungarian orders had shown their gratitude for their country being liberated: in the Diet of Pozsony in 1687 they relinquished their right to the free election of the king of Hungary and accepted hereditary rule through the dynasty's male line. At the same time, the gifts of land to foreigners, the Hungarian nobles gradually being forced into a disadvantageous position, the lawless ravaging of mercenaries, the open attacks by the Counter Reformation and the constantly increasing tax burden triggered major resistance from every social layer in Hungary. In 1703, the biggest landowner of the time, the Catholic Ferenc Rákóczi (II, 1675–1735), initiated an attack with French support. The resistance was successful: the Hungarian orders concluded a new compromise with the Viennese court (the Treaty of Szatmár, 1711), which remedied the most severe injuries suffered by Hungarians.

Above: Just like his father, Leopold I (1640–1705) was a talented composer. He wrote several hundred musical pieces, the majority of which were religious in theme. This painting, by an unknown artist, depicts the young ruler in Hungarian costume, and is a copy of an oil painting by Frans Luyckx (1604–1668) made in the 17th century.

Right: The European powers, united under the flag of the Holy League, recaptured Buda from the Turks in 1686.

In the meantime, the armed conflict over the Spanish inheritance came to an end: Philip V retained Spain and his overseas colonies, with the proviso that the lands of the Spanish and French Bourbons would never again be united. Naples and Milan gained their independence and the Netherlands were separated from the Spanish inheritance. Eventually, Charles (VI, 1685–1740; Holy Roman Emperor, 1711–1740; Charles III of Hungary, 1712–1740), the son of Leopold, joined this treaty in the name of the Holy Roman Empire and accepted all of its stipulations on 7 March 1714 in Rastatt. This marked the end of one of the most significant periods in the history of the Habsburgs. After a golden age that lasted for a century this far-flung empire came to an end. Up to this point the Habsburg family always kept its centre of gravity, at least figuratively speaking, somewhere in the centre of Europe. However, after 1713, this centre shifted eastward and found its new place along the Danube, and the group of countries that had earlier constituted a secondary property of the family now became their main estate.

The three leading male members of the family, Leopold I and his two sons, Joseph

Above: The European estates of the Habsburg family on an early 18th-century map. The inscription is surrounded by the coats-of-arms of the countries under the dynasty's rule, while on the left side is a family tree of the Habsburg rulers illustrated with their portraits with a bust-portrait of the emperor Charles VI at the top.

and Charles, signed a secret pact in September 1703. In the agreement Charles and Joseph agreed to forfeit the territories under Spanish rule (with the exception of the Principality of Milan) on condition that they would mutually inherit the other's estates through the male line in the event of one of them being left without a successor. Indeed, if there were no male members of the family left, the eldest daughter of the last male ruler would inherit the family's lands. After the Spanish struggles, and with Joseph's death in 1711, Charles VI, who moved back to Vienna in the mid 1710s, remained the only ruler with a male heir, who nevertheless died before his first birthday. However, in 1717, his daughter, the Archduchess Maria Theresa, was born. From this time onwards for the coming decades her father's policies increasingly focused on creating the conditions in the Monarchy to ensure succession through the female line. Maria Theresa chose to marry the young Lorrainian prince Francis Stephen, who had been driven out by the French and given the throne of Florence as recompense (Grand duchy of Tuscany).

After reoccupying the country from the Turks the absolutist politics of the Habsburg court oppressed the peasants and the nobility to an equal degree. As a reaction to this, in 1703, Hungary's biggest landowner, the Catholic Ferenc Rákóczi (II), roused every social class in a call to a war of liberation against Vienna. The military resistance came to end with the Treaty of Szatmár (1711). The king redressed the most extreme offences and promised to respect the rights of the orders to intervene in the governing of the country. The statue (above) of Ferenc Rákóczi (II) by sculptor János Pásztor (1881–1945) stands in front of the Parliament building in Budapest.

The family contract for the succession to be passed through the female line was made public on 19 April 1713, from which point on it was named *Pragmatica Sanctio* ('state sanction'). In addition to the order of succession, the document also contained the stipulation that the Habsburg lands had to be passed down *indivisibiliter ac inseparabiliter* ('indivisibly and inseparably'). The emperor had the orders of every country in the Empire accept the new situation (in 1723, in the case of the Hungarians), and used diplomatic avenues to obtain the consent of the great European powers. However, when the Prussian King Frederich II (1712–1786, king of Prussia 1740–1786) read the notice of the emperor's demise in 1740, he allegedly shouted, 'What's obligation worth when a good opportunity presents itself?' He immediately stormed into Silesia, one of the richest provinces in mines and industry of the Habsburg State, and the following spring he trounced the liberating Austrian army. Meanwhile the Bavarians, joined by the French court, also launched an attack, occupying Bohemia, Upper Austria and the Tyrole. Everybody was convinced that the fall of the emperor's daughter was imminent.

However, in the autumn of 1741 the Hungarian orders convoked a Diet in Pozsony (now Bratislava). Just how spontaneous the following scene was and how calculated its effect, later became a much debated issue: on 11 September the young and beautiful queen, still dressed in mourning dress, appeared in the council hall and asked for the Hungarian nobility's help to avert the extreme peril the dynasty was in. Her plea had the desired effect: the Hungarian lords jumped to their feet with enthusiasm shouting *Vitam et sanguinem!* in a gesture offering their lives and their blood to save the queen's throne. Reinforced by Hungarian hussars, Austrian troops turned the military situation around: in June 1743 the French suffered defeat and in September the electing princes elected Francis of Lorraine, Maria Theresa's husband, emperor.

The Treaty of Aix-la-Chapelle brought the war to an end in 1748. Maria Theresa lost almost all of Silesia, as well as Parma, Piacenza and Guastalla, but every other territory and all the conditions reverted to how they had been in 1742. Maria Theresa later declared on numerous occasions that the Hungarian orders and nobility had saved her throne. In fact, this gesture was probably made by the Hungarian orders because they greatly appreciated the Habsburgs' compliance with the compromise in 1711 that had brought an end to the Rákóczi War of Independence: the Peace of Szatmár ensured that Hungary could retain its feudal political mechanism while it remained part of the Habsburg Empire and supported the dynasty's western-oriented aspirations for power.

In the Seven Years' War (1756–1763), the Habsburgs made an unsuccessful attempt to avenge their defeat. At the same time Maria Theresa implemented a series of successful reforms through her internal policies. She continued her father's mercantile economic policy and modernised public administration, as well as the justice and education systems. This was followed by the modernisation of the army: the policy of recruiting mercenaries was replaced by the establishment of a standing army. The

Below: The Hungarian lords jumped to their feet with enthusiasm shouting Vitam et sanguinem!, *meaning they would offer their lives and blood to save the Queen's throne.*

empress was a deeply devout Catholic but she was convinced that the State had to bring the Catholic Church under its strict supervision, since working together was the only way of ensuring the common good. Her policy towards the peasants was also a pragmatic one, in which a humane approach was mixed with clear economic and power political objectives. 'You have to feed the sheep to sheer them', is an oft-quoted saying attributed to the empress. Indeed, she truly regarded it as important that the degree of exploitation carried out by landowners should be tempered by the State. To this effect she introduced the *urbarium* (an exact record of services rendered by serfs and peasants) in some countries, which was in conflict with the interests of the orders.

At first she tried to develop industry in the whole of the Monarchy but did not devote as much energy to this in the Hungarian territories, partly as a punishment for the Hungarian nobility's insistence on being exempt from taxes. The system introduced inflicted severe injustice on Hungary: if the Hungarian king (or queen) found the income from taxes insufficient, they could request an increase in taxes and introduce new ones. The money acquired in this way could only be spent on whatever was authorised by the orders in legal provisions even though the ruler insisted on 'automatic' taxes and other

Left: *Joseph II (1741–1790; Holy Roman Emperor 1765–1790) had a sharp intellect, decisiveness and an impeccable sense of decency. He was a resolute believer in the moderate form of Enlightenment, moderately religious, puritan in his habits and a true friend of the people. However, he held a deep-seated conviction that he had a mission to rule as an absolute monarch and believed that he had been chosen by providence to fulfil his role as a ruler.*

In the 400-year history of the Habsburg Empire, 1848 was a moment of great crisis. At the time the Habsburg Empire had an intellectually limited ruler, Ferdinand V, (right) at its helm.

income that could be spent freely. Naturally, the Hungarian orders were opposed to this since they had no intention of providing unlimited resources to sponsor the Habsburgs' dynastic policy in Europe. The agreement that thus came into being had to be adhered to by all rulers if they wanted to retain the possession of the Hungarian Kingdom; every ruler was obliged to take an oath before being crowned to keep this agreement. So, those that supported the unity of the empire (especially the ruler) may have criticised the Hungarian nobility for being penurious but – whether they liked it or not – every ruler had to stand by his promise stipulated in the diploma issued at their coronation.

Similarly to the empire's policy on taxes, the one on tariffs also introduced inequality. Since the territories given preferential treatment enjoyed advantages to the express detriment of the others, Hungary soon found itself in a disadvantageous position. The sale of Hungarian agricultural produce was kept within the empire due to the internal but especially the external customs frontiers while Hungarian goods were not allowed to enter better paying external markets and were even kept out of the Austrian–Czech territories if the given produce was in surplus supply there. The internal customs frontier did not allow Hungarian manufactured goods out of the country, while minimal customs tariff rates on Austrian–Czech mass-produced goods allowed them open access to the Hungarian market. Although the double customs system introduced from 1764 is not directly to blame for Hungary's declining economic performance, it clearly made the disadvantages that had already developed irreversible, since it resulted in the gradual disappearance of the great Hungarian export routes and Hungary was forced into the role of an agricultural provider and importer of industrial goods within the Monarchy. Of course spontaneous economic connections were woven between Hungary, which had better agricultural attributes, and the rich non-Hungarian provinces, which were more advanced in industrial production. This provided a wider framework for Hungarian economic relations in the coming century and secured some advantages. The problem lay in the disproportionate nature of central regulation that was only beneficial for one side.

In 1765, Joseph, Maria Theresa's youngest son, became emperor and co-ruler, but it was only after his mother's death, on 29 November 1780, that he really attained power. Characterised by a sharp intellect, strong decisiveness and a great sense of integrity, he was a devoted adherent of moderate enlightenment; was moderately religious and puritan in his lifestyle and was a true friend of the people. He held an extremely deep conviction that it was his mission to be an absolute ruler, however, and that providence had selected him for this monarchic task. He aimed to improve the lives of his subjects through the implementation of their objective interests (as he saw them), but at the same time ignored their subjective will. His reign of almost 10 years brought an accelerated programme of reforms in enlightened absolutism at a rapid pace.

Joseph's principal aim was to create the kind of modern state in which good decision-making made from above could be carried out in every sphere of life. He wanted to abolish the privileges and governmental practices inherited from the past and to implement unity and centralisation in every province and country. His first task was to transform Hungary's administration. To facilitate this, he refused to be crowned, hence his nickname 'the king without a

The principle objective of Chancellor Metternich's European policy was to secure the armed solidarity of the so-called Holy Alliance of conservative absolutist states against national and constitutional movements.

hat'. He did this in order to avoid making an unalterable oath at a public celebration to maintain the kind of institutions that he was about to liquidate. In 1785, he decreed the re-structuring of public administration in Hungary. In his economic policy Joseph expanded the approach of Charles VI and Maria Theresa in placing emphasis on the importance of agriculture. On 1 November 1781, a decree was issued to free the serfs, terminating the feudal law that had bound the serfs to the land. Joseph broke away from the Counter Reformation and the one-sided State support granted for the Catholic Church. On 13 October 1781, he issued the so-called 'Patent of Tolerance', which declared that adherents to the Protestant and Orthodox denominations would be granted the same civil rights that Catholics already enjoyed: they would have the same right to occupy public positions and suffer no disadvantages because of their denominational affiliation. The term 'Josephinism', referring to his measures aimed at the transformation of the State religion and the Catholic Church, was coined by his contemporaries.

During the decade of Joseph II's reign, changes became irreversible and, from the 1790s onwards, a new period began in the Habsburg countries and consequently in the history of Hungary. Emperor Joseph made a surprising gesture on his deathbed: on 26 January 1790 he signed his last decree which rescinded almost everything that had gone before. If he had not done this, various groups, dissatisfied with his policies and method of ruling, (the Hungarian, Czech, Austrian, Polish and Italian orders, as well as other leading groups who had secret relations with Prussia, which was ready to launch an attack) would probably have torn apart the nearly 700-year-old legacy of the Habsburg family. However, three decrees remained intact and these most faithfully reflected his intentions. They were measures to ensure better conditions for the serfs, political equality for Protestants and financial help for the lower clergy.

Joseph II's younger brother, Leopold II (1747–1792), arrived in Vienna from Florence to take up the helm of the empire. He had already proven himself in Tuscany, the 'model state' of the Habsburgs, as both capable and willing to improve the lot of his subjects through the implementation of legal, economic and educational measures of reform. His goals were identical to Joseph's, but since he set about achieving them in a far more flexible manner, and with a greater degree of diplomacy, he proved more successful than his impatient and often violent older brother.

Leopold managed to break the opposition of the nobles by granting them concessions and by employing the clever tactic of issuing threats; moreover, with his reform initiatives he truly strove for change. Through constitutional reform he wished to make it possible for groups in society that had been left without privileges to be represented in the Diet. This could be seen as a step towards establishing popular representation, even though his primary aim in granting these rights was to keep the aristocracy in check. Thus there was a real basis for those supporters of Leopold, who had previously been disillusioned by the opposition of the nobility, to hope for some tangible reform. However, on 1 March 1792, the ruler Leopold died unexpectedly aged barely 45. He was succeeded by his first-born son, the 24-year-old Francis (II, 1768–1835). The governing dynamism that had until now been characteristic of the

Above: *In 1795 Archduke Joseph was appointed governor by his elder brother Francis II, (king of Hungary 1792–1835; emperor of Austria 1804–1835), and soon after this he was elected to the position of palatine by the Hungarian parliament. The young man learned Hungarian, grew to love his new homeland and responsibly carried out the duties of his office over a period of 10 decades with a devotion to improving the welfare of the country and its people. He especially contributed to the expansion of Pest during the Reform Period. In Vienna he urged that the Hungarian territories be developed in tandem with the Austrian and Bohemian ones, but his ideas were rejected. This statue was made by Johann Halbig in 1869 and stands in Budapest, in the square named after the palatine.*

Right: *The defeat that Napoleon I (1769–1821) suffered at 'the people's battle' at Leipzig (1813) put an end to the French emperor's European hegemony.*

empire's leadership was replaced by political and social inertia. Emperor Joseph II had noticed long before Archduke Francis became a ruler that he was an apathetic, indifferent person who took no interest whatsoever in his environment. The *ars poetica* of the new ruler was limited to conserving what he had inherited. He was nevertheless a reliable bureaucrat and was always capable of following the affairs of state on a technical level without ever letting power slip from his hands. However, he always had close advisors and, after a time, the chancellor, Prince Clemens Lothar Wenzel von Metternich-Winneburg (1773–1859) was to become one of the most important of these. Francis II brought his father's plans for reform to a halt and gave up the idea of amending the constitution of the Hungarian nobles.

In 1798, Francis destroyed the Hungarian Jacobin movement sympathetic to the French Revolution but for the time being did not put pressure on the Hungarian nobles since they supported him in his war efforts against Napoleon by providing him with money from taxes, as well as with soldiers. This was a difficult period for Francis: he was not only humiliated by the numerous military defeats but also his young daughter Mary Louise married Napoleon in 1809. However, in the end the Habsburgs emerged as the victors, so much so that after the fall of the French Emperor, the congress held by the great powers to redraw the map of Europe was convened and celebrated in Vienna.

Above: István Széchenyi, the 'greatest Hungarian', was an ardent believer in, and supporter of, numerous important changes. The picture depicts him during the regulation of the Danube at Vaskapu (Iron Gates), a project in which he was the leading figure.

Towards the end of the Napoleonic wars, the Viennese court wished to free itself of State debt by devaluing the money that was already in circulation. This led to the disintegration of the earlier political agreement between the ruler and the Hungarian orders. The tension was beginning to escalate and the court finally agreed to convene the Diet. Posterity later symbolically named the political period dating from the Diet of 1825–1827 as the 'Reform Period', which laid the political foundations for social modernisation. This was the first time that István Széchenyi appeared before the public with his nationwide plans. These plans were primarily embraced by the most prominent circles of aristocratic liberal politicians in the counties. Miklós

Left: At a sitting of the Hungarian parliament in Bratislava on 3 March 1848 Lajos Kossuth, the leading spokesman of the opposition, presented his address to the Throne before his fellow delegates, which contained the most important objectives for constitutional reform from the preceding two and a half decades. Furthermore, he demanded the same constitutional changes in the empire's Austrian–Czech provinces too.

Wesselényi, who was a friend of Széchenyi's and developed his ideas further, organised the parliamentary reform opposition party from these circles, which filled the traditional framework of anti-Habsburg sentiments based on the injury suffered by the orders with a new – modern and liberal – content.

Francis was succeeded by his oldest son, Ferdinand (1793–1875; Ferdinand I of Austria and Ferdinand V of Hungary, 1835–1848) in 1835. Ferdinand suffered from epilepsy and had limited mental facilities, remaining peculiarly infantile for his entire life. A political advisory council of family members ran governmental affairs and it was only with their approval that it was possible to present any affair whatsoever to the otherwise kind-hearted and friendly emperor. Thus, the first half of the 19th century is deservedly recorded as the era of Metternich. On a European level, the chancellor primarily strove to provide armed solidarity to support a conservative absolutist system against national and constitutional movements. Upon his proposals the ruling authorities of the Holy League in Karlsbad suppressed the (mainly German) democratic movements. This decision was developed in 1820, when permission was given to use armed intervention against entire states if they rose up against the system of absolutism.

However, this policy could not continue in the 1840s. The Hungarian reform opposition further developed Széchenyi and Wesselényi's national modernisation programme. This concept did not set out to be in conflict with Hungary's position in the Habsburg Empire. The modernisation programme of Hungarian society primarily came into conflict with the policies of the Viennese court because things had fundamentally changed from the situation at the end of the 18th century. Back then a modernising emperor had had to contend with backward orders with a feudal mindset, but now a clearly modern, liberal reform opposition represented the interest of the majority against the conservative system of

Above: *A street scene from the March Revolution of 1848 in Vienna.*

Metternich. The Hungarian reform politicians recognised that they had to develop a new state structure in which all matters relating to political, economic, cultural and everyday life would be based on the individual and communal (national) rights of citizens. However, since this demand came into sharp conflict with customs tariff exploitation exercised in Hungary by the empire, the Hungarian reformers formulated proposals to improve the situation.

Although by this time Metternich had come to recognise that it was in the interests of the empire's future to allow some kind of controlled modernisation, he was unable to find the right social policy to facilitate such change. He used the ancient method of *divide et impera* when he supported the aspirations for relative independence by the little

Balkan States that were slowly freeing themselves from the oppression of the Ottoman Empire. However, this stirred up the jealousy of Russia with which he had sought to maintain solidarity against the revolution. While disregarding Hungarian aspirations, he encouraged the Croatian national movement and – to a certain extent – even gave some space to 'Illirism' (the Croatian-led southern Slav aspirations to unify), not least because he would have welcomed a Slav Catholic to lead the Balkan nations.

In the spring of 1848 there was a call to form popular mass movements for political change, which first resounded in Milan and Palermo on the Italian peninsula, and then the victory of the Paris revolution in February spread this call all over Europe, where many people recognised that the victory of the French Republicans was a blow to the supporting pillars of the Holy League, which had ruled over half of the continent since the Napoleonic wars. In the Hungarian Diet convened in Pozsony on 3 March, Lajos Kossuth, the opposition's leading spokesman, presented an address to the Throne, before his fellow delegates, which contained the most important objectives of their struggles spanning the previous two and a half decades. Furthermore, as a guarantee, he demanded

Below: *The symbolic and actual culmination of the struggle for freedom: the some 100,000-strong Hungarian Honvéd army recruited from liberated serfs reoccupies Buda Castle on 21 March 1849.*

effective constitutional changes in the empire's Austrian–Czech provinces too.

Protest spread rapidly across Austria too, and on 13 March the revolution in Vienna broke out. Barricades were erected and street disturbances began to spread across the city, culminating in one common demand: Metternich must go! The anxious archdukes finally persuaded the chancellor, who had been procrastinating stubbornly, to resign and he fled to London to avoid being held to account. The court agreed to abolish censorship and promised to allocate power on a constitutional basis (a parliament of people's representatives and an accountable government) and also consented to the establishment of a national guard. Representatives of the revolutionaries formed a Central Committee that gave orders to sections of the military. A new government came into power with Count Kolowrat as its prime minister, an erstwhile rival of Metternich but also the archduke's confidant – a fact which delineated the limits of the changes.

On 15 March both Pozsony and Pest responded to the changes in Vienna: Kossuth set off for the imperial capital with his more radicalised address to the Throne, while the crowds were led by the poet Sándor Petőfi. Through revolution (news of which assumed grandiose proportions) they also significantly contributed in the weeks that followed to the Hungarian demands being accepted by the leaders of the empire. Lajos Batthyány was appointed as the first Hungarian prime minister responsible to Parliament, and the acts that were passed after hasty negotiations were sanctioned by the king on 11 April. The Hungarian code of 1848 abolished serfdom and created a representative parliament, with its seat in Pest, that was elected by the people and established an independent government responsible to this parliament. The code also introduced the general and proportionate sharing of tax, abolished entailment and tithes to the Church, implemented equality of religion declaring a union with Transylvania, and framed the new press laws. From this point on every inhabitant of Hungary lived in a new, modern world.

The wave of revolutions spread further: on 18 March an anti-Austrian uprising broke out in Milan and, after a five-day battle, the crowds forced the emperor's military commander, Joseph Radetzky, to withdraw his troops from the capital of Lombardy. With the unity of Italy as his slogan, Charles Albert, the king of Sardinia (Piedmont) dispatched a declaration of war to Vienna. The pope, the king of Naples, and even Leopold II of Habsburg, Grand Duke of Tuscany, joined the war. On 25 April a new constitution was declared in Vienna, stipulating the calling of a single chamber parliament (imperial assembly) and the establishment of a government responsible to parliament. This constitution only applied to the provinces other than Hungary since Hungary's own transformation had been assured by the April laws mentioned earlier in this essay.

Following these events the two large parts of the Habsburg Empire as defined by constitutional law – Hungary and the hereditary provinces – became constitutional monarchies with two representative parliaments and two governments responsible to each of them. However, from the perspective of a dynasty that had striven for many centuries to retain the physical integrity of the family estates there did not appear to be a source of power to hold the two sovereign parts of the empire together. The Austrian constitution declared full equal rights for the nations living in the inherited provinces but it was not possible to know how the future would play out for the Germans, or to be more precise, for the Germans living in the Austrian and Czech provinces. From houses in Vienna and from the tower of Saint Stephen's Cathedral Dome the black-red-golden flags, the symbols of German unity, fluttered in the wind. Although not unanimously and not with the participation of the whole German population, the delegates for the German national assembly to be convened in Frankfurt were chosen. In other words, they wished to participate in the creation of a unified German State. The members of the Hungarian political elite supported this concept. What is more, if by any chance the Habsburgs were not to become the leaders of the German empire, they suggested that the dynasty move to Buda Castle since then Hungary would be the natural centre of the monarchy.

However, the tight little group at court (family members, military leaders, bureaucrats, aristocratic politicians), which up until the revolution had held power in their hands, saw all of this very differently. For this group – called the 'camarilla' by their contemporaries

– the main issue was maintaining the unity of the provinces. They envisioned that the task could be implemented in two steps: first, relying on the forces that had an interest in the maintenance of the former unity of the empire and secondly, the camarilla's influence and rule over these forces had to be made unlimited. Such interested forces were primarily the imperial army and the central civil service as well as the leaders of smaller nations with a moderate political disposition. The Czechs feared that they would become assimilated into a German national State, while the Croatians, the Romanians, the Serbs and the Slovaks feared Hungarian hegemony. Relations were sought with the Viennese court even by those that had ties with 'sister-nations' beyond the empire, since they realised that for the time being any unity with them was not realistic. Although the Poles and the Galician Ukrainians were not enthusiastic followers of the Habsburgs, they realised that the break-up of the empire would probably mean that they would come under Russian domination. For this reason the representatives of the Slav Congress, convened in Prague, committed themselves to maintaining the Habsburg State in the spirit of equal rights for all its nations.

The spring revolution was followed by counter revolutions in the summer, autumn and winter. The democrats in Baden had already suffered a defeat in April, and this fate was shared on 12 June by those supporting the uprising in Prague as well as those workers who went on hunger strike in Paris because they had lost their jobs. In July 1848, Italian troops suffered a resounding defeat at the hands of the Austrian army at Custoza, Lombardy. After these events the camarilla was now free to set about revoking the spring concessions granted to Hungary.

The Hungarians managed to re-occupy the historical capital of Buda for a short time and proclaimed in a Declaration of Independence that the Habsburg Empire had broken up and Hungary was able to take its place in the family of European States as an independent country. However, Hungary had no allies in Europe. Although the King of Sardinia (Piedmont) Charles Albert sent his troops at the end of March, he suffered immediate defeat near Novara at the hands of Austria's most skilful military commander, General Radetzky. After this only Venice continued to resist but the naval blockade by the Adriatic–Austrian fleet prevented it from sending or receiving reinforcements. After this the unfolding Russian intervention in Hungary, which took place with the tacit agreement of the great western powers, imposed the worst possible restrictions on self-determination for the peoples of Central Europe. The combined overwhelming superiority of the Austrian and Russian troops culminated in the summer of 1849 and within a few months the Hungarian resistance was worn down. The main body of the army laid down its arms on 13 August 1849, after which the castles and other military units surrendered. Then a merciless process of retribution ensued.

Even though the war of self-defence was lost against the overwhelming combined might of the enemy, the revolution itself did not fail. It was possible to destroy Hungary's self-determination but the most important key results of the transformation, namely the abolition of serfdom, the general and proportionate sharing of taxation and equality before the law, could not be revoked. The new prime minister, Prince Felix Schwarzenberg, sought to prepare the Habsburg State to play a leading

Above: A design for the uniform of the 'Bach Hussars', named after Alexander Bach, the minister for internal affairs, for whom the system of absolutism in Hungary after the suppression of the Revolution and Struggle for Freedom of 1848–1849 was introduced. In order to facilitate an easier acceptance of the new conditions of power, a traditional uniform reminiscent of Hungarian ceremonial attire was designed for State functionaries. As a reaction to this national public opinion derided representatives of the authorities by calling them 'Bach Hussars'.

role in the Germany which he would unite, and thus Austrian hegemony would triumph all over Europe. However, in the 1850s, the Habsburg Empire only had the means to exert regional power and it was not capable of maintaining this position entirely consistently. Although a restricted process of social modernisation was opened up by the empire's new form of autocracy, it nevertheless remained politically unstable since it rigidly blocked any chance of the self-determination demanded by national communities.

Above: 'The Sage of the Country' – the statue of Ferenc Deák in Budapest (by Adolf Huszár, 1882).

Having drawn certain conclusions from the events of 1848–1849, from the mid-1850s Hungarian and non-Hungarian contemporaries were preoccupied with the fundamental question of what form the relationship between Hungary and the Habsburg Empire should take. The starting point, which was agreed to by every important player, was that in 1848 Hungary had managed to rid itself of the shackles of feudalism but that in the self-defensive war waged for national self-determination in 1849 the country had been defeated. As Ferenc Deák and his followers saw it, the Monarchy was an indispensable protective power for the Hungarians wedged in between the Slav and German peoples. The task, therefore, was to reach an agreement with the court in order to maintain the status of Vienna as a great power. Deák thought in terms of an agreement that would not contravene the provision of Hungarian self-determination, which was based on a personal union (similar to the one established in 1848). Indeed, it was hoped that as a part of the Habsburg Monarchy, Hungary would be able to pursue its own 'imperial' policies to a certain degree, primarily in regard to the Balkans. Lajos Kossuth and his followers, both in Hungary and abroad, shared the basic proposition made by Deák but came to a radically different conclusion. They were also of the opinion that a protective power was needed against German and pan-Slav pressure, but they did not believe that Austria was right for this role. They regarded it as too weak, chiefly because it prevented the nations living within its borders from realising their aspirations for national progress. The solution was some kind of alliance of the smaller nations along the Danube. This alliance could then be developed into a confederation built on democratic principles.

Both concepts took the same European and Hungarian realities as their starting point. For example, it was clear that there would be no modern capitalist economy, nor any rapid material or intellectual growth, without foreign capital. The two divergent solutions outlining Hungary's future development actually provided an answer to the question of what should be the source of the capital inflow essential for Hungary due to an insufficient domestic capital accumulation. Those who believed in the future of the Habsburg Empire earnestly believed that Hungary's fate should be tied to the fate of the Empire and did not regard a certain limitation imposed on national self-determination as an unbearable sacrifice. On the other hand, those that had no faith in the Empire's future sought ways to be liberated from such bondage and were convinced that Hungary could only retain control over its own future if national self-determination was extended and developed into the country's full independence.

These two concepts offered true alternatives not only because of the different standpoints and values they embodied – one of liberalism and the other of democratism – but also because in the 1850s it was not possible to 'objectively' establish who would be right in regard to the fate of the empire. At the time, the Habsburg Empire projected an image which could be interpreted as one of stability and of instability alike.

Ferdinand I's nephew, Franz Joseph (1830–1916), who succeeded him in 1848, lost Lombardy in 1859, in the war between the Italians, the French and the Austrians. In the early 1860s it was becoming increasingly evident that the Hungarian political leadership were not seeking a way out of the crisis – resulting from the autocratic nature of the imperial regime as well as by Hungary's passive resistance – through an agreement with the minorities and the development of social reform, which meant that the majority wished to pursue the political direction proposed by Deák and not by Kossuth. In the third Hungarian representative parliament that assembled in December 1865 Deák's party won a clear majority. In March 1866 a 67-member committee convened to prepare the proposal of 'the common affairs', which delegated the task of dealing with the key issues to a 15-member sub-committee presided over by Count Gyula Andrássy, who had returned home from exile and was increasingly placed in the limelight by Deák.

On 3 July 1866, Franz Joseph finally accepted the proposal for a compromise from the Hungarian political leadership after the Austrian defeat at the Battle of Königgrätz. During the Austro-Prussian war, which had broken out to gain dominance over the German States, the Prussians even allied themselves with the fledgling Italian kingdom against Vienna. The Prussian divisions, which were better equipped and better led than their Austrian opponents, invaded Bohemia and won a decisive victory over the emperor's forces. The Austrian military failure marked the end of an historical process of six centuries: the Habsburg State was squeezed out of Germany once and for all. Franz Joseph was forced to accept the humiliation that Prussia had excluded him and his empire from German unification. Franz Joseph and his military clique, who were thirsting for revenge against the Germans, realised that entering into a compromise

with the Hungarians was an inevitable condition before further steps could be taken. The proposal had to be approved by parliament which reconvened for November 1866. The pivotal points of the agreement guaranteed the ruler's unrestricted command over the army and his right to pre-approve all proposals, i.e. in parliament his ministers were only allowed to submit bills which the emperor had approved in advance. Gyula Andrássy's appointment as prime minister dates to 17 February 1867 and three days after this the third government responsible to parliament in Hungarian history was formed; on 20 March the common affairs bill was passed by 257 to 117, in the absence of 22 representatives and the Croatian delegates.

Europe and the Austrians clearly classified the establishment of the Austro-Hungarian Monarchy as a political victory for the Hungarians. There was also no

Above: *Gavrilo Princip, a member of the Young Bosnia movement, being arrested after assassinating Franz Ferdinand in Sarajevo on 28 June 1914.*

Above: *'… I considered and thought through everything. I take the path of obligation with a clear conscience,' proclaimed Franz Joseph in his address to the people in regard to his decision.*

question that Ferenc Deák had done his utmost to ensure for Hungary what he had held to be 'a realistic 1848'. He regarded the system that had been established as the best one possible but not the one he truly desired, and hoped that the system could be flexibly corrected and amended in the future. Lajos Kossuth saw things differently. In the columns of his newspaper *Negyvenkilencz* (Forty-nine), sent from exile, he continued to write open letters expounding in detail how the Hungarian nation had chosen the worst and most difficult path in becoming a modern society when it had formed a pact with the emperor. He believed that the dualist agreement made the Hungarians accomplices in blocking the minorities' aspirations for self-determination and thus when the empire disintegrated it would drag Hungary down with it.

In the spring of 1867 a 19-year period of uncertainty came to a close in the history of the Habsburg Empire. In the spring of 1848 Hungary's state structure had transformed into a parliamentary democracy with a national parliament of people's representatives and with a government responsible to that parliament, which consequently meant that the country's population had become masters of their own fate. Never after this time in Hungarian politics were any concessions made in regard to this fundamental political achievement, which was symbolically marked by declaring 15 March, the day of the 1848–1849 revolution, as a national holiday. At first, this fundamental transformation in accordance with the stipulation of the April laws was approved and sanctified by the Hungarian king, who stemmed from the house of the Habsburgs. However, in the autumn of 1848 he unilaterally and illegally revoked what he had initially granted. When the Hungarian side did not wish to accept this, he launched a military attack against the country, and occupied it with Russian assistance. Then, apart from a few short periods, Hungary was governed by force through autocratic means that ignored both its constitution and its laws. Franz Joseph ruled Hungary but he was not a legitimate Hungarian king since he never fulfilled the legal conditions of a coronation and he was never even crowned according to centuries-old tradition. This created tension and conflict between the king and the country over a period of 19 years – which was only resolved by both sides reaching an agreement.

The subject of the agreement was the degree of Hungary's autonomy. In 1848 Hungarian politicians had wanted to establish a State that would have all the paraphernalia of sovereignty and one which would only be tied to the Austrian empire through the physical person of the ruler (the so-called personal union). This was the starting point on which a consensus eventually had to be reached in 1867: in return for parliamentary democracy being restored, which was stipulated in the laws of 1848, the Hungarians agreed that some very essential elements of political sovereignty (national defence, foreign affairs and the budgets pertaining to them) would be so-called common affairs. Compared to the period when the emperor had the power to use armed force to rule Hungary, there was every reason for Hungarians to regard the new situation as their victory, since from this point on Franz Joseph was only allowed to direct Hungarian internal affairs in co-operation with a government responsible to parliament. However, some Hungarian contemporaries regarded the concessions as too high a price to pay and feared that in the event of a new war leading to the collapse of the Habsburg Empire, Hungary would not have the most basic means to defend itself. This was the reason why the 'Hungarian victory' was far less popular at home, in Hungarian public opinion.

At the beginning of the 20th century the most serious military threat facing the Monarchy was represented by Serbia. This Balkan country, which was growing in strength, resented the Monarchy's occupation (1878) of Bosnia–Herzegovina immediately after the Russo-Turkish War and its subsequent annexation (1908). However, the nationalists dreaming of a greater Serbia, not only regarded the Neretva Valley as Serb territory to be liberated but applied this ambition to the southern Hungarian regions of Bácska and Bánság too. At the same time, the Hungarian political elite was unable to comprehend that granting rights of self-rule in areas of Hungary with a Serb population could put an end to Belgrade's separatist propaganda. The emperor and king would not hear of any concession in regard to the Balkans since this area of the world allowed him to experience the 'glory of the empire's expansion' which went some way to soothing the pain and humiliation wrought by the loss of the Italian territories.

The demonstration of a Bosnian military presence and Vienna's stubbornness were both clearly expressed in the environs of Sarajevo by the military manoeuvres held there in the summer of 1914, this event being honoured by visitors at the head of whom was none other than the illustrious heir to the throne, Franz Ferdinand. After a successful and spectacular military parade on 28 June, the royal couple were driving back to the Town Hall along the Miljacka River lined with crowds of people. Lying in wait among the crowd of on-lookers were desperate terrorists of the Young Bosnia movement who had been trained in Belgrade. One of them tried to throw a hand grenade at the procession but was caught by the police in time. The bomb failed to explode and the cyanide capsule with which the terrorist tried to commit suicide did not work. However, following this botched attempt and just a little further along, as the car was slowing down to take a turn, Gavrilo Princip jumped out from the crowd and used his revolver to kill Franz Ferdinand.

Both in Vienna and Budapest animosity towards the Serbs escalated, but cooler heads prevailed among the decision makers, who foresaw the dangerous consequences of declaring war on Serbia. The Monarchy principally looked to Germany as its main ally (the Duel Alliance, 1879), and to a lesser extent to Italy, which had already perceivably distanced itself from the Triple Alliance (1882), although this was still in effect on paper. In 1892 the French entered into alliance with the Russians against the Central Powers – named such because of their geographical location – and in 1904 the old adversaries England and France resolved their differences and formed an alliance based on a 'cordial agreement' (*Entente Cordial*, from which the name entante powers originated), as it was laid down in the introductory text of their agreement. When in 1907, England and Russia also formed an agreement, the 'Triple Entante' came into being. It remained a question which side the less powerful and smaller countries would take. There was no written alliance between Serbia and Russia, but Belgrade had every right to expect military assistance from St. Petersburg. The commitment of Bulgaria, Rumania and Turkey was open, as was Italy's position. At this point the overseas powers did not play a part in the plans of high politics.

Above: *The last Habsburg ruler, Charles IV, Empress-consort Zita and Archduke and Crown Prince Otto of Austria at Charles' coronation as king of Hungary.*

The most serious conflicts in the system of alliances developed over the issue of the colonies, with the focus of attention on the control over and the re-distribution of the sources of raw materials and the markets. At the same time, these problems were interwoven with the continent's 'traditionally' fundamental issues which chiefly pertained to the aspirations of minorities. At first Franz Joseph only thought of teaching Serbia a lesson and in his confidential letter on the matter he assured Wilhelm II that the conflicts with Belgrade would never come to an end. Finally, it was the German military leadership which recognised that the time was ripe for the world powers to settle their differences. German strategists were fully aware that the overwhelming military and economic strength of the Entante could only be successfully countered by a lightning war. Helmut von Moltke, the German chief of general staff, pointed out that procrastination had to be avoided since the balance of power was the most favourable at that point and would not remain so. The Germans urged Franz Joseph, the ruler of the 'piping days of peace' to take action and, because of Rumania's unreliability, also convinced the Hungarian prime minister, István Tisza, who had initially been against an immediate military response, of the same.

Above: *Food distribution for soldiers at a camp in Törökbálint. A postcard made from a contemporaneous photo.*

'It was my greatest desire during the last years of my life, granted to me by God, to devote myself to working for peace and to protect my peoples from the sacrifices and burdens of war. Providence would have it another way … I considered and thought through everything. I take the path of obligation with a clear conscience,' proclaimed the emperor and king in his address to the people in regard to his decision. One month after the assassination of Franz Ferdinand, a declaration of war was made to Serbia on 28 July and within a few days the other countries also entered the war in accordance with the solidarity expected of allies. Germany declared war on Italy and France, and when Belgium did not give its permission for the Germans to skirt north around the Maginot Line and the Germans invaded, Berlin received London's declaration of war. The Monarchy also declared war on Russia, Serbia on Germany, and this was followed by the arrival of the French and British declarations of war on Vienna. In the Far East Japan joined the Entante, while Central Powers won the alliance of Turkey.

The plan of the Central Powers was to apply German military strength in the west to overrun France in a projected six to seven weeks, while in the east the forces of the Monarchy would hold back the Russian and Serb forces, which it was believed would be slow to mobilise. After occupying Paris it was planned that German troops would be redeployed at lightning speed to the eastern front and their combined strength would be able to repel the tsar's divisions. Mobilisation was greeted by a mood of jubilation everywhere because everybody expected a quick and successful conclusion. As Kaiser Wilhelm II promised his soldiers, 'by the time the leaves begin to fall you will be home!'

In 1914, in the first year of the war, the Germans opened up the Western Front with the Schlieffen Plan, an attack across Belgium into Paris. In September they came to within 20km of Paris when the French counterattack was launched, turning back the German troops. The race for the sea remained unsettled and there was stalemate along the entire front. Meanwhile, on the Eastern Front, the Germans had met with failure because the Russians had mobilised much faster than Moltke had anticipated, and in order to prevent the tsar's armies from breaking through into Galicia and East Prussia, just before they were about to reach Paris, the best German troops had to be redeployed to the Eastern Front. However, at the end of August, the German Eighth Army, led by Paul von Hindenburg, almost completely destroyed the Russian Second Army at the Battle of Tannenberg, and in the middle of September the Germans repulsed the Russian First Army at the Mazury Lakes. In the meantime, the Monarchy was able to hold back the Russian advance (Limanova) in Galicia, in the Carpathians, although it was not successful in destroying the Serbian army on the Southern Front. Turkey's entry into the war improved the odds for the Central Powers to some degree, but at the same time the Germans' African colonies (with the exception of Tanzania) were occupied by British forces, while those in the Far East were captured by Japanese and Australian forces.

In May 1915, the Central Powers' combined armies broke through the Russian lines at Gorlice in Galicia and, by July, had managed to occupy territories in Eastern Poland and the greater part of the Baltic States. They also repulsed the British offensive in the Dardanelles and won Bulgaria over to their side. During the autumn the Austrian–Hungarian–German forces, swelled by the new Balkan ally, occupied Serbia and at the beginning of 1916 the Monarchy took Montenegro and two-thirds of Albania. However, in May 1915 a new front had opened up in the west: Italy entered the war on the side of the Entante since France and Great Britain had promised that Italy could keep South Tyrol, Trieste, the Istrian Peninsula, Dalmatia and part of Albania in the event of a victory. The 11 battles of the Isonzo, directed by Italian chief of general staff Luigi Cadorna, were fought for the possession of the County of Görz (Gorizia), and more specifically the town of Görz, the Doberdo Plateau, Monte San Michelle and Monte San Gabriele, after which a pincer movement attack was to be launched towards Trieste. The Austrian–Hungarian Fifth Army were entrusted with the defence and the attackers failed to break through.

In 1916 the German high command again concentrated on the Western Front, but instead of succeeding in their plan to overrun the fortress of Verdun a new war of attrition set in. In June 1916, the Russians broke through the front line in an unexpected counterattack and to exacerbate the situation Rumania joined the Entante forces in August, then pushed into Hungary and began the occupation of Transylvania. In June the British had launched a well-planned offensive along the River Somme. However, the Central Powers managed to halt every attack, and indeed even dealt a counterblow by occupying Bucharest and the rest of Rumania.

In 1916 Franz Joseph died and his death bought to an end an era in the history of Europe. In the Austrian half of the empire one of the reasons for the rising tensions in the internal political situation had been the ruler's refusal to summon the Reichstag after the outbreak of war and his insistence on governing without a parliament. The social problems and national aspirations were interwoven with anti-war protests to such an extent that dissatisfaction manifested itself in the most violent forms possible. This was attested to by the shocking assassination attempt on the life of Prime Minister Karl von Stürgkh, by the socialist Friedrich Adler. The new head of State, and the last true ruler of the Habsburg Dynasty (up to that point), Charles (1887–1922; Charles I as Austrian emperor 1916–1918; Charles IV as Hungarian king 1916–1918) finally reconvened the

Above: *An Austrian soldier at a sentry post set up in a glacier in Mount Marmolada in southern Tirol. Italian troops tried to advance primarily along the mountain ridge towards Punta Rocca, while the Austrian soldiers used explosives to blow tunnels in the ice in order to supply their military positions with ammunition and to help them build camps. As a result, an entire 'ice city' was formed within the glacier. The biggest avalanche accident of the wartime period is connected to the fighting here: on 13 December 1916, a snow mass came crashing down and buried the Austrian reserve camp at Gran Poz. 300 soldiers lost their lives.*

imperial parliament (Reichstag) in April 1917. However, even a succession of governments was not capable of slowing down the process of disintegration or of cooling Slav aspirations which increasingly failed to envision the future of their peoples within the old framework of the empire.

In Hungary, Count István Tisza became associated with the war and his dogged loyalty to the German alliance, and at the same time with the rejection of reforms. Being more aware of the necessity for change, King Charles dismissed Tisza but neither the cabinet run by Móric Eszterházy, nor the government of the old tactician Sándor Wekerle were able to prevent the growing unrest of the impoverished masses. Renewed conscription soon led to a serious shortage of manpower and despite introducing women into the workforce, production still fell. In 1915 bread rationing was introduced and from 1916 requisitioning was implemented; thus, by the end of 1918 there were 900 businesses being run by the military. Inflation soared and the black market assumed frightening proportions, while real wages fell by 50–70 per cent, all of which was mainly felt by small businesses, the workers and the urban poor.

In January 1917, Germany declared unrestricted submarine warfare to sever Britain's lines of supply by sea, leading the United States to enter the war on the side of the Entante. In the following period huge quantities of war material and some 2 million soldiers landed in Europe. Now all the Central Powers could hope for was that Russia, where the revolution was about to break out, would pull out of the war, which would allow them to transfer troops from the Eastern Front before the arrival of the Americans in order to snatch a final victory. The strategy shifted to active warfare on the Italian Front, too: in October 1917 the Central Powers now went on the offensive. This was the famous Caporetto breakthrough, which marked the first occasion that German troops had fought on this front, and also the first time that poisonous gas was used. The Fourteenth German Army and the First and Second Austrian–Hungarian Isonzo Army managed to get down to the Veneto Plain on 10 November, reaching the Piave River and thus cutting the distance between Trieste and Venice in half. However, it was here that the advance got bogged down: the new chief of general staff, General Armando Diaz, was able to prevent the pursuing enemy from crossing the river.

At the beginning of 1917, the Russian revolution swept away Tsar Nicholas II, yet the provisional government continued the war. It was only after the Bolsheviks took power that a peace treaty was signed on 3 March 1918, stipulating that Russia surrender the Baltic States, Belarus and part of the Ukraine. This finally allowed Germany to redeploy almost its entire army to France in 1918, although even with these reinforcements it was only able to pit 4 million soldiers against the Entante's army of 5 million (which was being continually reinforced). Military operations that were carried out in several stages took place along the entire length of the front stretching from the English Channel to Reims, but without any lasting success until the start of the Entante's counter-offensive on 18 July, which swept all before it. On 29 September, Bulgaria requested an armistice: this was followed by Turkey on 30 October and the Monarchy on 3 November. Finally, on 11 November 1918, Germany signed an armistice in a railway carriage in Compiégne Forest.

During the 4 year period of the war, 9 million soldiers were deployed from the territory of the Monarchy: 3.4 million from Hungary and Croatia. Out of this, 530,000 lost their lives, 1.4 million were wounded and over 830,000 were taken prisoner.

On 3 November 1918 the leaders of the Austrian–Hungarian armed forces on the Italian Front became signatories to a ceasefire on the dictate of the Italian general Armando Diaz, and the Monarchy lost the Great War. However, when a republic was simultaneously declared in Vienna and Pest, the history of the Habsburg Empire truly, spectacularly and symbolically came to an end but a new chapter commenced in the history of the Habsburg family.

Right: The allegory of the Compromise on the plinth of the Ferenc Deák statue in Budapest.

John C. Swanson

The Body of the Empire

The Compromise – the *Ausgleich* or *kiegyezés* between the emperor and the Magyars of the Empire – defined the political world of Austria–Hungary from its inception in 1867 to the Monarchy's dissolution in 1918. The debate continues as to its success or failure. Did it hasten the Monarchy's demise or did it succeed in establishing a sound, perhaps not ideal, but stable political and constitutional system that possessed the potential for change. The problems of the Compromise are often highlighted, especially in English-language literature, but one should not forget that the agreement lasted 50 years, longer than most settlements in Central Europe. None of the Monarchy's successor states endured such longevity.

The agreement of the Compromise occurred in the aftermath of the Austrian Empire's military defeat at Königgrätz (Sadova, also spelled Sadowa) in 1866 to Prussia. Austria had been forcibly removed from the German world, as well as obliged to surrender Venetia to Italy, and therefore needed to settle its differences with at least one of the major nationalities of the empire. It settled on the Magyars. At the time the Magyars were proposing a dualist arrangement, whereas the Czech federalists called for the division of the Monarchy into five units: two in the Alpine lands, Bohemia–Moravia, Galicia, and Hungary–Croatia. The Hungarian statesman Ferenc Deák, realising the advantageous position for the Hungarians, declared after hearing of Austria's loss on the battlefield: 'We lost the war! … we are now victorious.' In all actuality a compromise between the emperor and the Magyars had already been long underway by 1867; the outcome of Königgrätz simply left Franz Joseph with less negotiating power. The Magyars did not change their demands. Their terms were exactly the same as they had been before the Austrian defeat. The Emperor, reluctant to give in, received encouragement to agree to a settlement with the Magyars, both from his wife, Empress Elizabeth, who in her own right had become a Magyarphile, and Friedrich Ferdinand von Beust (an anti-Prussian, anti-Bismarkian Saxon), the man who would be appointed Austrian Foreign Minister.

For the other nationalities of the Monarchy the new political and constitutional arrangement was a bitter pill, yet not entirely unexpected. Nevertheless, a number of Czech, Croat, Ruthenian, and Slovenian politicians, led by Frantíšeck Palackyȩand F. L. Rieger, travelled to Moscow at the time when the Compromise reached the Austrian Parliament, in order to demonstrate their disapproval and their belief that Slavic salvation would be led by Russia. In 1869, Rieger also approached Napoleon III for French support of the Czech cause, but the French were not interested. The Croats were quelled with a separate compromise, the Nagodba, modelled on the terms of the Ausgleich, passed by the Croat Diet in 1868. It guaranteed Croatian as the official language of the region and permitted some autonomy in non-economic affairs. Yet it stipulated that the Croatian Ban – the Croatian leader – be appointed by the Hungarian King, who was also the King of Croatia as well as the Austrian Emperor, upon the advice of the Hungarian Prime Minister. Other nationalities, such as the Poles, voiced opposition, but their

Above: *The joint coat-of-arms of the Austro-Hungarian Monarchy, 1915. After long decades of debate the solution appeared as a combination of two coats-of-arms of equal ranking arranged side by side.*

Left: *The coronation ceremony of Franz Joseph took place on 8 June 1867 in Budapest. The city was awoken at 4 a.m. by a 21-cannon salute. The king rode across the city wearing Saint Stephen's crown and carrying his sword. In the Pest parish church Franz Joseph held a crucifix in his right hand and raising three fingers of his left hand towards heaven swore an oath to respect and uphold the Hungarian constitution and to protect the territorial integrity of the country.*
Opposite: *the abutment of the Chain Bridge on the Pest side, location of the symbolic sword stroke.*

concerns were not recognised, and eventually Poles would discover the advantages of being pro-Compromise, mainly because of the advantageous position they received in Vienna. Probably the biggest mistake made by the Slavs in Austria was their retreat from the parliament in protest during discussions of the Compromise, thereby providing the German Liberals with the opportunity to define the new Austria as they saw fit. The Slavs only returned to parliament when dualism was already in place.

Even if we understand the Ausgleich as a victory of the Magyars in their negotiations with the Crown and a done deal handed to the Austrians, one should not forget that the other victors in 1867 were the Liberals in both halves of the Monarchy. The Compromise created a world in which many of their goals could be achieved, even if the Austro-German Liberals continued to object to their exclusion from the larger German realm, especially after the creation of the German Empire in 1871. The so-called liberal era in Cisleithania, up to 1879, however, was fragile. Franz Joseph accepted their demands for liberal legislation on church and school matters, but he would not share control of his army or foreign affairs. The emperor-king would rather cooperate with Slavic and Magyar elements to stabilise the Monarchy than give in to encroachments on his power. This explains perhaps the success of the Taaffe era (Count Eduard Taaffe was appointed Prime Minister in 1879 and would rule until 1893), which will be described later (*see page 86*). In the Hungarian half, the Liberals under Kálmán Tisza would come to power in 1875 and struggle with an opposition that continued to attack the Compromise. In essence, one could argue, as historian Robin Okey does, that: 'The history of Dualist Austria thus becomes a study in the erosion of German liberal hegemony and the emancipation from it of the non-German nationalities.'

Austria–Hungary – the Dual Monarchy – has been described as the embodiment of 'the good old days' as well as a 'prison of the peoples.' Simultaneously it calls forth praise and condemnation. Sometimes these opposing perspectives are delineated by a person's ethnic background, but often they are more clearly defined by the time period in which they are voiced. Most historians after World War I were very critical of the multinational dynasty, yet post-1945 descriptions have become more favourable, looking for a positive alternative to the cold war settlement imposed by the iron curtain. And much of the recent literature finds many positive aspects of what others have described as an anachronistic, feudal entity. In the following essay I try to avoid either extreme; my goal is to present the Monarchy and all its territories as a modernising state (or states), not unlike many other states in Europe at the time, caught up in the many inherent political, economic, and social struggles of the late 19th and early 20th centuries.

The majority of this chapter looks at the forms of the Monarchy – what has been referred to as the 'body of the Empire': its demography, political institutions, economy, cities, leaders, and society. My understanding of Austria–Hungary is not as a living, organic entity, yet the metaphor proves useful in envisioning its full character. Approaching the Austro-Hungarian Monarchy as a body allows me to describe the integral parts of the political space of Austria–Hungary, but it does not imply that the Habsburg Monarchy had a natural life cycle from birth to eventual death, just like a person. Austria–Hungary was in reality a spatial unit held together by the Habsburgs and the state apparatus that had been created in their domains.

The theme throughout the chapter is the continual struggles that represent life in the Monarchy. One often thinks of Franz Joseph representing the 'old' in constant conflict with the new – the bourgeois world of commerce and modernity. One needs only to turn to Franz Joseph's description of himself to Theodore Roosevelt in 1910 as the 'last European monarch of the old school'. He told Roosevelt that he wanted to meet him in order to see how the new movement felt and thought. But things were not so simplistic.

Above: *Many people regarded Franz Joseph as the embodiment of the 'old' in constant conflict with the 'new', the latter being represented by commerce and the modernity of the bourgeois world. Others believe that the most accurate description of his character is the one he made about himself to Theodore Roosevelt in 1910, according to which he was the last European ruler of the old school. He said that the reason he wanted to meet Roosevelt was to find out how the new generation felt and thought.*

The struggle was not just between old and new or between Western and Eastern European state models, which some scholars have emphasised. The West in the 19th century was seen as based on constitutional and centralised states, the East on dynasty with particular and feudal privileges. By 1867 the two halves of Austria–Hungary had become constitutional monarchies, and both struggled to centralise their respective halves, yet both were led by a dynasty with strong feudal undercurrents. Perhaps one of the real defining conflicts was that between centre and periphery. Even the infamous and on-going nationality conflicts of the Dual Monarchy can be understood as struggles between a German- or Magyar-speaking centre and the nationalities on the periphery.

The difficulties and many struggles of the Monarchy have been illuminated in memorable images of Austria–Hungary given to us by expressions like 'muddling through' (*fortwursteln*) and *Kakania*. *Fortwursteln* refers to the unofficial policy of Count Eduard Taaffe, Prime Minister in the Austrian half of Austria–Hungary between 1879

Below: The overview map of the Dual Monarchy in German. Cisleithania is shown in pink and Transleithania in pale yellow.

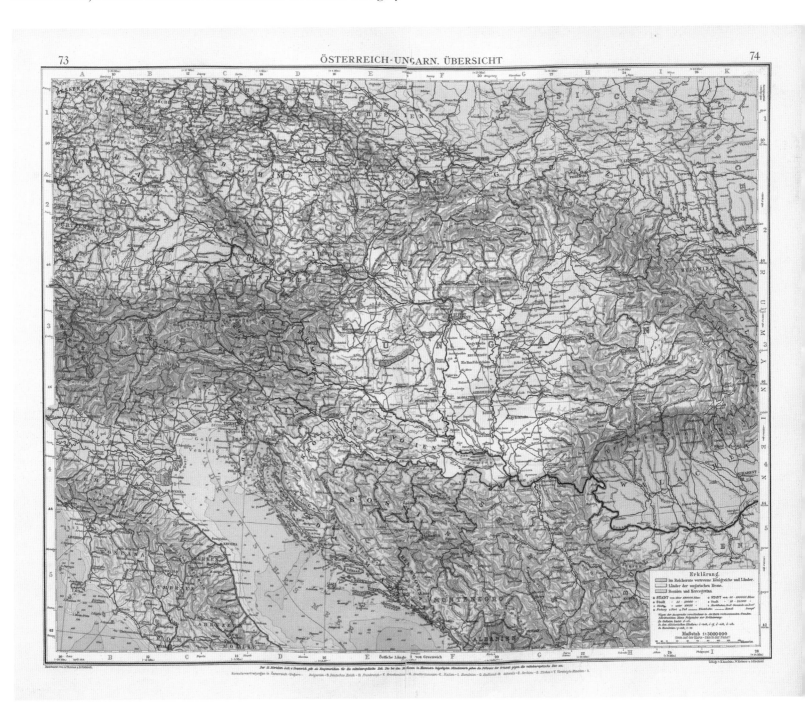

and 1893. The expression was used by his critics, but he accepted it and even employed it himself. The idea was to keep things moving forward – to keep the machinery working and the Monarchy intact – by maintaining contending interests, mainly those of the nationalities, in a state of 'well-tempered discontent.' It might have been 'muddling through,' but Taaffe did it with considerable adroitness. His coalition of the Iron Ring and the absence of majority governments held things together in Vienna until the 1890s, when obstructionism and the government's emergency decree, paragraph 14, became common practice.

If *fortwursteln* and its consequences represent the hobbling along that many describe as typical in Austrian politics, the expression *Kakania* symbolises the criticism that many had of the entity known as Austria–Hungary. It was first coined by Robert Musil in his novel, *Mann ohne Eigenschaften* (*The Man without Qualities*) to refer to the state of mind of the Monarchy, and today is often employed in reference to the old Monarchy, often in a kind of tongue-in-cheek way. *Kakania* comes from K. K. or K. und K.: *Kaiserlich Königlich* or *Kaiserlich und Königlich* (Imperial and Royal), a designation adorning to all common governmental institutions and buildings in Austria–Hungary.

Below: *Franz Joseph, who lived a disciplined and almost bureaucratic life, indulged in very few passionate pastimes, one of which was hunting.*

But the word 'kaka', existed before Musil's invention, in German and international nursery language with the meaning of Shiteria or Shitland. Therefore, speaking of the Dual Monarchy as *Kakania* not only reminds us of the Imperial and Royal aspect of the Habsburgs' rule, but also of the utter nonsense it supposedly stood for.

Austria–Hungary was a dynastic monarchy, consisting of two rather different states, ruled by one man, Franz Joseph. It was modernising – economically and socially becoming a state that needed its middle class and its workers. It was a constitutional monarchy, with a monarch who never totally lost his absolutist control. It was a liberal state in which the great landlords, especially in the eastern half, held on to their power. It was a state centralising power in the hands of the federal governments, in Vienna and Budapest, by suppressing the desires of the periphery, especially the non-German and non-Magyar nationalities. It was not a state of contradictions, it was a state experiencing the struggles of becoming modern.

Territory, Physical Characteristics: Demographic Composition

The Habsburg realm, in its last incarnation as the Dual Monarchy, from 1867 to 1918, was geographically the second largest country in Europe after the Russian Empire, and the third most populous after Russia and Germany. Yet the Danubian Monarchy lacked any clear territorial or physical unity: no body of water and no mountain range to define its borders. Historian A. J. P. Taylor described it as 'geographic nonsense', while historian Oscar Jászi considered it a 'species of medieval entail held together by the same imperial will, and by the same insatiable desire for consolidation and expansion'. Whatever its shape, it was without doubt geographically awkward. Since the middle ages, the House of Austria had built its empire through the policy of marriage: *Bella gerant alii, tu felix Austria nube!* ('Let others make wars, thou happy Austria, marry!'), and by the 16th century, under Charles V (1500–1558; Holy Roman Emperor, 1519–1556), it had become a world empire, with territories in Central Europe, Spain, the Netherlands, and the New World. Charles V's final wishes separated the realm into Spanish and Central European entities, and by the late 19th century Habsburg Europe was confined to the region of East Central Europe.

In 1867 the Habsburg Monarchy stretched from Bohemia in the northwest to Galicia in the northeast, from Transylvania and the Banat in the southeast to Tirol and Vorarlberg in the west. And with the 1878 occupation and subsequent 1908 annexation of Bosnia and Herzegovina the Habsburg territory expanded southward. The Ausgleich in 1867 may have divided the region into two halves – creating the Dual Monarchy of Austria–Hungary – but in many ways the Habsburg Monarchy continued to be the potpourri of lands over which the Habsburgs were sovereigns, such as Bohemia, Moravia, Lower Austria, Upper Austria, Styria, Tirol, Vorarlberg, Carinthia, Carniola, Istria, Galicia, Bukovina, Hungary, Croatia–Slavonia, and Transylvania, to name some of the major regions. The dynastic legacy, even if somewhat exaggerated, still held sway, with the head of the House of Austria formally representing the 'Emperor of Austria, Apostolic King of Hungary, King of Bohemia, of Dalmatia, Croatia, Slavonia, Galicia, Lodomeria and Illyria; King of Jerusalem, etc.; Archduke of Austria; Grand Duke of Tuscany and of Cracow; Duke of Lotharingia, of Salzburg, Styria, Carinthia, Carniola, and Bukovina; Grand Duke of Transylvania; Margrave of Moravia; Duke of Upper Silesia and of Lower Silesia, of Modena, Parma, Piacenza, and Guastella, of Auschwitz and Sator, of Teschen, Friaul, Ragusa, and Zara; Princely Count of Habsburg and Tyrol, of Kyburg, Görz, and Gradiska; Duke of Trient and Brixen; Margrave of Upper and Lower Lausitz and in Istria; Count of Hohenembs, Feldkirch, Begrenz, Sonnenburg, etc.; Lord of Trieste, of Cattaro, and above the Wendish March; Great Vojvod of the Vojvodina of Serbia, etc. etc.'

Above: The family vested imperial power in the hands of the 18-year-old Franz in the hope that the young ruler would be able to strengthen the Monarchy and basic monarchic principles.

This dynastic hodgepodge still defined the Zeitgeist in the late 19th century, even though some of the titles were no longer being bestowed on the Habsburg sovereign. The Habsburgs still dominated life in much of Central, Eastern, and parts of Southern Europe. Franz Joseph always considered himself a German prince, and Italy occupied a central place in Habsburg Europe. Yet the 19th century witnessed territorial modifications to the Empire. Austria surrendered most of Lombardy to Italy in 1859 and lost Venetia and the rest of Lombardy in 1866. Also, in 1866, Austria was expelled from the German Confederation, and in essence gave up its central position in the German world to Prussia after the military defeat at Königgrätz (Sadova/Sadowa). The Turkish provinces of Bosnia and Herzegovina were added to the Monarchy in 1908, and there were other territorial readjustments. The 1867 compromise returned Transylvania to the Crown of St Stephen (the Kingdom of Hungary), and the former military border, originally established in the 18th century along the southern frontier and governed from Vienna, became part of Croatia–Slavonia, all under Hungarian control.

The Dual Monarchy of 1867 had no capital, even though Vienna continued to be regarded as such. There were two centres: Vienna and Budapest, between which the emperor-king was to divide his time. The majority of the people lived in the Austrian half (55 per cent, 28,571,934) compared to Hungary (40.6 per cent, 20,886,487). The remainder inhabited the recently acquired lands of Bosnia–Herzegovina (3.8 per cent, 1,931,802). This territorial restructuring left Austria–Hungary in the ambiguous region of East Central Europe; as A. J. P. Taylor so aptly put it, the Monarchy continued to lack clear natural borders. Vorarlberg, for instance, is geographically part of Switzerland and Tyrol of southern Germany. Carinthia and much of Styria belong with Carniola and the Adriatic hinterland, not with the lands of the Danubian valley. Slovenia also is geographically separate, and Dalmatia really has no connection to Austria. Between Bohemia and Moravia sits a line of hills. Galicia was also set apart from Austria, and Bukovina was far, far away from Vienna. The eastern half of the Monarchy was a little less problematic. Most of Hungary comprised the great plain of the middle Danube. This did not, however, include Croatia, which was more geographically aligned with Carniola or Bosnia.

The demographic awkwardness of the Dual Monarchy is not only visible in its geography, but also in its ethnic composition. It is one thing to look for natural borders or social and economic connections, but it is another to try to comprehend the unity of a multi-national state such as Austria–Hungary. There were approximately 11 different major nationalities and a handful of smaller ones in post-1867 Habsburg Europe, yet one needs to be very careful about how these groups are understood and counted. Our modern world of nation-states and ethnic categories was in its infancy in the 19th century. One must not forget that the old medieval sense of the nation representing nobles, that is a class category, not an ethnic one, was still present in many places in Central and Eastern Europe at the time. Rural people, even in the late 19th century, often described themselves as members of a certain province, county, region, not as members of a nation. A division of the region into discernible nationalities and nations often results from the rhetoric and actions of nationalists of all colours. Nevertheless, no study of the Habsburg Monarchy and Austria–Hungary would be complete without a demographic breakdown of the various nationalities.

Below: Franz Joseph at military manoeuvres in Bohemia.

The image of this 'national' – or more accurately 'linguistic' – composition of the Monarchy was and remains vague. Census reports were first carried out in the area in the mid-to-late 19th century, and most of them were conducted by local officials often as part of a conscious or unconscious political battle. The question utilised to categorise nationalities simply inquired about the 'language of communication' – that is, the language usually used – which meant, for example, that in 1910 *The Times* correspondent in Vienna was counted as German, since that was the language he used while shopping. It is important to point out that the census reports in the two halves of the Monarchy asked different questions that would be used by Habsburg officials and historians to determine the number of nationalities. There was no specific question asking for national affiliation. Hungary introduced it first in 1941. The Austrians asked about 'language of communication' (*Umgangssprache*), and the Hungarians inquired about the 'mother tongue' (*Muttersprache* or *anyanyelv*). This might lead one to conclude that the Austrians were more accepting of assimilation, but one should never forget that the Hungarians needed converts to maintain the facade of a Hungarian nation-state. In both halves it was not uncommon that the local official determined the language and thus the nationality of individuals, as well as of whole villages. (This explains some of the dramatic shifts in rural areas that historians, as well as nationalists, describe as assimilation, when in reality it was often nothing more than the decision of the census taker.) This is, of course, most unfortunate, since some of these census battles would be employed as objective criteria for the post-1919 divisions in the region.

Despite the blurred data of census figures, linguistically the Monarchy was a mosaic of peoples, and perhaps the best way to get an introduction to this composition is to look at the two halves of the Monarchy separately. The Austrian half was comprised of approximately 35 per cent Germans, 23 per cent Czechs, 17 per cent Poles, 12 per cent Ruthenians, 4 per cent Slovenes, 2.8 per cent Serbo-Croatians, 2.75 per cent Italians, and 0.98 per cent Romanians. The core provinces of Cisleithania, such as Vorarlberg, Salzburg, and the duchies of Upper and Lower Austria were overwhelmingly German. There were some Italians in Vorarlberg and some Czechs in Lower Austria. The city of Vienna, located in Lower Austria, contained many Germans, but was not a national city; it was an imperial one, with representatives of many of the realm's nationalities, especially a large Czech minority. Other provinces contained German-speaking majorities, such as Tyrol, Carinthia, and Styria, with Carinthia and Styria containing a significant number of Slovenes as well. Tyrol, south of the Alps, was heavily inhabited by Italians. Carniola was Slovene; even German speakers identified themselves as Slovene there.

Below: King Charles IV, Queen Zita and the child Ottocar at the funeral of Franz Joseph.

The free city of Trieste contained a majority of Italians, but also a growing minority of Slovenes and Germans. The Slovene majority was growing faster than the Italian population in the province of Gorica, while in Istria the Croats were in the majority. The three coastal regions were clearly Southern Slav. Dalmatia, a region acquired in 1815, was exclusively Serbo-Croat, except for a small urban-based Italian minority. Yet even the Italian city dwellers were losing out to an increasing number of Slavic labourers migrating to the cities.

Rudolf, Crown Prince of Austria and Heir to the Throne

Above: Mária Vetsera.

Rudolf, the only son of the imperial couple, was highly popular throughout the Empire. As the heir to an empire comprised of over 11 nationalities his intelligence and flare for languages became a distinct advantage. He rebelled against traditional court life and he sought out his friends among artist circles, liberals and Jews. He publicly criticised Franz Joseph's conservative policies, the emperor's insistence on forming an alliance with Germany and Austrian Bosnian participation.

Rudolph's marriage with Princess Stephanie of Belgium was not a happy one, and Rudolf had numerous mistresses. Rudolf was found dead with one such woman, referred to as the Baroness Mária Vetsera, on 30 January 1889 in the hunting castle at Mayerling, near Vienna. A suspected double suicide, the circumstances of the tragedy have never completely come to light since the details of the event were immediately covered up.

Elizabeth, Queen of the Hungarians

Above: The young emperor and empress.

In accordance with family tradition, Franz Joseph's mother, the ironhanded Archduchess Sophie, planned that her son would marry his cousin, Helen of Bavaria. However, when the young ruler travelled to Bad Ischl in 1853 to visit his bride-to-be he fell in love with her 16-year-old younger sister, the beautiful Elizabeth, known in her close circle as 'Sissi' or 'Sissy', who was passionately drawn to the arts, literature and sports. The attraction was mutual. They became engaged one day after they had met on Franz Joseph's 23rd birthday. They were married in April 1854.

The atmosphere of the court at which Elizabeth found herself was quite anti-Hungarian, an antipathy especially felt by Grand Duchess Sophia, Elizabeth's mother-in-law. Perhaps because of this, Elizabeth embraced the Hungarians and even learnt their language. Her constant lady-in-waiting, Ida Ferenczy, played a significant part in this. The queen was an ardent supporter of Ferenc Deák's ideas, which later became the basis for the Compromise.

In 1866, the queen left Buda on an excursion to Gödöllő and enchanted by the building's beauty and environs asked her husband to buy the castle, which had originally been built by Antal Grassalkovich. In the following years she spent a great deal of time there. Franz Joseph also liked to spend time here and their mutual interest in nature, riding and hunting drew the married couple closer together. Although the emperor and king sought physical comfort in the arms of other women, the passion and love he felt towards his wife never abated.

Above: The royal couple and their children in the garden of Gödöllő Castle.

Sissy was a free spirit and travelled (often incognito) all over Europe. She wrote poems and her favourite poet was Heinrich Heine (1797–1856), whose voice can be detected in Sissy's poetry. In honest recognition Dezső Mészöly wrote, '... for Elizabeth writing poetry was truly creative and not just a way for a dilettante to pass the time. Her restless soul could not have endured without some form of self-expression.' (Seagull in the Castle, Balassi Publishers, 1995.)

After the death of her son, Rudolf, Elizabeth wore black and remained in mourning for the rest of her life. She travelled extensively. One of her favourite destinations, other than Vienna, was her castle in Corfu.

Her tragic death occurred in Geneva on 10 September 1898, while she was walking with her lady-in-waiting Irma Sztáray. A young man ran at them, stabbing Elizabeth in the heart with a sharpened file. The queen collapsed but with her companion managed to quickly reach the boat that was already waiting for them. Since she lost consciousness soon after the boat set off, it was turned back to shore. The doctors, who hurried to her hotel, were able to do nothing more than pronounce her dead.

Today 'Sissi' attracts almost as much attention from the tourist industry as her husband.

Right: The final photo taken of Elizabeth.

The northern Austrian provinces, the lands of the Bohemian Crown – Bohemia, Moravia, and Silesia – had majority German populations in compact areas, such as the mountainous region along the Austrian and German borders, and in a number of towns. Germans also dominated in Silesia with a population of 281,000 Germans, 178,000 Poles and 129,000 Czechs. Bohemia was 62 per cent Czech and 38 per cent German, Moravia 70 per cent Czech and 30 per cent German. Prague had been 40 per cent German in 1855, but that number fell to 7 per cent by 1910. A similar development occurred in the Moravian capital of Brno as well.

Galicia could be geographically split into a western and an eastern half, with Poles enjoying a slight majority in the west, and sharing the east with a large minority of Ruthenes. The landowners were Polish, which helped the Poles remain dominant in the region. The large number of Jews in Galicia, especially in cities such as Lemberg (Lwów in Polish, Lviv in Ukrainian, and Lvov in Russian) was often counted, especially in 1910, as Poles. Bukovina was also a very ethnically mixed region – a real mosaic of peoples, with Ruthenes in the north, Romanians in the south, and a large number of Germans, Poles, and Magyars, as well as many Jews, who had never been separately counted.

Jews in Cisleithania and in the Kingdom of Hungary were not counted, that is not recognised as a separate nationality. According to confessional statistics, in 1910 4.4 per cent (2,258,013) of the Monarchy's total population were Jewish. Linguistically, and therefore nationally, they were often counted as members of the dominant nationality: German in the west and Magyar in the east. In places such as Galicia they were counted as Poles.

The Hungarian half of the Dual Monarchy has been described by historians as more ethnically harmonious, in comparison to the Austrian half, but this is not quite so obvious. Hungary, Croatia, and Transylvania – the 'lands of the Crown of St Stephen' – were clearly multinational. In 1910, Hungary, excluding Croatia–Slavonia, but including Transylvania, was 54 per cent Magyar, 16 per cent Romanian, 10.7 per cent Slovak, 10.4 per cent German, 2.5 Ruthenian, 2.5 Serbian, and 1.1 per cent Croatian. (Including Croatia–Slavonia the Magyars were a minority in their own state: representing 48 per cent of the total population.) The Jews, approximately 5 per cent of the population, were usually counted as Magyars. Yet these figures have been described as manipulated by half a century of magyarisation; they clearly differ from census figures taken by the successor states, with different agendas, after 1919.

Although the Magyars lived throughout the kingdom, they resided mainly in the centre, with the other nationalities inhabiting the outlaying regions. Upper Hungary was heavily Slovak, the northeast Ruthenian, the east Romanian, and the south Serbian. Croatia–Slavonia was mainly Croatian, with Serbians in the region of Slavonia, and Magyars serving as state officials and businessmen. Germans were in the north, east, south, and the centre. In the early 19th century, the various towns that would form Budapest in 1873 were heavily German; by 1910, because of migration and assimilation, the Magyars were dominant, comprising 80 per cent of the city. The 3 million Romanians in Hungary were primarily located in Transylvania and the Banat, the majority living under rural conditions, yet by the end of the 19th century more had migrated to the larger towns.

Bosnia and Herzegovina, the new addition to the Monarchy in 1908, belonged to both halves equally; it was not a constituent part of the Austrian provinces or the Hungarian Kingdom. It was officially administered by the joint minister of finance. Primarily Slavic: 1,800,000 Serbo-Croats (96 per cent of the population), the annexation greatly increased the number of Slavs in the Dual Monarchy. The remaining 4 per cent of the new inhabitants was divided between Germans and Magyars. A little more than a quarter of the population was Moslem.

Above: *Franz Ferdinand met Countess Sophie Chotek while doing his military service in Budweis (Budejovice), Bohemia. The married couple's favourite residence was the castle in Konopiste, Bohemia. According to the inscription, this picture was given to its owner on 22 March 1901.*

This ethnic distribution was complicated by the fact that many peoples had co-nationals in several provinces as well as outside the Monarchy. Germans were everywhere, in the Austrian and Hungarian halves, as well as in Germany and Switzerland. Serbo-Croats lived in southern Hungary, Croatia–Slavonia, Bosnia–Herzegovina, the Adriatic littoral, Dalmatia, the independent Serbian Kingdom, and the Ottoman Empire. Religiously the Monarchy was also heterogeneous. Approximately four-fifths of the regions were members of the Roman Catholic Church, one of the major centrifugal forces that held the Monarchy together until 1918. In addition, there were large numbers of Uniates in the Ruthenian area, Orthodox in the East and southeast, and Protestants, both Lutheran and Calvinist, mainly distributed across Hungary. Jews could be found in most large cities such as Vienna and Budapest, in Galicia, and also throughout the countryside, especially in Transleithania. Many Hungarian villages had at least one Jewish family.

The Skeleton: Political and Institutional Systems

The Compromise divided the Austrian Empire in half and created two separate entities under one ruler (the emperor-king); it established the Dual Monarchy of Austria–Hungary. Both halves were to be ruled separately; in Vienna and in Budapest would sit two respective cabinets and two Prime Ministers, as well as two separate parliaments (both of which had a lower and an upper house). The two halves would share three common ministers: foreign affairs, war (sometimes translated as defence), and finance. All three were appointed by the Monarch, and all three ministries remained in Vienna. The army would be a joint body controlled by Franz Joseph himself. (Token forces – the Honvéd in Hungary and the Landswehr in Austria – were also set up and placed under separate Hungarian and Austrian ministries of national defence.) There were other common interests, such as various economic issues, including inherited state debt, tariffs, currency and certain indirect taxes. These affairs, as well as the quota fixing each state's share of common expenses, would be agreed upon and renegotiated every 10 years. (Hungary initially paid 30 per cent of the common expenses, but this figure continually went up during the decennial re-negotiations.) The Habsburg sovereign continued to wield a great deal of power and control. He retained complete control of the common army, his prize possession, and he dominated foreign policy issues. One need only remember that the foreign minister's appointment and dismissal rested solely in Franz Joseph's prerogative. At least in the first years after 1867, important questions were sent to the Crown Councils, represented by the three common ministers, the two Prime Ministers, and sometimes others.

The terms of the Compromise were mainly the result of negotiations between the Austrian Emperor – who was also the Hungarian King – and the Magyar upper classes. Since both sides wanted a quick agreement, more than they wanted clear and fair terms, most of the articles were speedily agreed upon or simply left without proper definition. On 29 May 1867, the Hungarian Diet accepted the results of the discussions as Law XII of 1867, with 257 votes in favour and 110 opposed. And Franz Joseph, who had not been crowned King of Hungary in 1848 upon assuming control of the Habsburg realm, finally was granted the honour of receiving the Hungarian crown on 8 June 1867. On 28 June he gave his Royal sanction to Law XII. Only after this pomp and circumstance was the Austrian Parliament's (the Reichsrat's) assent to the compromise sought, in December 1867. It was already a fait accompli for the Austrians, yet a settlement that favoured the Germans in the Austrian half was to some extent welcomed by the German Liberals, since the Liberals were at the same time able to get a number of constitutional revisions through the parliament as well. For them it was a better settlement

Above: *The gold crown was legal tender until 1927.*

than any other one, especially one that would have meant sharing power with the Slavs. Others, however, such as Alfred Skene, the German Centralist leader, described the laws as 'Austria's domestic Königgrätz.'

The difficulties embedded in the new entity created in 1867 are symbolised in a way by problems of designation. The Eastern half was the Kingdom of Hungary (actually two kingdoms: Hungary and Croatia, in addition to the newly re-added Transylvania), and the Western half was officially known as 'the Kingdoms and Lands represented in the Reichsrat.' (The Reichsrat, the Imperial Council, was the parliament in Vienna.) For simplicity, the Austrian half also was called Cisleithania, referring to the small Leitha River (Lajta in Hungarian) that separated the two halves of the Monarchy. In this context Hungary was also known as Transleithania. It is true that, in the beginning, Franz Joseph had hoped to carry the titles 'Emperor of Austria, King of Bohemia, etc. and Apostolic King of Hungary; for short, Emperor of Austria and Apostolic King of Hungary.' And the Dual Monarchy was to be known as the 'Austro-Hungarian Monarchy' or 'Austro-Hungarian Empire (Reich).' Yet these proposals displeased certain subjects, especially the Magyars, and were eventually abandoned in favour of 'Austria–Hungary,' which in essence was the official name of the Dual Monarchy. Franz Joseph retained the title Emperor, but there really was no Empire. Franz Joseph's successor Emperor Charles, however, sanctioned the name 'Austria' for the Western half in 1917; providing this new Austria with a lifespan of one year. One should never forget the fact that despite the

Below: *In 1867 the borders of the Habsburg Monarchy extended from north-western Bohemia to north-eastern Galicia, from south-eastern Transylvania and the region of Bánát to northern Tyrol and Vorarlberg. Habsburg territory spread yet further southwards with the occupation of Bosnia and Herzegovina in 1878 and its annexation in 1908.*

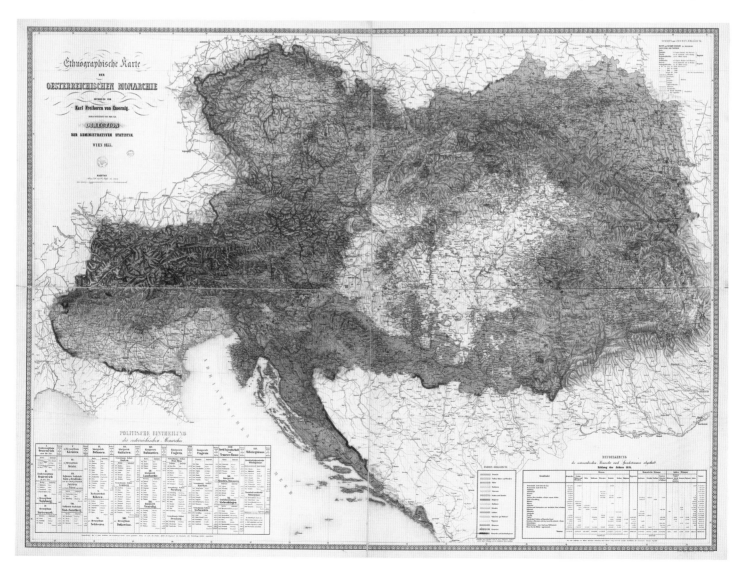

erroneous use by many scholars of the word 'Empire' to refer to the Dual Monarchy, Austria–Hungary was never officially an Empire, although it may have acted as one.

The problems with naming this 1867 creation continued with the struggle of how to refer to common services and common bodies. Initially the common institutions, instead of being simply imperial (*kaiserlich*), became *kaiserlich königlich*, 'Imperial-Royal' (imperial in reference to all of the Monarchy, and royal to Hungary). In 1889 the word *und* (and) was inserted into the designation of the armed forces to create the *k. und k. Armee*, and the foreign minister became *k. und k.* in 1895. The Minister of Finance, who in 1867 retained the title Reichsminister, lost the *Reichs* (imperial) in 1868 and was simply referred to as 'common' (*gemainsamer, közös*). The Minister of War kept the title 'Reichskriegsminister' until 1911, at which time he also became *k. und k.*

In the Austrian half the 'Basic Law' of 21 December 1867, which approved of the Compromise, was accompanied by other

Above: *Franz Joseph, who was the 'first civil servant' of the Monarchy, was all too happy to take part at the frequently held official openings and unveiling ceremonies of the period. This photograph was taken in 1896, at the opening of the Museum of Applied Arts in the museum's iron structured, glass roofed great hall. The building, which is on Üllői Road, was designed by Gyula Pártos and Ödön Lechner, the latter of whom was accredited as being the Hungarian representative of the Secession. In the tender they put in for the work in 1890 the plan for the museum bore the title 'Hungarian to the East', which said much about their style.*

laws (fundamental laws, which could only be altered with a two-thirds majority vote) that transformed Austria into a kind of constitutional monarchy. The new liberal state of Austria – Cisleithania – became a *Rechtsstaat*, a state based on law. At the same time, the new, or not so new, Kingdom of Hungary did not change its political structure (just like Austria, it was comprised of a bicameral parliament, with a lower and an upper house). The members of the Hungarian upper house were, before 1886, selected exclusively by birth, later they could be nominated by the king. The Hungarian parliament of 1867 was in essence the diet of 1865, originally elected to reach agreement with the Crown, not to transform Hungary into a new entity. Whereas Dualist Austria struggled with many problems, which will be explained later in this chapter or other parts of this book, the Hungarian parliament concentrated its time on the so-called 'Issue of Public Law' (*a közjogi kérdés*): the relationship between Hungary and the Crown, which had been the sole business of the Hungarian Diet for centuries.

It may be questionable how much constitutionalism was introduced in either Austria or Hungary in 1867. Oscar Jászi considered the entire settlement: 'sham constitutionalism,' mainly for not representing the interests of all inhabitants of Austria–Hungary. The feudal aristocracy still dominated in both halves, even if we consider the Compromise a victory for German and Magyar liberalism. Austria maintained the Curia system until universal suffrage was introduced in 1906. (The Curia system will be explained in more detail later in this chapter; *see page 84*.) Hungary, however, did not change at all; it retained a limited franchise until the end of World War I.

In Cisleithania, political issues continued to be divided between questions affecting all of Austria and local questions. The first came before the central parliament and the others before the various provincial diets (*Landtage*), which were still dominated by landowning interests. In larger provinces (*Länder*) there were further subdivisions into circles (*Kreise*). The Kingdom of Hungary was also divided into component parts since its inception under St Stephen, and these counties (*vármegyék*) were led by a representative of the Crown. In the late 19th century this person carried the title of Lord Lieutenant (*föispán*). Most counties were also further divided into districts (*járások*), similar to the Austrian *Kreise*, but the *járások* were simply subdivisions of the county, not separate units. In the Hungarian half of the Monarchy, the autonomy of the counties was much stronger than in Cisleithania, but also more clearly representative of the interests of the upper and middle nobility.

In spite of the autonomy of the provincial administrations and the democratisation of political life, more so in Cisleithania than in Hungary, the Habsburg sovereign remained supreme. Franz Joseph continues to dominate the story, in a discussion of the political institutions in Austria–Hungary. However, I have left out any detailed discussion of the emperor-king in this overview of the governmental systemm, as he will receive more attention in a later section. The emperor-king's control and that of the landowning classes continued to dominate the political and institutional system established in 1867, and the structure of the Dual Monarchy remained more or less unaltered until its collapse in 1918. The only major change was the inclusion of the newly acquired territories of Bosnia and Herzegovina, as an occupied region in 1878 and then as annexed territory in 1908.

Above: *A Saxon family from Kereszténysziget (Szeben County). Photo taken by Béla Révész in 1908.*

Circulation: Economy, Transport, Migration, Urbanisation and School

Economy

Oscar Jászi has argued that 'one of the most powerful forces which upheld the Habsburg Monarchy was, without a doubt, the growing capitalistic penetration of its economic organisation' led by the German bourgeois class centred in Vienna and the Bohemian industrial regions, as well as more and more by Jews throughout the Monarchy. Economic interests may have helped to hold the Monarchy together, especially since the economic health of both halves was essentially good. The standard story describes sharp economic growth until the stock market crash in 1873 and slow recovery until an upswing began in 1896, continuing until World War I. Yet some scholars would argue that expansion began earlier than 1896, rather in 1879, and more recent scholarship has tended to portray an overall healthy economy in the late 19th and early 20th centuries, despite the 1873 crash and depression. This view, of course, emphasises growth in Cisleithania, where much of the capitalistic, industrial activity took place, but it also holds true in Hungary, which in addition to its agricultural base experienced rapid industrial growth.

The economy in the Monarchy after 1867, in reality after the defeat by Prussia in 1866, greatly benefited from the extra currency issued to finance the war – a short, seven-weeks' war. The transition to a new status quo, an end to the struggle for control of Germany, the introduction of constitutionalism in Austria, and the settlement with Hungary were welcomed by financial powers. Austria became a place for foreign investment, while the currency remained strong and did not depreciate. Another benefit for the financial circles was the fact that throughout the Monarchy, from Vorarlberg to Bukovina, the currency was the same. Since 1754 the population of the Austrian Empire and subsequently of Austria–Hungary used the Gulden (forint in Hungarian), which was based partially on the silver standard. In 1892, as part of an effort to put the Monarchy on the gold standard, Austria–Hungary introduced the Krone (korona in Hungarian) at the rate of 2 Kronen for 1 Gulden. The Gulden had been divided into 60 Kreuzer (the forint into 60 krajczár). The introduction of the Krone was accompanied by a new division of the main unit into one hundred parts: 100 Heller in one Krone or 100 fillér in one korona. The Krone bills were printed in German on one side and Hungarian on the other. In small print, on the German side, not the Hungarian one, the amount was sometimes listed in other languages of the Monarchy, such as Czech, Slovak, Polish, Ukrainian, Italian, Slovenian, Croatian, Serbian, and Romanian. The paper money also carried images of fictional people, female and boy models, sometimes allegories of sciences and industry. This demonstrates that the complaints against the non-national and fictional images on the more recent Euro bills were unfounded, since such currency designs had already been tested in Austria–Hungary.

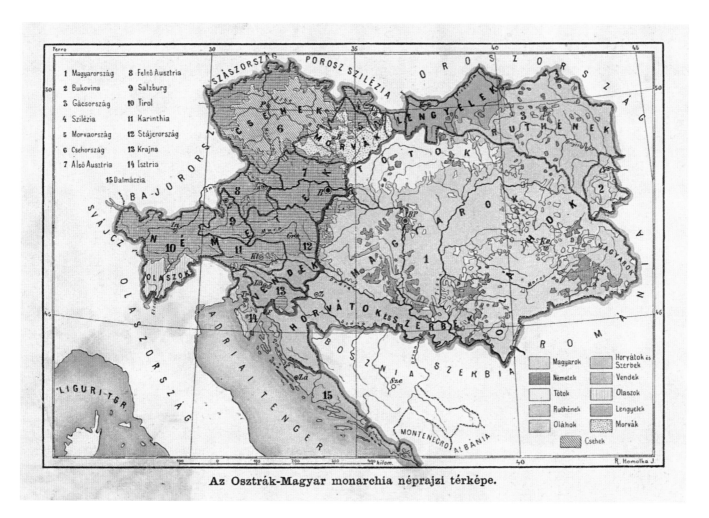

Az Osztrák-Magyar monarchia néprajzi térképe.

Economically the two halves of the Monarchy were held together in a customs union, as part of the Compromise agreement. Not only did goods travel freely throughout the Monarchy, but similar products and shops could be found in many places, sometimes with slight modifications. The owner of the Austrian grocery store chain Julius Meinl, for instance, was known as Meinl Gyula in Hungary. (In Hungarian one's last name always proceeds one's first name.) There was clear economic integration in the Monarchy during the dualist period, but it is perhaps easier to describe the economic conditions by looking at the two halves of Austria–Hungary separately.

Above: *A contemporaneous map. It can clearly be seen that the location of political borders and ethnic groups do not overlap.*

The period between 1867 and 1873 in Cisleithania, the so-called Gründerzeit, reflects the industrial advancement led by heavy industry and an increase in the number of banking institutions willing to finance this growth. The crash of 1873 brought the Gründerzeit to an end, and has been described as a period of plunging share prices, panicking crowds, runs on banks, and a surge in registered suicides (152 suicides that year). Yet by the 1880s, or as early as 1879, the Austrian economy began to recover, with the help of 'universal banks' and the growth in the number of cartels (around 200 by 1912), which regulated prices, output, as well as market shares. Much of this growth was led by German speakers, but Czechs and Poles also occupied leading positions.

Hungary was more of an agrarian state, a major exporter of corn and flour. In the mid 1870s, half of Germany's flour imports came from the Monarchy, mainly from Hungary. Yet Transleithania was industrially not far behind its western counterpart; iron production in Hungary, for instance, was on par with other European states. The argument by Hungarian nationalists that Hungary was treated as a colonial possession of Austria, especially because of the stipulations of the customs union, does not prove true. There were, of course, problems in the customs union as far as Hungary was concerned. Some stipulations focused Hungarian exports on agricultural products and supported uneven economic conditions within Hungary. Things improved in the early 20th century, however, when Hungary achieved some sort of an emancipation within the framework of the customs union. Hungary started to produce more of its own rails and railroad cars as well as found investment beyond Austria. Nevertheless, Hungary – or one could argue, the Monarchy as a whole – was an agrarian state. In 1910, 53 per cent of Austria's working population was still employed in agriculture, with 26 per cent working in mining and industry. In Hungary at the time 60 per cent were working in agriculture compared to 18 per cent in mining and industry.

Transportation

Transportation during the compromise period was dominated by waterways, roads, and more and more by the railroad. Waterways, mainly shipping via the Danube River, but also the Rivers Sava and Tisza had helped boost economic growth since the late 18th century, especially benefiting Hungarian agricultural exports to Austria. Roads were still few and far between in 1867, but increasing. At the same time, the expansion of the railroad, the symbol of the ever-expanding industrial revolution, transformed transportation in Austria–Hungary during the late 19th and early 20th centuries.

Above: *A large illustrated article in* Vasárnapi Újság *(Sunday Newspaper) about an ethnographical exhibition in Prague.*

Even before 1867 the length of railway lines throughout the Monarchy had increased, but during the dualist period the expansion was dramatic. Historians emphasise the role the spreading railroad played in economic growth in the second half of the 19th century. The economic historian David Good argues that railways lowered transportation costs and created demand for certain goods, such as timber, coal, iron, and steel. A look at the increase in the length of railway tracks in the Habsburg realm will demonstrate the growing importance, of the railroad after 1867. In Cisleithania there were 3,698km of tracks in 1865; in 1913 there were 22,981km of tracks. The centre, Vienna, had been connected to all the outlaying areas: to Innsbruck, to Pilsen, and to Prague, and provinces were being connected with each other. In Transleithania – the Hungarian half of the Monarchy – there were only 35km of tracks in 1846; that increased to 2,285 in 1867 and to 22,084 in 1913. Budapest occupied the centre of this network, as it still does today. In the Compromise period, the numbers of passengers travelling by train multiplied. In the Austrian half 32 million people travelled by train in 1877 and 301 million in 1913. During the approximate same time (1867 to 1913) the number of train travellers in Hungary grew from 9 million to 166 million.

Above: *The Secessionist synagogue in Szabadka (Novi Sad).*

Migration

The growing population in both halves of the Monarchy began to pose new problems, mainly regarding access to resources. Cisleithania had, by the turn of the century, reached a population of 26 million, and by 1910 this number had further increased to 28.5 million. The number of people in Galicia, for example, had grown quite rapidly, and Galicia became the most populated province with over 6.5 million inhabitants. Second was Bohemia with 5.8 million. The German Lands experienced slower growth, with the exception of Lower Austria, which ballooned because of the rapid expansion in Vienna and its suburbs. Hungary, including Croatia–Slavonia, had reached a population of 19.25 million by 1900, and 21 million by 1910. These demographic changes put stress on the social and economic structure of society not only in the two halves of Austria–Hungary, but throughout all of newly industrialised Europe.

The increase in population was most intensely felt in the countryside; rural overpopulation was common. Industrialisation, the expansion of factories, and rural migration to industrial centres helped to relieve some of this tension. Yet it remained extremely critical in the Cisleithanian regions of Galicia and Bukovina, where industrialisation was not as intense, and in Slovak-inhabited Upper Hungary. Other areas throughout Hungary were also affected by rural overpopulation, especially where inheritance patterns favoured division of the land between the offspring, instead of the custom of many German speakers, who left the homestead intact to one child, while the others were sent off to work in the cities or for the Church.

Industrialisation helped to ease the pains of a growing population, but so did emigration. Before 1880, emigration from the Monarchy had been negligible, perhaps a couple of thousand people a year. There were cases of Czechs going to Russia in search of land as well as instances of German miners from Bohemia going to the Klondyke during the gold rush. But after 1880 there were more and more emigrants setting out for the New World. In the year 1880, around 20,000 left the Monarchy; by 1890 the annual number had increased to 40,000. Subsequently, registered overseas migration had reached 120,000 in 1903. It was common that 20 to 25 per cent of the emigrants would return, either because they had achieved what they set out to, or because they had not. The overwhelming majority of these emigrants were landless men or dwarf-holders, many of whom came from overcrowded rural areas such as Galicia or Bukovina. There were also well-to-do Jews, some from Vienna, who left for the USA, England and Germany.

The provisions of the Compromise came into being as a result of negotiations between the Austrian emperor – who was also the Hungarian king – and the Hungarian aristocracy. Since both parties were more interested in reaching a speedy agreement than the application of clear and accurate terminology, most of the clauses were written quickly as an agreement often lacking accurate definitions. On 29 May 1867 the Hungarian Parliament accepted the conclusion of the negotiations and from it framed Act XII of 1867 (see the cover of an edition de luxe to the right) by 257 votes in favour to 110 against. Franz Joseph, who had not been crowned Hungarian king when he came to power in 1848, finally had his coronation on 8 June 1867. Following this, the ruler sanctified Act XII on 28 June. It was only after this, in December 1867, that the Imperial Council was asked to enact it in Austrian law.

In addition to migration to the New World there was also some intra-European movement, as well as internal migration within the Monarchy. Between 1880 and 1910 nearly 300,000 Hungarians went to Austria, the majority being German speakers from West Hungary, migrating to the cities of Graz and Vienna. Also, 42,000 people left for Germany, and 102,000 for Romania; most of those going to Romania were Romanian speakers, as well as a large number of Szeklers (a Magyar-speaking ethnic group, located mainly in Transylvania). There was also significant Jewish emigration from the Monarchy to Western Europe, as well as internal Jewish migration from Galicia to other parts of Austria–Hungary, especially to Vienna and Budapest.

Urbanisation

The changing economic and social structure in the Dual Monarchy led to a redistribution of classes and to increased urbanisation in both halves of Austria–Hungary. Growth in urban populations was caused by work opportunities in surging urban industries, but it was also the obvious outlet for victims of rural congestion as well as of agricultural depression. More recent scholarship on Budapest has also demonstrated that the rapid increase in the city's population can be partly attributed to simple natural multiplication, which caused perhaps as much as one third of the population gain. Urban migration was typically a one-way street, yet it was not unheard of for unemployed factory workers to return to the countryside or for migration to occur in the reverse direction during economic slumps. Notwithstanding, city and town populations were growing and so were the number of individuals working in non-agricultural occupations.

Above: *The Austrian central coat-of-arms from 1915–1916.*

Both halves of the Monarchy were essentially agrarian at the turn of the century, but rapidly modernising and becoming a society in which industry and trade played a larger part; Austria a little faster than Hungary. The Monarchy was still agrarian, but in the last decades of the 19th century, especially from 1890, industry was expanding, mainly in regions such as Bohemia and Lower Austria. The percentage of agricultural workers was especially high in Bosnia–Herzegovina and in Galicia and Bukovina.

Some of these changes were, of course, influenced by the rapid increase in the overall population both in Cisleithania and Hungary. Cisleithania had reached a population of 24 million by 1890; before 1848 there were only 17.5 million, and then 20.5 million in 1869 and 22 million in 1880. Hungary had fewer people, but the numbers were growing faster. In 1850 there were 13 million inhabitants, in 1869 15.5 million. By 1890, Hungary's population had reached 17.5 million and continued to increase. This growth was sustained even with outward migration to the New World and Western Europe.

Urbanisation was the logical outcome of the growth of industry as well as of an increase in population. The number of individuals in Vienna rose between 1869 and 1910 from 600,000 to 2 million. Budapest, which became one city with the unification of Pest, Buda, and Óbuda in 1873, experienced a growth from 270,000 to 913,000 during the same time period. Prague, in contrast, had only reached 450,000 in 1910. Within Europe, Budapest's rapid growth was only outpaced by Berlin. The majority of other towns and villages throughout the Monarchy remained small. In Cisleithania most communities were small and semi-rural; the overwhelming majority had fewer than 5,000 inhabitants. Only about 150 contained populations between 5,000 and 10,000. The situation was similar in Hungary; at the turn of the century there were few (60) larger villages, and even fewer (7) cities. In 1900, Budapest housed 700,000 individuals. After Budapest, the second largest town was Szeged with a population of 118,000 in 1910. The third largest town was Szabadka (Subotica, today in Serbia), with 94,000 people and then Pozsony (today's capital of Slovakia – Bratislava) with 78,000. The largest city in Croatia was Zagreb, which remained less 'developed', with just over 50,000 inhabitants.

Education

Education was very important to the health and development of Austria–Hungary. Mass education, even if we are only talking about mass elementary education, had a major influence on social and political conditions. Through education students learned about the outside world, began to understand how a society works, and formed a larger entity to be mobilised for political or even military issues. This was a common occurrence in European countries, but the speed at which it took place in Hungary, and even in parts of Cisleithania, created tension. A literate population, not allowed to participate freely in governing themselves, will look for alternative avenues through which to voice their opinions, such as by creating national oppositional organisations.

With the Ausgleich in 1867 civic education in Austria and Hungary began to differ. Austrian education remained centred around the emperor and the dynasty, Franz Joseph's portrait adorning the walls of every classroom, and Austrian history portraying the personal history of the Habsburgs, with an emphasis on victory and success. In non-German regions of Cisleithania teachers may have presented the party line, but they also extolled the national aspirations of their particular peoples. As for the Hungarians, the Compromise gave them a chance to define education apart from the wishes of Vienna. Whereas education in Austria pushed a kind of 'dynastic religion', Hungary employed civic instruction as the major instrument in a policy of magyarisation, aimed at assimilating the non-Magyar nationalities and building a centralised, modern state.

In Cisleithania education had become the object of the state with the three 'confessional laws' of May 1868. The Catholic Church no longer retained privileges in the sphere of education, even though it continued to struggle to exert its influence. Elementary education was officially under the supervision of the ministry of education, yet actual control rested with the provincial governments. Each province contained a school council, filled with the local governor and local political and religious representatives, and the council decided on the subjects and language of instruction. This explains how the Czechs had been able to establish a school system in their mother tongue by 1914. It should also not be forgotten that most schools were still staffed with graduates of the Catholic seminaries.

The May 1868 school law in Austria also confirmed that eight years of primary education be compulsory, even though in practice the length of school days and school year varied from province to province. It was quite common that rural dwellers did not support eight years of schooling. Austrian education did succeed, however, to improve the

Below Top: The Austrian parliament building was built on the Ring from 1873–1883 in the Neo-Classical style and was designed by the Danish architect Theophil Hansen.

Bottom: The Hungarian parliament building, designed by Imre Steindl, was built on the bank of the Danube in the Neo-Gothic style. Construction commenced in 1885 and the building was inaugurated in 1904.

ratio between literate and illiterate subjects, especially in German-language areas and in Bohemia. The worse cases were in Galicia, Bukovina, and Dalmatia, yet even there, in 1914 less than 10 per cent of school-age children were not attending school.

In Hungary, education remained in the hands of the Church yet there was an increasing number of state schools. Many of these new schools were established in non-Magyar areas, with the objective to magyarise the nationalities. The new Hungarian administration made schooling mandatory for children between the ages of 6 and 12, in 1868, and where parishes did not maintain schools, the state stepped in. Every community with at least 30 school-age children was obliged to have an elementary school. According to the 1868 Nationality Law, instruction in elementary schools could be conducted in the language of the local population, yet this liberal policy was not always adhered to and it was slowly dismantled over time. In 1879 the teaching of the Magyar language in elementary schools was made mandatory, and in 1907, the *Lex Apponyi*, named after the minister of religion and education, Count Albert Apponyi, placed all teachers, including those in Church schools, under the control of the state. All teachers had to read, write, and teach Magyar, and their non-Magyar pupils had to be able to

Above: *Young Bohemians disrupted a sitting of the Reichsrat by creating a riotous noise on 8 June 1900. This print based on a drawing was published in the newspaper* Das Interessante Blatt.

express themselves in the state language by the fourth school year. As in Austria, more and more children in Hungary were receiving an education. By the early 20th century, around 80 per cent were attending school. The regions of northern and eastern Hungary, however, continued to lag behind.

Higher education was also expanding: in Austria, secondary schools (*Mittelschulen*) were administered by the province or were private, and attendance was optional and expensive. Often students would study at secondary schools for an additional eight years, normally in preparation for the university or technical colleges. In Hungary, secondary schools often had religious affiliation; others were created by the state after 1867. Graduates, as in Austria, were prepared to either attend university, enter a profession, or begin an official career. Most secondary school students in Hungary were Magyars, which included assimilated Jews and Germans, and the language of instruction was always Magyar, except in Fiume. There were few universities; those in Vienna and Budapest being the most well-known. The medical faculty of Vienna was actually one of the leading institutions of its kind in the world. During the Compromise era, new universities were created throughout the Monarchy: in Kolozsvár in 1872, in Zagreb in 1874, and another in Czernowitz in 1875.

Heart of the Empire: Vienna, Budapest, Prague, Zagreb
Cities occupied an important position in the struggle between a dynastic world and a

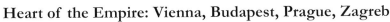

national one in the 19th century. Vienna would in many ways remain an imperial city, but other urban areas began to take on more modern and more important roles as newly defined national centres by the late decades of the century. The cities mirrored the national, as well as the economic and social changes: they became, in the words of the architectural historian Ákos Moravánszky, 'political monuments'. Throughout Europe, and especially in Central Europe, urban centres were restructured and extended in order to demonstrate their new or redefined roles. The former feudal relationships between villages, towns and cities, usually founded on local loyalty, were slowly replaced by a modern, capitalist world with clear administrative centres and often these new centres would or would attempt to take on a national meaning as well.

The three obvious hearts of the Monarchy in the late 19th century were Vienna, Budapest, and Prague, yet Zagreb, as the main city of Croatia–Slavonia, also deserves its place among the them. There were, of course, other principal cities, such as Cracow, Lviv (Lehmberg/Lwów/Lvov), Trieste, Bratislava, Klausenberg (Kolozsvár/Cluj) that could be mentioned, but they were all considerably smaller than the major centres. Yet these other cities do share a common characteristic with Zagreb, more so than with Vienna, Budapest, or Prague: they were cities very much tied to their local environment, not to other capitals or urban centres in the Monarchy or in Europe.

The focus in the following description is on buildings and roads in some of the hearts of the Monarchy. Such architectural landscapes are what today's tourist sees and understands as the history of the Dual Monarchy; objects and places, such as Vienna's Opera and Budapest's Parliament. For the historian, these buildings point to the progress of urban development in the late 19th century as well as highlight the continued struggle as to what these urban centres were supposed to represent. The struggle between historicism and modernism in the building styles is quite obvious in almost all the cities of the Monarchy, and it highlights the continued tension in the Monarchy for control of the future.

Vienna

Historically, Vienna had been a market place, a battlefield, a fortress, the residence of princes, and a site of peace settlements. A visitor to Vienna today may get caught up in the maelstrom of coffeehouses, pastries, wiener schnitzel, and Mozart's life story, but he cannot avoid the impression of being in an imperial city – located in a tiny alpine republic. Vienna has not lost its grandeur, it has only lost its empire. Much of what one sees today, from the Ringstrasse to various objects of Habsburg nostalgia, represents memories of Compromise Austria.

Vienna's location at the point where the Danube River, the only major European river running west to east, exits the Alps and enters the Vienna Basin as it begins to descend through the Hungarian Plain on its way to the Black Sea,

Below: The population of the Austrian Empire – and later the Austro-Hungarian Monarchy – had used the forint, which was partially based on silver, as legal tender since 1754. In 1892 the Monarchy introduced the crown in the Austro-Hungarian Monarchy, which was part of the process of converting the Monarchy to gold cover; the exchange at the time of the conversion was one forint for two crowns. The forint had earlier been divided into 60 krajcárs. With the introduction of the crown one unit was divided into 100: one crown equalled 100 fillers. The new banknote was printed in German on one side and Hungarian on the other. Sometimes the denomination would appear in small letters in other languages of the Monarchy, i.e. Czech, Slovenian, Polish, Ukrainian, Italian, Slovene, Croatian, Serbian and Romanian on the German side of the banknote, but never on the Hungarian side. Figures from literature were placed on the banknotes, as well as boy and girl models and sometimes allegories of science and industry.

was determined by geographical conditions. There is evidence of trade routes passing through the area of Vienna as far back as 1,000 B.C.E. The history of the city itself began with the Roman camp of Vindobona, built to protect the empire from Germanic and other hostile tribes. Yet the Romans eventually were overrun and then retreated. In 976 the Babenberg family received the region from the German King, Otto I, and during the 270 years of Babenberg rule the city flourished and the territory of Ostarrichi, first dated in 996, expanded. In 1246 the Babenberg dynasty died out, and a new family, the Habsburgs arrived and besieged the city in 1276. They would remain for 640 years.

The city became the centre of Habsburg Central Europe as the House of Austria expanded its realm throughout much of the region. The Habsburgs, sitting in Vienna, fought for the maintenance of Roman Catholicism against all reformers. In 1804 the city took on a new role as imperial capital, when Franz I proclaimed the Austrian Empire. It also served as the centre for the diplomatic settlement in 1814–1815, when Europe was reorganised after Napoleon's defeat. And in 1848, in the midst of a revolution demanding change that also spread across the streets of Vienna, Franz Joseph inherited the reins of the Monarchy. The new emperor took back the city and re-established an absolutist state in the years after 1848.

The new Vienna, the Vienna of historical memory, the one that most tourists seek, is the Vienna built by Franz Joseph after 1848. His call for the dismantling of the old city walls would allow the incorporation of many of the suburbs to join the city as new Viennese districts and this new metropolis is best defined by the Ringstrasse. The three-decade long construction began with an imperial decree in December 1857, but not without aesthetic and strategic objections. Some argued that the city walls had been useful in March 1848, when the city's gates could simply be closed to help control the revolution. Nevertheless, architects began work on a broad avenue that would be magnificent and militarily prudent. Yet a focus on grandeur sometimes resulted in simple mistakes: toilets

Above: *The railway station of Érsekújvár (Nové Zamky).*

were not installed in the *Rossauerkaserne* (Rossauer military barracks) that still stand along the Ring today. They had simply been forgotten.

The first public building completed on the Ringstrasse was the Court Opera House, finished in 1869 and criticised for its style by the Viennese public and even by Franz Joseph. Eduard van der Nüll, one of the architects, was so bothered by the criticism that he took his own life before the official opening of the building. Legend has it that this tragedy caused Franz Joseph thereafter to refrain from public criticism and to always issue the same standard phrase on all occasions: *Es war sehr schön. Es hat mich sehr gefreut.* (It was very beautiful. I liked it a lot) Later, before World War I, the young Adolf Hitler swooned with reverence at the sight of the Viennese Opera and other Ringstrasse buildings.

Along the Ringstrasse numerous other public buildings and public monuments were built: the Parliament, the twin museums of art history and natural history, new wings to the Hofburg (the imperial palace), the Court Theatre, the city hall, the building of the University of Vienna, as well as other public buildings and private dwellings. The buildings represent an eclectic conglomeration of many architectural styles, whose mixture became a style of its own: the Ringstrassenstil. And in the late 19th and early 20th centuries this new Ringstrasse style was imitated in many public buildings (post offices, theatres, train stations, apartment houses) throughout the Monarchy.

*Below: Newly built railway stations were a favourite theme of the picture postcards of the day.
The Bahnhofplatz in Brno,1908.*

The Ringstrassenstil and the world represented by the grand avenue also called forth its opposite. Austrian architects rebelled against this pompousness. Divergent voices, such as Camillo Sitte, the 'romantic archaist,' and Otto Wagner, 'the rational functionalist,' found much to reprove in the new Viennese style. As Carl E. Schorske has argued, Camillo Sitte criticised the builders for 'their betrayal of the tradition to the exigencies of modern life,' whereas Otto Wagner denounced 'the masking of modernity and its functions behind the stylistic screens of history.' Architects, such as Wagner, instigated a different style, a modern, art nouveau style, that not only opposed the Ringstrassenstil, but put forth an alternative, that for many scholars and tourists is also characteristic of Franz Joseph's fin de siècle Vienna. Wagner's Postal Savings Bank, sitting on the opposite side of the Ring from the grand Ministry of Warfare, may not be the first site visited by a tourist in Vienna, but it is high on the list of art nouveau fans. Perhaps Wagner's greatest influence is

Above: Keleti (Eastern) Railway Station in Budapest.

epitomised in his designs of the Stadtbahn transit system and the dams and quayside installations along the Danube Canal. Most of his other plans, for museums, ministries, bridges, monuments, churches, and city districts, were not put into effect.

Budapest

The city of Budapest can be found on many maps and in many histories of 19th-century

Left: The railway station of Gyékényes.

Above: Factories were constructed along the railway line and the country's chief means of transport gave a boost to the economy wherever it progressed.

Europe, yet the union of Buda, the royal centre of power, Pest, the booming industrial city, and Óbuda, the agricultural and market town as well as former Roman centre, only took place on 17 November 1873. At that time Budapest became Hungary's capital, and only from that date forward can we really speak of one unified city. The revolutionary government in 1848 had been interested in union, but such plans never came to fruition. However, in the years following the failed revolution several projects prepared the towns for unification. The famous Chain Bridge (Lánchíd) was erected in 1849, connecting Buda and Pest. A Capital Public Works Commission for financing and managing city development was set up in 1870, and perhaps the most important event that influenced the creation of Budapest was the 1867 Compromise itself.

A Hungarian statesman in 1848 had voiced the opinion that Budapest was not Hungary in the same way that Paris was France, but that attitude changed by the end of the century, when most people agreed that 'Budapest is the heart of Hungary.' By the late 1800s Budapest had become a major city and the capital of half the Habsburg Monarchy. Its path to city-status was not as smooth as that of Vienna, which had already established itself as a privileged burgher town in the Middle Ages. The growth and development of Pest–Buda was stunted at the turn of the 15th and 16th centuries and halted by the Ottoman occupation in the early 16th century. Things only began to change for Pest–Buda in the 18th century, especially during Maria Theresa's reign. Even before her ascent to the throne in 1745, the royal court had moved from Pressburg to Pest in 1723. A university was established in Buda in 1777, and Maria Theresa's son, Joseph II, set up his administrative seat in Buda. Many commercial interests were based in Pest, and new buildings were built there. The city grew, just like Vienna. It received the status of capital town with a royal residence in 1892. By 1910 there were 1.1 million inhabitants.

A modern-day visitor to Budapest will not find an exact equivalent to the Ringstrasse of Vienna, but many of the roads and boulevards defining Pest do call forth similarities. Perhaps the closest in grandeur and elegance is today's Andrássy út, originally named Sugár út (Radial Road). Construction started in 1871, even before the unification of

The period of construction, i.e. the Gründerzeit, and that of civic pride. This self-esteem and confidence manifests itself in the postcards of the period.

Right: The building of the Museum of Applied Arts on Üllői Road was one of the most outstanding achievements of the Hungarian Secession.

Far right: The main square in Koblenz was almost completely covered with café tables.

Below: The centre of Kolozsvár with the building of New York Hotel.

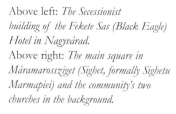

Above left: *The Secessionist building of the Fekete Sas (Black Eagle) Hotel in Nagyvárad.*
Above right: *The main square in Máramarossziget (Sighet, formally Sighetu Marmapiei) and the community's two churches in the background.*

Pest–Buda, when the city began to demolish 142 old houses in the Terézváros district of Pest. When designing and building the Sugár út the goal was to create a road that would be, in the words of Péter Hanák, 'imposing, a broad, spacious promenade expressive of Budapest's status as a great city.' Its construction was meant to help centre the new twin city in the heart of Pest. And it was under Andrássy út that continental Europe's first electric subway was put into operation in 1896.

Another major thoroughfare in Budapest was the Nagykörút (Grand Boulevard) that opened in 1896, during the millennial celebration of the Hungarians' arrival in the Carpathian Basin. It took more than two decades to build the Nagykörút's two and three-quarter-mile length from Boráros square to the Margaret Bridge. Whereas the Ringstrasse in Vienna demonstrated the grandeur of Franz Joseph, the Nagykörút served an economic and social purpose, connecting the inner and outer districts of the city. Péter Hanák argues that in contrast to the Ringstrasse, the Nagykörút had 'a combining and levelling nature, binding together the inner area and the rapidly integrating outer areas.' It also did not possess the grand buildings of the Ring, other than the National Theatre and the Vígszínház (Gaiety Theatre).

The architectural style found along the Nagykörút and the Sugár út also differed from that of the Ringstrasse. The Ringstrasse mixed styles and developed its own style, which in many ways represented the pomp of the emperor and the growing *haute bourgeoisie* (the high middle class defined by money and achievement). In Budapest the style was also mixed, negatively described by some as the work of an upstart *haute bourgeoisie* unable to master their own ideas. Others have characterised the Budapest style as 'eclectic.' Perhaps the real difference between Vienna and Budapest was that the Ringstrasse

Left: *A kindergarten in Holešovice (one of Prague's quarters), around 1900. Photo by J. Eckert*

was lined with representational structures, unlike the Sugár út or the Nagykörút. Sugár út, with its residential buildings, was a show street. The Nagykörút's goal was to improve traffic flow and connect parts of the growing metropolis.

In addition to thoroughfares and houses, the Budapest leaders also began to build grandiose structures to demonstrate Budapest's capital status in the late 19th century. Budapest was to be seen as an equal to Vienna. As mentioned, the Chain Bridge (Lánchíd) had been built in 1849, and in the late 19th century five more bridges were constructed in order to connect Buda and Pest better: four bridges for road traffic and one for the railroad.

At the millennial celebration of 1896, Franz Joseph laid the foundation stone for the Royal Palace, a reconstructed building that would consist of 860 rooms. The magnificent Parliament, in neo-Gothic style, was built along the Danube in Pest, and in 1904 it replaced the earlier seat of parliament in the Sándor Utca Palace (today the Italian Institute in the Bródy Sándor utca). The Gothic style of the Parliament was not only influenced by the neo-Gothic Parliament building in London (constructed between 1835 and 1860), but was also meant to recreate a style from Hungary's golden age.

Above: *Schoolboy in Jablonec, around 1890. Photo by A. Ulrich*

Budapest also differed from Vienna in another important aspect. Péter Hanák has argued that 'Pest was a city of factories, not gardens: the workshop of Hungary's bourgeois development.' Vienna, on the other hand, was a 'green' city: first to the land-owning magnates and then to the city fathers. 'Vienna is truly a garden city.' But because Budapest sped forward trying to catch-up, little thought was given to future problems of urbanisation. One obvious case in point is the high density of buildings. Even in the inner part of the city rows of houses stretched for long distances, without cross streets. 'The city has no emphatic centre, few spacious squares, and relatively little green open space, at least in the seven inner districts of Pest, where the proportion of open space is a tiny 1.3 per cent of the built-up area.' At the time the Városliget (city park) and Népliget (people's park) were on the edge of the city, and Margaret Island was closed to the general public. (The Buda side of the river, however, has more green spaces, and did not experience the affects of industrialisation to the same degree as Pest.)

Prague

The Dual Monarchy had two unofficial capitals: Vienna and Budapest, but other regions of Austria–Hungary also developed urban centres. By the late 19th century there were in actuality at least three centres of gravity in the region: the Alpine hereditary lands (today's Austria), Hungary, and Bohemia. The centre of Bohemia, Prague, could still be described as a 'provincial backwater' in 1895, with a population of less than 350,000. But, like Vienna and Budapest, it was growing at lightning speed. Unlike Vienna and Budapest, however,

Above: *Schoolboy, around 1878. Unknown photographer.*

Prague was the capital of a single crown land, Bohemia, not half of Austria–Hungary. Its local role was a strong element of its identity as compared to other cities.

Prague had established itself as an important trading centre, but it had begun to decline by the time it fell under Habsburg rule in 1526; and subsequently it became subservient to Vienna. For a short time under Rudolph II (1576–1612) the Habsburgs

Spacious, large-scale, sunlit schools with wide corridors and modern gymnasiums were built throughout the Monarchy.

Right: *This school built in 1910–1912 in Budapest on commission from the capital was designed by Ernő Balázs.*

Below: *A detail from the mosaic ornamentation on the façade.*

Above: *The main building of the Viennese University on the Ring (1877–1884).*

moved their court to Prague, but upon Rudolph's death returned it to Vienna. The tension always remained high between Prague and Vienna. The 1618 revolt of the Bohemian nobility sparked the Thirty Years' War, which would clearly define Prague's secondary position in the region, under the domination of Vienna. Prague, as most of Bohemia, would feel the affects of industrialisation and a growing Czech nationalism during the 19th century. The city and its inhabitants would begin a real battle with authorities in Vienna for equal representation, some form of autonomy, and respect for their new national ambitions.

As the other urban centres mentioned above, Prague had been a multilingual city with a large German-speaking population in the 19th century. Vienna was, of course, a German-speaking city, but with Czech, Slovak, and Magyar immigrants, the majority of whom were too politically and economically weak to counterbalance the dominant German speakers. Budapest, as well, had been a German-speaking city in the early part of the 19th century. This only changed because of magyarisation efforts encouraging assimilation to Magyardom in the second half of the century. Prague was also mainly German speaking. In the mid 19th century there were more than twice as many German speakers in Prague as Czech speakers. (Jews were also overwhelmingly counted as German speakers.) Some of these German speakers were descendants of German immigrants, but the majority of them were people of various backgrounds who had adopted the German language and culture as part of the modernising trends in government, education, and commerce. The layout of Prague is similar to that of Budapest, with the Vltava River instead of the Danube River running through the centre. The narrower Vltava actually allowed the two halves, one with the castle hill and the other a flat area just like Pest, to be more closely integrated than Pest and Buda. Yet whereas Budapest responded to city growth in the late 19th century by incorporating neighbouring suburbs, Prague faced political obstacles. Subservient to Vienna, Prague often suffered from the empire's objection to increasing the city's political position in Cisleithania. Prague's wish to incorporate outlaying areas into the city

Above: *Girls skating in the courtyard of the Erzsébet School for Girls (now Teleki Blanka Secondary School). At its opening in 1872 it was a teacher training college for ladies and one of the pioneering institutions in female education. It has been a secondary school since 1928. The building was designed by Sándor Baumgartner and Zsigmond Herczegh.*

was rejected by Vienna in 1849. At the time, nearby towns also voiced opposition to joining an expanding Prague. The city, therefore, would not be able to incorporate many neighbouring areas until it became the capital of the independent Czechoslovak state after World War I.

Nevertheless, population growth forced Prague to act and Vienna to accommodate in some way. From 1873 and continuing into the 1880s, the city leaders demolished the city's remaining ramparts and destroyed the densely packed Jewish quarter, infamous for fires and epidemics. In their places new buildings and streets were erected, mixing historicism and art nouveau. These changes were expensive for Prague, since the city had to buy the wide esplanade of its baroque fortifications from Vienna, and Vienna was not interested in selling it cheap as it often had in German-controlled municipalities. As a consequence, the city was forced to subdivide the land and sell lots to developers and contractors, which prevented the building of a tree-lined avenue as in Vienna.

Prague's street design also made it difficult for city planners to imitate Vienna's Ringstrasse or Budapest's Andrássy út. One could argue that the 'Golden Cross' in the centre of Prague was an attempt to build a 'metropolitan promenade.' This consisted of three streets, Na Příkopě, Národní třída and Wenceslas Square (Wenceslas Square, the city's former horse market, is in many ways more of a broad boulevard itself than a real square.) One could also consider the Pařížská Avenue, named after the city of Paris, as an elaborate boulevard in the spirit of Vienna's Ringstrasse. Pařížská clearly became the focus of redevelopment activity in the modernised centre of Prague. Instead of serving as a bridge between the historical centre and the Letná Plain, as it was initially imagined, Pařížská Avenue was eventually lined with ornamented apartment blocks and shops, leaving it looking much more modern in style than the Ringstrasse.

Above: *The Institute for the Blind, built in 1901, is situated next to the Erzsébet School for Girls and was also designed by Baumgarten and Zsigmond Herczegh.*

Prague differs today from both Vienna and Budapest in its lack of emphasis on the Habsburg past. In the other cities one cannot avoid images of the ruling family, perhaps more so in Vienna than in Budapest, but in Prague the Habsburg era is simply one of many historical periods. The visitor to Prague may also see the city as more medieval or more baroque than other Central European cities, but that is not the case, if one veers off the tourist path. Prague was a centre for modernism, and it experienced the effects of the architectural struggle between historicism and modernism during the Dual Monarchy.

Zagreb

In addition to Vienna, Budapest, and Prague, there were a number of other growing urban centres in the Monarchy, such as Zagreb. Today Zagreb, sitting between Mount Medvednica and the Sava River, is the capital of the independent country of Croatia, but the city and region had existed under foreign and domestic rule for centuries. At the beginning of the 12th century, the Croatians recognised the Hungarian King as the common ruler of Hungary and Croatia, and in 1526 this common kingship was inherited by the Habsburgs. At the same time, the encroaching Ottoman Empire began occupying Croatian-Slavonian territory, and much of the region fell under Turkish control. The Habsburgs recaptured all of the territory of Croatia–Slavonia in the late 17th century, and by the 19th century the city of Zagreb began to take on an even more important position in the semi-autonomous region of Croatia-Slavonia within the Kingdom of Hungary.

Similarly to Prague, Zagreb planners also had difficulties voicing their opinions regarding Zagreb's urban expansion. Most decisions rested on the will of the Austrian and Hungarian authorities. When a plan arose in the late 19th century to emulate the grand boulevards of the Monarchy, such as the Ringstrasse in Vienna and Andrássy út in Budapest, problems were expected. The planners, however, avoided direct confrontation by creating numerous fait accomplis; they built skating rinks, soccer fields, tennis courts, and a university building along what would later become a series of squares shaped in a U, facing the old town. This grand boulevard design could not be curved, like a ring street, since the streets of Zagreb followed a fairly strict grid, with only slight irregularities. It was in the end lined with parks and public buildings along the three (eastern, southern, and western) sides. There were similarities with the Ringstrasse of Vienna, mainly in its local grandeur, but it did not serve the same purpose of a grand boulevard in the imperial centre. Today the visitor to Zagreb cannot avoid this U-shaped series of parks and promenades now referred to as the 'Green Horseshoe,' since along its sides sit most of Zagreb's squares, parks, cultural institutions, and museums.

With the decree to tear down the old city walls the ruler made it possible for numerous outlying areas to become part of Vienna as districts.

Right: *a detail of the city wall.*

Above: *In 1874 the university observatory was built on this site. The huge building was designed by the prominent Viennese architects Ferdinand Fellner and Hermann Hellmer, who were renowned in the Monarchy for theatre design.*

Head of the Empire

The leadership of the Dual Monarchy rested in the hands of its sovereign, the Emperor of Austria and the King of Hungary. After 1867 the emperor-king also kept many of the titles of earlier times, but it was his control over the lands of Cisleithania (the Kingdoms and Lands represented in the Reichsrat) and the Kingdom of Hungary, including Croatia–Slavonia, that defined his rule. For all but the last two years of the period under investigation Franz Joseph held this position. He led the Monarchy into the 20th century and into the Great War of 1914. Charles, Franz Joseph's great-nephew, succeeded Franz Joseph and officially ruled for only two years, until the dissolution of his realm. 'Officially', since Charles never abdicated. He died in 1922 in exile, after two failed resurrection attempts in Hungary.

It may have become unfashionable to focus on political leaders – the great men of history – but no story of a dynastic state, such as Austria–Hungary, can avoid it. We may want to call both Austria and Hungary constitutional states, but they remained in the hands of one leader: Franz Joseph. Certain aspects of state, especially the military, were exclusively under his authority. His decisions would affect all segments of society, from the aristocracy to the rural peasants.

Guidebooks and tourist objects, the kind one finds today in Vienna, portray Franz Joseph as the grand old Emperor. His life spanned the rule of 18 American presidents. The image of Franz Joseph, similarly to the view of the Habsburg Monarchy in general, has become more amiable in the second half of the 20th century, as compared to the very critical studies of him written and published during the interwar years. The earlier anti-Habsburg and anti-Franz Joseph rhetoric common in public opinion often died down, as most of the successor states by the 1930s proved to be even more intolerant and authoritarian. A positive Habsburg myth has more recently taken hold.

Franz Joseph became Emperor of Austria on 2 December 1848, in the middle of a revolution. At the time, the Habsburg family was sitting in Olmütz, as it had fled Vienna because of the revolutionary unrest. The family chose to pass the throne to the 18-year-old Franz with the objective of strengthening the Monarchy and the monarchical principles. Franz chose on that day in December the imperial title 'Franz

Below: The Royal Opera House was the first public building to be constructed on the Ring in 1869 and it immediately drew the criticism of the Viennese public and that of Franz Joseph. Edward van der Nüll, one of the building's architects, was so embittered by what the critics said that he committed suicide even before the official opening. According to popular legend, it was Franz Joseph who caused the tragedy and from this point on he refrained from expressing any kind of public criticism. This is supported by the fact that on every such occasion where his opinion was expected he would only repeat the same phrase: 'Es war sehr schön. Es hat mich sehr gefreut'. (It was very beautiful. I liked it a lot). Later the young Adolf Hitler would swoon with admiration at the sight of the Viennese Opera and the other buildings on the Ringstrasse.

Far left: *The Kunsthistorisches Museum (Museum of Art History) opened its gates to the public in 1891. The monumental building in the Italian Neo-Renaissance style was designed by Gottfried Semper (1803–1879) and Karl von Hasenauer (1833–1894), as was the Naturhistorisches Museum (Natural History Museum) that stands opposite it at the other side of the square.*

Left: *The Rossauer Barracks (Kaserne) built in 1887 on the banks of the Danube channel.*

Above: *The Burgtheater, designed by Semper and Hasenauer, was the national theatre of Austrians. Its façade is ornamented with the busts of famous poets (Calderon, Shakespeare, Moliere, Schiller, Goethe, Lessing, Halm, Grillparzer and Hebbel).*

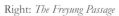

Right: *The Freyung Passage*

Right: *Otto Wagner (1841–1918), who had a fundamentally classical education, designed his own villa on the crest of a hill using classical architectural elements. Huge pillars are set in front of the building's covered entrance and the steps are lined by decorative, cast iron railings.*

Below right: *He and his fellow architects, then later his students, significantly renewed Austrian architecture and applied arts. In addition to the Viennese metro station and other structures he also designed the metro's building on Karlplatz.*

Left: *Typical Viennese street scene.*

Wagner and similar architects inspired the creation of a completely different, modern art nouveau style, which not only followed another direction than the style on the Ringstrasse but provided an alternative that in the eyes of many researchers and tourists became typical of Franz Joseph's Vienna at the turn of the century. Wagner's Post Office Savings bank stands opposite the huge building of the Ministry of Defence on the Ring, and although it is perhaps not the first port of call for tourists coming to Vienna, it is nevertheless to be found somewhere at the top of the art nouveau fan's list.

Left: *Another one of his well-known works is the Wienzeile apartment house complex that rises up behind the market (Naschmarkt).*

It is perhaps the case that Wagner's approach and influence are best shown in his design of the city's tram network as well as in the works of art along the Danube-channel's dams and wharfs. He drew up other designs for museums, ministry buildings, bridges, monuments, churches and whole city quarters but they were not realised.

Right: *It would appear that when designing the imperial station in Schönbrunn, Wagner made certain compromises to accord with the emperor's taste. However, Franz Joseph never used the building that was constructed especially for him and decorated with his initials.*

Right: *In 1870 the Municipal Public Works
Council was established with the objective of
developing the city. Its president was the
prevailing prime minister but the actual work
of the council was directed by the deputy-
president. From 1873 until 1905 this
function was performed by Baron Frigyes
Podmaniczky. As a young man Podmaniczky
was mainly interested in women and grand
balls. However, after the failure of the
revolution and upon his return to Pest in
1856 he was shaken by the extent of the
neglect and poverty in the city. As he later
wrote, 'I pledged that … I would set myself
the aim of improving our capital as the central
ideal of my life.' He was true to his oath and
in his capacity of deputy-president of the
Municipal Public Works Council he did a lot
for Budapest's development.*

Joseph I' in recognition of his grandfather, Franz
I (II), and his great uncle, Joseph II. Franz Joseph
had been educated in the spirit of the court, thus
he believed that his family had been chosen by
God to do his bidding, and that they should live
their lives in his service. The role of the sovereign
was to serve the people, a goal that Franz Joseph
maintained throughout his whole life. He saw
himself as the 'first servant' of his peoples. Yet in
this light, it was Franz Joseph who knew what
was best for all; no one else enjoyed the right to
decide what would make them happy.

After putting down the rebellions throughout
the Monarchy in 1848 and 1849, followed by the
execution of 13 Hungarian generals at Arad, Franz Joseph implemented a kind of neo-
absolutism characterised by censorship, police control, strict laws, and tough measures.
He gave the Catholic Church in the 1855 Concordat certain rights over education and
marital matters. Franz Joseph, as well as his controlling mother, grew very unpopular,
and in 1853 there was an attempt on his life. Yet during this era of tight control, Franz
Joseph also began to implement reforms and tore down the Vienna walls to build the
Ringstrasse and its numerous imperial buildings.

In 1854 Franz Joseph married his first cousin Elizabeth of Bavaria by whom he had
four children (*see page 45*). He loved the army and was a German military man receiving
his first uniform when he was 3 and his first regiment at 13. The army belonged to him,
and he rarely appeared in public without a military uniform. Yet, unfortunately, every

*When the new 19th-century
Budapest was built the medieval and
even classical city of the beginning of
the century disappeared.*

Right: *In the top picture is
Ferenciek Square before the 1880s
with the building of the University
Library, still standing, on the left
and the classical building of
Atheneum Printers, subsequently
demolished, on the right. The
building housing the famous Café
Central was built soon after, on the
site of the ground floor level of the
house in the background. The
locality in the lower picture has
changed little.*

military endeavour in the mid-19th century
ended in defeat or isolation for Franz Joseph
and the Austrian Empire. The Crimean War,
1853 to 1856, left Austria isolated. The
conflict with Sardinia and France, which
Franz Joseph led himself as Generalissimus,
ended in defeat at Magenta and Solferino, the
only two battles of the war and the defeat by
Prussia in the Seven-Weeks' war in 1866
ended Franz Joseph's hopes of an Austrian-
led Greater Germany, even though he never
gave up on the thought of himself as a
German prince.

With the unity of the Monarchy as his
primary goal after 1866, Franz Joseph went
about reorganising his lands. Despite the
Czech proposal of a federalist solution, he
signed an agreement with the Magyars in
1867 creating the Dual Monarchy. This
agreement, which he considered final, even
though the Magyars viewed it as the starting
point for further negotiations, defined the
last stage of Franz Joseph's realm until its
dissolution in 1918. It allowed Franz Joseph
to be finally crowned King of Hungary, a title

that the Habsburgs had held since 1526. (He was never crowned King of Bohemia.) The ceremony took place in Budapest on 8 June 1867. The city awoke at 4 a.m. to 21 cannon shots proclaiming coronation day. The spectacle was unprecedented. Large crowds awaited the king, who rode through the city wearing the sword and crown of St Stephen. In the parish church of Pest, Franz Joseph, holding a crucifix in his left hand and raising three fingers on his right hand, swore to uphold the Hungarian constitution and preserve the territorial integrity of the country.

The last decade before the turn of century was very difficult for Franz Joseph. His son Rudolf, the heir apparent, committed suicide in 1889, and his beloved wife Elizabeth was assassinated by an Italian anarchist on the quay in Geneva on 10

Left: *The location of the Nagykörút (Great Boulevard) was once occupied by one of the Danube's river branches. When it became necessary to join the already built avenues the idea arose to construct a navigable channel that would run within Budapest, but this idea was later abandoned. The road cut across many still existing but, at the time, haphazard streets (Király Street, Dob Street, and Fűzfa/now Dohány Street) sweeping away the numerous one-floor buildings in its path. It primarily became a residential area and trade route on which rows of hotels (e.g. the New York Hotel, and the Royal Hotel) were also built throughout the decades. Various sections of the Great Boulevard were later named after members of the royal family out of respect, so there was an Elizabeth Boulevard, a Joseph Boulevard and a Franz Boulevard. Originally almost all the buildings on the road had been built in the Eclectic or historical style.*

September 1898. (His brother Maximilian had been court-martialled and shot by Mexican revolutionaries in 1867.) Franz Joseph may not have had a deep devotion to his son, but his tragic death was difficult for him as it was for his wife Elizabeth. Sisi's assassination was even more devastating for the emperor-king. Typical of his character, he simply replied upon hearing of her death: 'Is nothing spared me on this earth?'

Franz Joseph was a solitary man. He adored his wife, but she preferred to be out of Vienna and consequently not near her husband. He was not interested in members of his family, except perhaps his youngest daughter Maria Valerie and her children. He was not fond of his brother Ludwig Viktor, who became heir for a short time after Rudolf's death. Franz Joseph liked some, but not all his fellow European monarchs; his only close friend being Albert of Saxony. The emperor-king did grow close to the Burgtheater actress, Katherina Schratt, yet their almost daily meetings never evolved beyond a platonic friendship.

Franz Joseph was a simple and diligent worker; he slept in an iron bed and was at his desk by 5 a.m. every day in order to start going through documents. At 8 a.m. he began receiving audiences with his ministers. He never took a break and would work into the evening. His days, especially after 1890 focused more and more on the governing of the Monarchy, and he became more willing to leave the minutiae to his ministers. Twice a week Franz Joseph held general audiences with anyone who wished to speak with the

monarch. This, however, was more about his public image than about remedying the ills of the common man, and his frequent visits to the provinces were also more for the purpose of representation and pomp than for actually investigating the needs of the people. Franz Joseph lived an ordered life; he did not like disruption or disturbance. Even on the day he died, 21 November 1916, he spent the morning working at his desk. Upon retiring to rest in the afternoon, he asked for 'a little water,' and these were his last words.

Rudolf and Franz Ferdinand

Franz Joseph and Elizabeth had four children: three daughters, of whom the eldest died in infancy, and one son, Rudolph. Rudolph was born on 21 August 1858; he was intelligent and well liked. He had a gift for languages, which was an advantage for the heir to a realm of more than 11 nationalities. Unlike his father, but more like his mother, he rebelled against traditional court life and found friends in artistic circles, among Liberals and Jews, yet there was little hope that Rudolph would have become a Liberal Monarch. Relations with his father were tense. He openly disagreed

Above: *The Neo-Renaissance building standing opposite the opera had formerly housed the famous Dreschsler Coffee House.*

Above: *The first underground railway in continental Europe was built under Andrássy Road.*

Right: A huge Hungarian coat-of-arms made out of mosaics can be seen on the side of Várhegy (Castle Hill).

Below: The construction of Andrássy Road began in 1871 – even before the Pest–Buda unification – with the demolition of 142 houses in the Terézváros district. At the time when they were planned and built the avenues were of elemental beauty and importance. In Péter Hanák's words, 'It was a wide and spacious promenade, which was symbolic of Budapest's status as a big city'. By building the road a new twin city centre was created in the heart of Budapest. 'Andrássy Road stretched across Budapest like the Danube stretches across Hungary. Nobody could just pass by it, live without it or ignore it. Nobody could compete with Andrássy Road in Pest, it was the city's hope,' wrote Gyula Krúdy.

Below: Franz Joseph Bridge (now Szabadság híd – Liberty Bridge) was opened up to traffic in the year of the millennium. It is Budapest's shortest bridge and it links together Vámház Square and Gellért Square. On the Buda side looms Hotel Gellért, which was built in the Secessionist style in the same period. One of the typical features of the bridge is its portal ornamented with the historical Hungarian coat-of-arms and the mythical eagle of the ancient Hungarians set atop its pillars.

Left: The Post Office Savings Bank (now the Hungarian National Bank) building designed by Ödön Lechner, the most well-known representative of the Hungarian Secession, is located in downtown Budapest. Lechner's name is associated with the creation of the Hungarian Secession and the use of eastern motifs, as well as the ornamented majolica with Secessionist Hungarian motifs, or to be more precise the architectural application of the pyrogranite created by the Zsolnay factory. Lechner also designed the Museum of Fine Arts and the Institute of Geology buildings (both of which are in Budapest) and public buildings, private houses and churches were constructed all over the country based on his designs (Pozsony, Kecskemét, Miskolc).

with Franz Joseph on the emperor-king's anti-liberal policies, his continued adherence to a close relationship with Germany, and Austria's Bosnian activities. Franz Joseph, therefore, ignored his son and excluded him from any serious role in public affairs.

On a personal level, Rudolph suffered in his love life. On 10 May 1881, he married the Belgian Princess Stephanie, who failed to live up to his unfulfillable expectations, and he sought refuge with a number of mistresses. One of them, the Baroness Marie Vetsera, was found dead next to him on 30 January 1889 in the hunting lodge of Mayerling, just outside of Vienna. The tragedy was never entirely cleared up, since the details of the event were immediately declared classified. Yet today most accounts agree that it was suicide. Rudolph chose to end his life and convinced his young lover to join him.

Rudolph and Stephanie only had one daughter, so his death left Franz Joseph's brother, Karl Ludwig, heir to the throne. But Karl Ludwig died in 1896. His eldest son, Franz Ferdinand, was thus next in succession to the throne. Born in 1863, Franz Ferdinand was a military man. He had served in the Austrian infantry and cavalry, during which time he developed an intense aversion to the Hungarians. In 1898 he became acting deputy to the emperor in all military matters, yet Franz Joseph was reluctant to give his nephew any real power. At the time of his assassination in June 1914, Franz Ferdinand was Inspector General of the combined armed forces, and it was in that capacity that he was attending military maneouvres in Bosnia.

Franz Ferdinand had an unhappy youth plagued by ill health. Things were so severe that certain circles assumed an early death and therefore began to court his younger brother, Otto. Franz Ferdinand has also been described by historians as 'a very nasty man.' He was clearly a troubled soul. He, like his uncle, had an interest in hunting, but, unlike Franz Joseph, this hobby did not reflect his fairness or sympathy for animals. Hunting was not a sport, but rather a sign of his superiority. He often boasted that he had shot over 200,000 wild animals, including hundreds of tigers. Instead of enjoying the sport of the hunt, Franz Ferdinand just liked to shoot animals. He would have stags driven in front of him in order not to miss. He also had fattened, slow pheasants put up in front of him, again to assist him in attaining quantity in his shoot.

His relations with the emperor were further strained when he chose to marry Countess Sophie Chotek, a member of the Bohemian aristocracy, but not of equal rank to the Habsburgs. Franz Joseph gave his blessing to their union only after Franz Ferdinand agreed to a morganatic marriage, preventing any of their offspring from gaining rights to the throne. Sophie Chotek was not an equal; she did receive the title 'Princess,' but this was a far inferior rank to that of Archduchess. It is interesting that the two men who treated Franz Ferdinand's bride with full deference, the German Emperor and the King of Romania, received Franz Ferdinand's friendship in return.

Left: *'Golden Crossroad' is perhaps the only promenade that conjures up a big city atmosphere. It is here that three 'streets'– Na Příkopé, Narodni třida and Vencel Square – come together. The latter, which was formally a horse market, rather gives the impression of being a wide road than a square.*

The alliance with Germany was key to his foreign policy.

Franz Ferdinand set up base in the Belvedere Palace in Vienna, which became a kind of second court in the last decades of the Monarchy. His disagreements with the emperor led him to begin creating his own policies from the Belvedere. In his shadow government Franz Ferdinand was apprised of activities throughout the realm and established close contacts with domestic and international parties and individuals. As future sovereign of Austria–Hungary, his ultimate goal was not unlike Franz Joseph's: to maintain the integrity of the Monarchy. Even his unsympathetic views of Hungary, Italy, and Serbia, were more about their positions as disruptive elements to the status quo. Any suspicion of a pro-Slav sentiment on his part is disproven by his clear dislike of Poles and Czechs, notwithstanding his wife's background. It is possible that his intense aversion to the Hungarians may have been inspired by his inability to learn the Hungarian language, as he was a poor linguist. In addition to a close friendship with Germany and its Emperor, Franz Ferdinand was fond of imperial Russia, and it would have pleased him to have recreated the *Dreikaiserbund* (Three Emperors' League).

Charles, the great-nephew of Franz Joseph and nephew of Franz Ferdinand, inherited the position as heir presumptive on Franz Ferdinand's assassination in the summer of 1914. Charles had been born in Lower Austria in 1887 and received a very strict Catholic, aristocratic, and military upbringing. He, like Franz Joseph and Franz Ferdinand, believed in imperial destiny and the need to hold the Monarchy together. Also like his uncle, he was a military man; he began his military career in 1905 in the Austrian cavalry. But unlike his uncle, he veered away from politics. In the decision-making process in the summer and autumn of 1914 Charles was absent, but in August 1914 he took over the Army high command in Teschen and later in March 1916 he became field marshal-lieutenant of the 20th Battalion.

Above: *Central Hotel, one of the pearls of Secessionist Prague.*

Charles, Zita and Otto

After the death of Franz Joseph, Charles inherited the throne on 21 November 1916. Charles's main interest was in ending the conflict. At the end of 1916 Charles attempted through his wife's brother, Prince Sixtus von Bourbon-Parma, to open channels for peace discussions in France. The letter to Sixtus made clear that France's demand for the return of Alsace-Lorraine would be honoured. Even though France and Britain welcomed these advances, they were stopped by the Italian objection, since Italy's

Above: *The historical centre of Prague, which has been a World Heritage site since 1992.*

*Zagreb – a detail (*right*) of the famous 'green horseshoe', and a beautiful passage connecting to a bank. (*below*)*

interests were not being addressed. Later peace feelers, via the Pope, the King of Spain, and the King of Belgium also got nowhere, since Austria–Hungary continued to be viewed as an extension of Germany. The Dual Monarchy's participation in the peace with Soviet Russia in March 1918 and its occupation of Ukraine led the allies not only to refuse to negotiate with Charles, but also to support the carving up of the Monarchy into national parts.

More so than any of his predecessors, Charles was a reformer, but always within the framework of a united Monarchy. He tried, but failed, in 1917, shortly after the February Revolution in Russia, to convince the Hungarians to expand the franchise in Hungary. Also in reaction to the illusion of a democratic revolution in Russia, Charles and his advisers decided to reconvene the Cisleithanian parliament, which had not met since 1914. (For three years Cisleithania had been ruled without a parliament; decisions were passed according to paragraph 14 of the 1867 constitution.) Charles also pardoned many political prisoners. In a last ditch effort to save the Monarchy, or at least the western half, Charles issued what became known as his *People's Manifesto* in October 1918, which was to transform the Austrian half of the Monarchy into a federal state of autonomous national units. (On the same day, Hungary ended the Ausgleich.)

At war's end Charles was forced to resign his powers and leave Austria. Anti-Habsburg laws were passed in the new Austrian Republic in April 1919, deposing Charles I. Charles attempted twice in 1921 to retake his throne, which he had never officially abdicated, but he was turned back, the second time after a small battle on the outskirts of Budapest. On 6 November 1921, Hungary passed laws dethroning the Habsburgs, but leaving open the possibility that in the future a Habsburg could be elected king. Charles died a lonely death on the island of Madeira on 1 April 1922. His wife, Zita, lived until 1988, at which time she was buried with full pomp and circumstance in Vienna.

Charles's legacy is a complicated one. He only ruled for two years. Helmut Rumpler of the Austrian Academy of Sciences has described Charles as a 'dilettante, far too weak for the challenges facing him, out of his depth, and not really a politician.' Yet after the Second World War, beginning in 1949, Charles's interest in peace and reform, as well as his role as a 'Christian statesman' has led to a campaign for his canonisation. In October 2004 he was beatified by Pope John Paul II, and currently one more documented miracle is necessary for his canonisation as a saint in the Roman Catholic Church.

Tissue of the Body, Society and Politics

The political climate of the Dual Monarchy was determined by balancing the maintenance

Above: *The Karácsonyi Palace (built 1883–1884), now the presidential office building on Stefania, in the centre of Pozsony.*

Below: *The building of Jagelló University in Krakow, constructed in the Neo-Gothic style.*

Above: *Lviv (Lemberg), the capital of Galicia. Its main square, the Market (Rinok), is flanked by beautiful palaces in varied styles. The famous 'black house' (Anczewsky house) now houses the Lemberg Museum of History.*

of stability with satisfying the desire for change. The era began with a sense of calm, with new conditions. The regimes of Eduard Taaffe in Cisleithania and Kálmán Tisza in Hungary also reinforced a sense of stability, but there were newer movements afoot, especially those resulting from mass politics. The growing wishes of new political parties and of the nationalities not represented in the Compromise, as well as of those who were (Germans and Magyars), began to put more pressure on the ruling elites. In Cisleithania, the solution was to expand the franchise, to allow more people to vote. The Kingdom of Hungary, on the other hand, did not change its electoral laws, but rather worked toward centralisation during the Compromise period, a characteristic seen as modern in the history of Western European states. The common theme after 1867 was the slow decline of aristocratic control, faster in Austria than in Hungary; and taking the leading role in these changes were the ideas of liberalism.

In the late 19th and early 20th centuries, the political conflicts permeating society were those between conservatives and liberal-minded reformers (together with various new mass organisations that preached all forms of something new). Liberalism was central to the political, social, and cultural society of Austria–Hungary, so an explanation of what it stands for is in order. 19th-century Liberals were mainly middle class, but it was not uncommon for aristocrats to be among them. Liberal aims were thus often those of this new growing bourgeoisie opposed to any form of absolutism and the feudal privilege that absolutism represented. Liberals usually supported an efficient bureaucratic state, run by themselves, and pressed for intellectual freedom, including freedom of the press and the end to censorship. Many promoted equality among all peoples, at least among educated men, and championed anti-military and anti-clerical measures. Belief in science replaced religion. Yet for their very progressive positions, many liberals in the Monarchy and throughout Europe also took on nationalist goals. German Liberals in Cisleithania wanted a German-led state, and Magyar Liberals supported assimilation of nationalities. They were often hostile to the lower classes – those who, in their view, needed an education before they could participate in any form of society. Liberals in the late 19th century may have often supported expanding the franchise, but rarely to all men, and almost never to women.

Below left: Kálmán Tisza was appointed as prime minister in 1875 and he filled this position for the next 12 years. His party, the Liberal Party, maintained a majority for the next 30 years. (The Liberal Party – from 1910 it was named the Party of Work – to all intents and purposes held power from 1875 to 1918 and was only forced into opposition between 1905 and 1910.) Tisza's nickname was the 'general' and this name was an apt one since he dominated parliament and made all the decisions. Similarly to previous governments, the Liberal Party supported the Compromise between the Crown and Hungary in the spirit of constitutional law, especially after the measures of renewal of the economic compromise.

Above right: Eduard Taaffe, a childhood friend of Franz Joseph became Prime Minister in 1879. He established a government dubbed the 'Iron Ring', which included the participation of clericalists and German conservatives, as well as Polish and Bohemian representatives. Taaffe's government has often been called a coalition government, which in many respects it was. However, his true loyalties were to the emperor and not to the government. He called his government 'supra-party'. His government served the interests of agriculture before those of industry and put clericalist interests before liberal ones, supporting the stance of the Slavs over that of the Germans.

The Initial Years

The new government in Cisleithania after 1868 – the so-called *Bürger-Ministerium* (Burgher Ministry) composed of men drawn mainly from the German middle classes, many of them from German-Bohemia – represented the beginning of a liberal era in Austria, as officials began to put into effect the general principles spelled out in the Fundamental Laws of 1867. (Franz Joseph accepted this ministry against his wishes. It was the first and last time he would do such a thing during his reign.) The Ministry of Police was abolished, and laws weakening the power of the Church were also approved. The general trend in Cisleithania was towards more centralisation, which did not sit well with the non-

Germans, especially with the Czechs, who were angry that they had failed where the Hungarians had succeeded in establishing a new order in their favour. Yet by 1871 the experiment in liberal politics, which had formed a kind of constitutional monarchy in Cisleithania, had been curbed, though never abandoned, and a great deal of power reverted back into the hands of the Emperor, with the Reichsrat becoming an advisory body to the Crown.

In Hungary the mood after 1867 was optimistic, but the government was faced with many problems, generally graver than in Austria. It had to create a new working political structure. It had to create arrangements with Croatia and with the nationalities, neither of which was finalised until 1868. Hungary also had problems with the incorporation of Transylvania and the Military Frontier, as well as with defining the relationship between federal and provincial authorities. The Kingdom of Hungary after 1867 suffered from constant regime change and the ongoing attempts by each succeeding government to completely undo the work of its predecessor. The political situation was complex and chaotic.

Nevertheless, the initial years after the Compromise witnessed a number of liberal reforms in Hungary, even if they were not as far-reaching as the ones during the failed revolution of 1848. The government recognised the principle of equality between the churches, Jews were granted civic and legal equality with Christians, and the 1868 elementary education law obliged all children between 6 and 12 to attend school. Most western European states had centralised or were in the process of centralising their administrations, and Hungary followed their lead to rationalise and modernise the administrative system by weakening the traditional autonomy of the provinces. The initial momentum for change, however, dwindled somewhat and in some cases even reversed itself by 1869. This was caused by bad harvests and a financially strained government. Also, the grand old men who had negotiated the Compromise were fading from public life; Gyula Andrássy became foreign minister, József Eötvös died, and Ferenc Deák retired. Then the economy crashed in 1873.

Even before the economic catastrophe, tensions were rising in Hungary. The Nationalities Law of 1868 had calmed the fears of many nationalities, but an outburst of Magyar chauvinism in 1872, partially in reaction to Franz Joseph's flirtation with the Slavs in Cisleithania, added fuel to the fire and put many nationalities on the defensive again. Kálmán

Below: *Revolt of the opposition in parliament, 13 December 1905.*

Above: *František Palacký (1798–1876) was a Czech historian, politician, writer and one of the proponents of Czech scientific and public life, as well as a prominent figure in the cause of Austroslavism.*

Tisza, who was emerging as a major political force, concluded that Hungary had to both cooperate with Franz Joseph, in order to prevent the emperor-king from allying himself with the Croats and the other nationalities, and simultaneously implement an energetic programme of assimilation – that of Magyarisation. Hungarian politicians may have emphasised the need to modify the Compromise in favour of Hungarian interests, and the public agreed, but the government chose to work in accordance with the Compromise while criticising it in public.

In a way this policy, which may seem inconsistent, was not unusual. It was perhaps simply part of a Hungarian struggle to maintain the status quo and demand change at the same time. In Hungary during the late dualist period one could find a portrait of Franz Joseph and one of Lajos Kossuth hanging on the same wall. Despite the obvious contradiction, it was acceptable, just as loyalty to the Habsburg King was also strong among those whose rhetoric could be considered anti-Habsburg.

Franchise

As in much of Europe at the time, the franchise throughout the Monarchy was extremely restricted. (At the turn of the century the percentage of people who elected government representatives ranged between 22 per cent in Germany, 28 per cent in France, 16 per cent in England, 8 per cent in Italy, 27 per cent in Austria and 6 per cent in Hungary.) Before 1907 Cisleithania possessed a Curia system: an electoral class system in which public life was represented by four separate interest groups (the so-called Curias): the great landlords, the chambers of commerce, the tax-payers in the towns, and the tax-payers in the villages. Each Curia had a set number of reserved seats in the Parliament. Until 1873 the Curias would select representatives for the county diets (Landtage) and the diets would send representatives to the Reichsrat in Vienna.

In April 1873 a new Franchise Act was passed, yet it did not extend the Franchise. As before, only 5.9 per cent of the population could vote, and the system of Curias remained, yet now each Curia in each Land elected and sent a representative directly to the Reichsrat, thereby bypassing the provincial diets. The change also increased the number of representatives from the towns and decreased those from the great landlords. In the end, the number of representatives in the Reichsrat was raised to 353. The great landlords sent 85, the Chambers of Commerce 21, the urban constituencies 116, and the rural constituencies 131. These changes also favoured the German speakers.

With the new government of Eduard Taaffe in 1879, and the Czechs somewhat reconciled and back in the Reichsrat, another franchise reform act was passed in 1882. This time the vote was extended in urban and rural constituencies, thereby giving the vote to more peasants and to the petite bourgeoisie. The result of the next election in 1885 was a swing to the Right. Increasing the franchise pleased the nationalities, but it often meant an increase in votes by and for the 'little men', mainly craftsmen, small shopkeepers, etc., and this newly enfranchised constituency had a disposition to vote for the German nationalists, such as Georg von Schönerer with his anti-Semitic policies.

Other developments led to new plans for the continued expansion of the franchise. Franz Joseph was convinced that the national struggle was a middle-class struggle and a democratisation of the suffrage would give power to the lower classes, which he believed were not corrupted by national yearnings. These lower classes were seen as sound. Their interests were social, not national; they were loyal to the dynasty, reliable, and easy to rule. However, a new bill to extend the third and fourth Curias did not go over well. It incited many vocal opponents. The German Liberals, the Christian Socials, and the Social Democrats all rejected the bill.

Nevertheless, a fifth Curia was added in June 1896. The earlier four remained intact, other than that the property qualifications for the third and fourth were lowered. The new fifth Curia voters needed to have reached their 24th birthday, needed to be literate, and have lived at least six months in a constituency. This new Curia would send 72 representatives to the Reichsrat. These changes increased the number of lower- and middle-class representatives in the parliament, but it never completely eliminated the control of the great landlords. The Curia system continued to grant them more representatives, even though their percentage in relation to the whole was declining.

By the early 20th century demands for suffrage reform intensified, especially from the Social Democratic Party. After the Russian Revolution, demonstrations in Austria persuaded the Prime Minister to promise electoral reform. Franz Joseph was also convinced of the need for universal suffrage and not only in Cisleithania; he wanted franchise reform in both halves of the Monarchy. On 1 December 1906, a bill was adopted to abolish the Curia system and introduce universal suffrage for every male citizen above 24 years of age who could demonstrate one year residency in a constituency – this applied only to the Reichsrat, not to the Austrian provincial diets (*Landtage*). The number of constituencies was also raised from 425 to 516. The new franchise bill officially came into law in January 1907, and the first election took place on 14 May 1907, resulting in a parliament representing almost all classes of Cisleithania. Over 30 parties returned candidates. It was a victory for the Social Democrats, whose representatives increased from 11 to 87. The number of Christian Socials also increased from 27 to 67. Other victors were radical nationalist parties of all forms. The extension of the franchise may have introduced some democracy to Austria, but it made it almost ungovernable at the federal level. The provincial diets continued to function, partly because they had not been affected by the franchise reform.

The electoral system in the other half of the Monarchy, in Hungary, remained in the hands of the great landlords – the nobility – until the very end. Oscar Jászi argues that the only difference between the upper and lower house of the Hungarian parliament was that the lower house had a louder voice and less aristocratic manners, but it was no less of a feudal body than the upper house. Those who sat in the lower house were aristocrats, the attorneys and officials of the aristocrats, or other segments of the Hungarian nobility. There were from time to time some representatives of the peasants and petite bourgeoisie, but never a representative of the city workers or the agricultural labourers. In the eyes of the government, the limited franchise kept the poorer classes and the nationalities in check. No one, not even Magyar politicians, wanted the peasantry to vote, no matter what language they spoke. In Hungary the franchise did not change between 1867 and 1914; one could argue that the Hungarian franchise actually became more restrictive. The rampant electoral corruption (purchasing votes, forgery, intimidation, preventing voters from reaching the polling place) that was very common in Hungary maintained the status

Above: *Contemporaneous caricature: Palacky with the Czech lion.*

quo and prevented any change. The tradition of open ballots allowed local administrators a great deal of influence over the voters. (One should not overlook the fact that there was also intimidation in Cisleithania, especially in Galicia.)

Eduard Taaffe and Kálmán Tisza

The German Liberals had done well for themselves after 1867 in Cisleithania. The 1873 franchise law benefited them by increasing the representation of the German middle class, but the 1873 economic crash caused a slow decline of liberal politics in Austria. Their real downfall, however, occurred because of their position on Bosnia and Herzegovina in 1878: they were against the addition of more Slavs to the Monarchy. Their failure to vote the money needed for the administration of the new provinces led to the collapse of the government in 1879 – the collapse of the last purely German ministry in Compromise Austria. Eduard Taaffe, a boyhood friend of Franz Joseph, became Prime Minister in 1879 and formed a cabinet of clericals, German conservatives (feudalists), together with Polish and Czech representatives – known as the 'Iron Ring'.

Right: *Oszkár Jászi was a liberal social scientist, editor and politician.*

The bloc controlled 168 seats in the Reichsrat, while the Liberals only 145. Taaffe's government is often described as a coalition government, but in fact Taaffe served the emperor, not the government. He described his government as standing 'above the Parties.' His government favoured agrarian interests over industrial ones, clerical interests instead of liberal, and Slavs more than Germans.

Instead of favouring the German speakers, Taaffe and the Iron Ring focused on winning over the Czechs – who were divided more and more into 'Old' and 'Young Czechs,' with the latter demanding more radical reform – and ironing out some of the nationalities problems. It was agreed that the first objective should be language equality, mainly that Czech, alongside German, be permitted within the Bohemian administration. This did not sit well with the Germans in Bohemia, and as time went on, the Germans and the Young Czechs became increasingly militant. Failing to find a compromise between Czechs and Germans, the Taaffe government fell in October 1893, and its 14-year rule has been described by historians as the 'last stable regime before the war.'

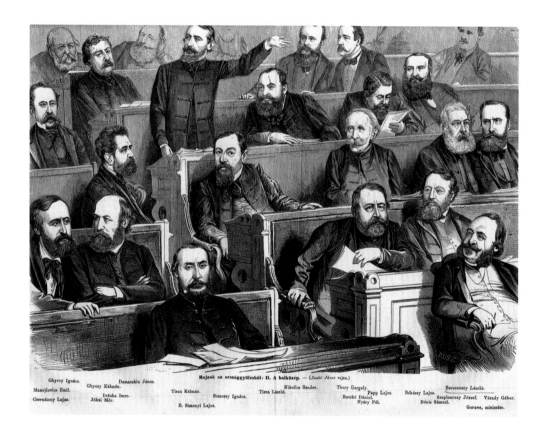

Above: *A contemporaneous drawing of the centre left in parliament. The man in the second row and second from the left is Mór Jókai, the most well-known and popular Hungarian writer of the period.*

A similar development took place in Hungary under Kálmán Tisza between 1875 and 1890. Tisza created the Liberal Party in early 1875 by brokering a deal between two existing parties, and in the 1875 elections secured 333 out of 408 seats for this new political formation. On 20 October Tisza was appointed Prime Minister, a position he would hold for 15 years and which the Liberal Party would control for the next 30. (The Liberal Party ruled Hungary in essence from 1875 to 1918, with the exception of the years between 1905 and 1910.) Tisza, who was referred to as the 'general,' commanded the parliament; he was the man who made decisions – the grand patriarch. The focus of the Liberal Party, not unlike earlier governments, was on the relationship between the Crown and Hungary – the interpretation of the Compromise, especially during the renewals of the Compromise agreement in 1877, 1887, 1897, 1907 and 1917.

Unlike the 'Party of Independence and 1848', the Liberals continued to support having some relations with Cisleithania, yet there was a clear move toward establishing a centralised, free-standing Hungary. Under Tisza, Transylvanian Saxon autonomy was curbed, areas outside the county system were incorporated into the county structure, and the county leader, the *főispán*, whose powers were increased, became a political representative of the government. The Liberal Party also implemented reforms in the area of mixed marriages, civil marriages, and the status of Jews, thereby bringing Hungary in line with reforms that had taken place in Austria 30 years earlier.

Mass Politics in Cisleithania

As mentioned earlier, the political changes in both halves of the Monarchy, in Austria more so than in Hungary, were leading to an era of mass politics, in which the masses, or at least a higher percentage of the masses, could participate in political life. The liberal movements and liberal parties, most of which supported progressive policies, were often catalysts for more radical changes. The liberal fight against the feudal order occasioned the creation of other movements and parties, whose positions were often anti-liberal. The Austrian liberals' support of a centralised German state, led to Slavic nationalists demanding autonomy, and when the German liberals lightened up on their nationalist rhetoric, they were considered traitors by the German petite bourgeoisie. And since this lower-middle class often equated liberalism with capitalism and capitalism with Jews, anti-Semitism was always on the rise within this segment of the

The Linz Programme
The first attempt to establish a purely national political agenda in Austria came about with a meeting of intellectuals in Linz in September 1882, resulting in the so-called Linz Programme, which sought to save the Germans from being overwhelmed by the Slavic peoples. The manifesto advocated that it was essential that the non-German territories of Cisleithania, as well as Galicia, Bukovina and Dalmatia be ceded to Hungary or given complete autonomy. Thus, the German-language area that was to come into being would form close ties with Germany and its relationship with Hungary would only be in the form of a personal union. Many Linz participants made successful careers for themselves in other movements such as Viktor Adler (left) and Georg von Schönerer (right).

population. A liberal emphasis on laissez-faire economics was answered by Marxist programmes for collective ownership. The liberal anti-Church position was fuel for the fire for disgruntled, religious peasants and artisans. This Europe-wide development of mass politics in many ways provoked a crisis of liberalism.

Thus liberalism and the Liberal Party were on the wane in Cisleithania by the early 1870s. Many former Liberals as well as non-Liberals moved in the direction of a more nationalist position. Perhaps the first attempt to clearly define a national programme in Austria was during a meeting of intellectuals in the city of Linz in September 1882. The result, the Linz Programme, proposed a number of ways that the Germans, who they believed were drowning in a Slavic sea, could be saved. First of all, non-Germanic areas of Cisleithania, such as Galicia, Bukovina and Dalmatia, were to be detached, given to Hungary or made autonomous. The German-inhabited territory of Cisleithania was then to intensify its connections to Germany and the relationship with Hungary would continue solely in the person of the emperor. This programme was not popular, but many of its signatories were influential men, such as Georg von Schönerer and Viktor Adler, both of whom would go on to occupy major positions in other movements.

Liberal legislation of earlier governments had alienated the peasants, who throughout the Monarchy, were the single largest social group. Protective – that is restrictive – provisions (typical of the pre-liberal era), had been removed by liberal politics, leaving peasants to fend for themselves. In both Austria and Hungary peasant movements began to arise, but it would take more time for actual peasant parties to form. By the late 19th century, peasant representatives were getting elected to various Cisleithanian county diets and even to the Reichsrat, but a real successful peasant movement was hampered by the general structure of the Monarchy. Peasant programmes were usually anti-liberal; they stood for agricultural protection, restrictions concerning the division of land and interest rates, and an increased role of the churches in the schools. At times they did mirror liberal ideals as they fought for 'education, thrift, and temperance.' The perceived enemy of many peasants was the liberal businessman, and since he was often a Jew, anti-Semitic sentiments became common in rural movements.

The artisans and small shopkeepers, the so-called petite bourgeoisie, had initially been aligned with the wishes of the Liberals, but as time went on they became more reactionary and anti-capitalistic. (Many historians see this segment of society developing into the supporters of later fascist movements.) After the 1882 extension of the franchise, these individuals were major beneficiaries, and they often gave their vote to the German nationalist and anti-Semite, Georg von Schönerer. On the other hand, while they may have agreed with Schönerer's anti-Semitism, they usually did not support his anti-Clerical and even anti-dynastic position.

A discussion of the growth of mass politics in Austria–Hungary often centres on Cisleithania for the obvious reason that it was there that political participation was expanding. The Kingdom of Hungary, as we know, kept the majority of the population distant from political involvement. It was not easy for any group to form a political party. By the late 19th century, Hungary insisted that any form of association remain non-

Below: A report in Vasárnapi Újság *(Sunday Newspaper) on a demonstration in Budapest demanding the right to vote.*

political. Many of the reforms implemented after 1867 also strengthened the federal government's position and weakened the possibility for other groups to voice alternative views. The modified re-organisation that put some county officials under the control of the Ministry of the Interior and made villages subordinate to the counties made it all but impossible for the rural population to actively participate in any form of political life. It also fuelled nationality tensions, since non-Hungarian peasants then looked for non-rural ways to voice their opinions. Nevertheless, alternative political parties were also created in Hungary. Hungarian peasants were no longer willing to accept social inequality; literacy and the railroad had shown them a new world. Ill treatment led to bloody riots and military reaction in the 1890s. Agrarian socialists managed to organise and even to get two representatives elected to parliament by the end of the century.

Industrial workers in Hungary had organised a Trade Union (under the cover of a mutual benefit association) before the Compromise in 1861, yet later developments were hampered by government opposition. There were small, minor steps taken in the 1860s and 1870s and in 1868, following the tenets of Ferdinand Lassalle, the father of the German socialist movement, the Comprehensive Association of Workers was established. In May 1880 a United Workers' Party of Hungary was proclaimed. The new party struggled not only against the government, but also against many radicals in Hungary who did not approve of the party's 'legal means' and connections to the petite bourgeoisie. These developments led eventually to the creation of the Social Democratic Workers' Party of Hungary in 1890. The party was strong, and as Gustav Gratz has argued, after 1896 it was only the Social Democrats who could call out the masses. Yet the party was never able to win a seat in a parliament dominated by Liberals.

Both halves of the Monarchy also had ethnic parties – parties that defined themselves by their nationality. In some cases, such as with the Czechs, the nationality was divided between radical and more accommodating individuals: between Young Czechs and Old Czechs. The Poles, because of deals with the establishment, usually were fairly cooperative with the ruling Germans. In Hungary, ethnic parties began to organise in the mid-1890s. Education and the railroads had shown the Slovaks, Romanians, and Serbs the world. They then made their own demands, or at least what their leaders convinced them were their demands.

The 20th Century

The key issue in Cisleithania was almost always language, specifically equality between the German and the Slavic languages. Taaffe had failed to broker an agreement between the Czechs (both Old and Young Czechs) and the Germans. After Taaffe's 14-year rule, there were more incidents demonstrating the intense strain on relations between nationalities, especially over language use. The Slovenes in southern Austria demanded more schools in their own language, and the tensions erupted in June 1895 in the town of Cilli (Celje) in southern Styria. The town was German, but in a Slovene countryside, and the German inhabitants rejected the idea, which the government in Vienna supported, of parallel instruction in both German and Slovene in the local elementary school. (The Cisleithanian government's support of the language decree led to its collapse.)

What happened regarding Cilli was repeated on a larger scale in the late 1890s. The Prime Minister, Count Casimir Badeni, a Polish noble, sought a solution to the Czech-German dispute, while at the same time trying to secure the Young Czech vote, which he wanted before the upcoming decennial revision of the Compromise. He therefore made an offer to the Czechs. (Badeni was attempting to rule without the emergency measures of Paragraph 14, which in the late 19th century was still a measure Austrian Ministers avoided.) On 5 April 1897, Badeni made the Czech language equal to German

Above: *Count Casimir Badeni, who placed the German and Czech languages on an equal basis by decree, on 5 April 1897, in every administrative and legal process in Bohemia and Moravia. By 1901 every official functionary in the two territories was obliged to use both languages. For the Germans in Bohemia and the other German communities of Cisleithania this was all unacceptable and they sought to obstruct this decision, which they held to be unjust, by violent means. However, their efforts failed. The seriousness of the situation is indicated by the comment of an Austrian historian according to which the decision was tantamount to a death sentence for the Habsburg Empire. In November 1897 Franz Joseph had to accept Badeni's resignation and finally had to repeal the decree in October 1899.*

in all administrative and judicial matters in Bohemia and Moravia. All officials in those provinces would have to command both languages by 1901. This was unacceptable to Bohemian Germans as well as to Germans throughout Cisleithania, who turned to violence and filibustering in order to stop what they saw as injustice. Yet they failed. Conditions were so grave that an Austrian historian has argued, 'from this moment the Habsburg realm was doomed.' Franz Joseph was forced to accept Badeni's resignation in November 1897 and to finally repeal the decrees in October 1899.

The Reichsrat never recovered after the Badeni crisis; obstructionism became the norm, as politicians fought for their individual Party interests and against one another. By the end there were often more than eight nationalities represented in the lower house of parliament, most of them divided into rival political camps. The Monarchy had basically returned to neo-absolutist rule under Franz Joseph and his bureaucracy. Not even the 1907 introduction of universal male suffrage remedied this. Austrian Prime Ministers in the 20th century were no longer political leaders, they were all civil servants selected by the emperor. Their ministries were rarely based upon a majority and when the parliament could not function, the emperor always had paragraph 14 of the 1867 constitution – an emergency measure allowing him to enact laws when the Reichsrat was not in session. Universal suffrage had been granted, but the Reichsrat ceased to function. In 1913, Prime Minister Karl Stürgkh, who would be shot by Victor Adler's son, Friedrich Adler, in October 1916 for supporting the war, dissolved the Bohemian Diet and placed the province under the control of an imperial commission. In March 1914, he dismissed the Reichsrat. This left Cisleithania at the outbreak of World War I governed as it had been after the 1848 revolutions: by Franz Joseph.

The Kingdom of Hungary may not have experienced as many political ups and downs during the Compromise era, since it had never modified its feudal character, as Cisleithania had. Political and societal changes in Hungary were toward a unified, centralised state, which over time began to distance itself more and more from Vienna. The central theme of Hungary's political life in the early 20th century, as it had been since 1867, or even earlier, remained the 'issue of public law' (*közjogi kérdés*), that is defining Hungary's relationship with its king. Many Prime Ministers and governments had realised the need to maintain a close relationship with Franz Joseph, yet beginning in 1889 Hungary started to take a different position regarding its connection to the Crown. And it was not, as one might have expected, the Party of Independence and its leader, Ferenc Kossuth (the timid son of Lajos Kossuth) who took the lead, but rather Count Albert Apponyi, a former opponent of the Liberals, who later chose to join them. According to Apponyi, Hungary was an independent state. In his opinion, neither the Pragmatic Sanction nor the Compromise had curbed Hungary's sovereignty.

Hungary then began to focus on itself as a Magyar nation state, implementing policies of magyarisation considered by the nationalities as chauvinistic and highly criticised by historians. The real turn against all forms of liberal ideas happened during the government of Dezső Bánffy (1895–1898). His was a government of the 'strong hand', and he did everything to quell the wishes of the non-dominant classes: the lower classes, the peasants, the workers, the socialists. Judit Frigyesi argues that 'Parliament became increasingly an empty facade, its debates theatrically affirming the political power structure but ignoring the issue of much-needed economic reform.'

The Activity of the Body: Society and Everyday Life

But what was life like in the Empire; how did people live? What did people do? The answer to this question often depended on a person's social standing, and in the late 19th and early 20th centuries one's social standing no longer referred to one's order (clergy, nobility, or other), but to the increasingly important social class, mainly the various forms of nobility, middle class, working class, as well as the peasantry. This new focus on social class was the result of urbanisation and other changes in society already discussed above. Of course, the transition was not straightforward anywhere in the Monarchy, or in Europe for that matter. Newer works avoid focusing on labelling the class structure of the Dual Monarchy as pre-modern. Nevertheless, the role of the classes in Austro-Hungarian society remains crucial for a better understanding of the Monarchy and for comprehending the everyday life of its inhabitants.

It is, of course, true that class struggles differed from region to region. There were conflicts between classes, between one or more class and the emperor-king, and between groups and various nationalities. In some areas the nobility participated in the ethnic struggle against either Vienna or Budapest. In Bohemia, for example, it was not uncommon for German-speaking nobility to side with the Czech cause against further Germanisation. The Hungarian nobility – more the middle nobility (the gentry) than the more Habsburg-loyal upper aristocracy – also lived in constant conflict with the Crown. The middle class will receive greater coverage, since their world of coffeehouses, newspapers, tourism, modern clothing, etc., came to dominate the spirit of the times and these are the images one often thinks of as characteristic of the 'gold old days' of the dualist period.

Above: *Hunting was one of the great pastimes of the aristocracy. Franz Joseph was happy to participate in hunts. The picture shows the park of the hunting castle in Köröserdő.*

Nobility

The nobility in Austria–Hungary was not a homogeneous group. Some of the differences between various levels of the nobility had faded by the late 19th century, yet there were still a few clear lines of demarcation. The so-called Hochadel, those with titles such as Prince, Duke, Count or Baron, were at the very pinnacle of society, even allowed to socialise with the Monarch and his family. There were all in all a few hundred great families – magnates – in this upper strata, some of the most famous being: Liechtenstein, Esterházy, Batthyány, Lobkowitz, Schwarzenberg, and Windischgrätz. (21 families within this group also enjoyed the privilege to marry into the Imperial family.) Magnate families owned large tracts of land in every part of the Monarchy. Below the magnates stood the middle nobility: the Ritterschaft of the German lands, the Ryttersgwo of Bohemia–Moravia, and the *nobiles bene possessionati* of Hungary. (In German this group was sometimes marked with a 'von' in their names.) They may have been nobles, but their land holdings, their wealth, and their privileges were insignificant compared to the Hochadel. In addition, every region also had a number of minor nobles.

In the Monarchy as well as across Europe at the time, the nobility usually dominated the land, politics and the army. Yet, as in all of Europe by the end of the 19th century, the nobility of the Dual Monarchy had lost some of its power. Their role in politics changed, but in places such as Hungary the nobles continued to dominate both the upper and lower houses. Even in Cisleithania the Prime Minister's position was reserved for a member of the noble class until the 1890s, the last being Prince Adolf III Windisch-Graetz, who served from 1893 to 1895. Yet, more middle-class elements were entering these formerly noble arenas. The Austro-Hungarian artillery and navy began to be dominated by the bourgeoisie at the turn of the century.

A major aspect of the everyday life of a noble was the belief in 'honour.' This was a characteristic that had defined noble life for generations. For example, in the 18th century Hungarian nobles were honour-bound; when a crime was committed by a noble, he remained free until his trial. He could never be compelled to give evidence; 'his word of honour sufficed.' This kept the act of duelling alive, even after it was outlawed by the Austrian authorities. The defense of honour by duelling was most common in the higher echelons of the Austro-Hungarian military, and it was a way for the nobles as well as some non-nobles, especially army officers, to distinguish their class from others. It obliged one to defend his and sometimes others' honour by challenging the offender to a duel. One of the most famous literary examples of duelling was in Joseph Roth's *The Radetzky March*, when the Jewish medical doctor was compelled to challenge his fellow officer, an aristocrat, to a duel with pistols for anti-Semitic remarks. (Both would die in the end.)

Duels were meant to protect honour, they were not for pleasure or for sport. The degree of insult determined the severity of the duel, with physical assault calling for the most serious encounter. Actually, the rules of duelling had taken on a 'ritualistic rigidity' by the 19th century. Once honour had been affronted, the opponents exchanged visiting cards, then seconds (two for each) were selected. A protocol was drawn up and a location was chosen. At the actual duel, witnesses were necessary as were surgeons for the wounded. Duelling took various forms; in the military the sword and the pistol were

Above: *This cream-coloured silk evening gown with purple georgette was made in Vienna around 1905. The sign on the belt shows that the company that made it operated on the Graben but had an affiliated firm in Trieste too. (Museum of Applied Arts, Budapest)*

recognised. Duels with the sword could involve slashes or slashes and thrusts, and the duel could end with 'first blood,' after an agreed-upon time limit, at the sign of 'total exhaustion,' or when one participant was dead. Pistol duels were just as ritualistic. They could begin from a fixed position, with participants firing freely or on command, or with participants moving toward one another. The number of bullets allowed was predetermined.

The life of the nobles was also defined by their social activities. In Hungary, the National Casino, first established by Count István Széchenyi in 1827 as a club for magnates, served as a centre for gatherings and meetings of this class. Balls – dances – were important social events of the noble class. At some balls, such as at the charity balls before Lent, the upper nobility and the lower nobility actually mingled, not a common occurrence at other times of the year. These elaborate events usually took place in urban palaces or the ballrooms of hotels, and were for invited guests only. Balls played a symbolic role in delineating the nobility from other classes, as well as separating the various levels of nobility themselves. They also fostered the propagation of this closed society (or societies), since balls served as a place for the young to meet. (It was also common within this class that marriages were arranged.)

The activity of the nobility kept it isolated from the outside world. Their living quarters separated them not only from other classes, but also from many aspects of life. Some families possessed palaces in Vienna or Budapest, but many castles and palaces were located in a village or small town. Everyday activities in the noble household were taken care of by a population of servants. The noble was free to associate with his class, in hunting outings or various gatherings. Of course, the degree of isolation depended on the individual and the status of the family. As more and more middle nobles joined the ranks of politicians and as members of the middle class, including Jews, were ennobled, an increased interaction between the classes occurred. It is likewise true that most nobles, including the aristocracy, spent some time away from their outlying rural castles and palaces and frequented their urban dwellings. City experience exposed them to the changing urban world of the time.

Middle Class

Since the late 18th century, the growing middle class in all regions of Europe played an important role in social, economic, and political life. But what exactly is the middle class? Examinations of Austria–Hungary, or of Europe in general, cannot escape discussing this social group, but its definition has created confusion for many. First of all, the English term 'middle class' does not carry the same meaning as its French, German, Polish, or Hungarian equivalents (bourgeoisie, Bürgertum, Mieszczanstwo, polgárság), for example. In German the word *Bürgertum* can refer to 'burgher,' that is an urban dweller in medieval and early modern towns, or 'bourgeoisie', as well as

Above: *György Klösz's photos of cities and castles paint a unique picture of the period. This photo shows one of the rooms of a palace owned by the Erdődy family.*

Left: *Klösz not only worked in Budapest but also photographed many castles in the provinces too, included among which was Solymosy Castle in Loós.*

'citizen.' The Hungarian word 'polgár' or 'polgári' can mean bourgeois or urbanite, and it can include all types of individuals under this category, including the impoverished middle nobility, leaving the Hungarian word for 'middle class' to really designate: all people not engaged in agriculture. Judit Frigyesi has argued that by the end of the 19th century the use of the word polgár in Hungary was not about describing some kind of a bourgeoisie, rather the expression simply referred to a certain ideology, culture, and lifestyle. Middle class ideals stressed achievement, education and the goal of creating a modern, secular, civil society.

Despite the ambiguity surrounding the meaning of 'middle class' and doubt concerning unity within this so-called group, the term usually suggests merchants, manufacturers, bankers, capitalists, entrepreneurs, managers, rentiers, doctors, lawyers, ministers, scientists, professors, teachers and bureaucrats. At times, other groups such as artisans, retail merchants and innkeepers, who in the 18th and early 19th centuries had been seen as middle class, came to be separated from the new sense attached to this group and were often labelled as the petite bourgeoisie (lower middle class). Besides members of the noble class, the middle class also excludes peasants, manual workers, and other lower-class individuals. When we think of the middle class, or the bourgeoisie, during the time of the Dual Monarchy, both in Austria–Hungary and throughout Central and Eastern Europe, we are actually talking about a fairly small group, especially in comparison to the influence they wielded in society. In many places they comprised perhaps 5 per cent or less of the total population.

'Tourism' became a magic word in the Monarchy. People generally went on holiday in summer and it was not without example that people travelled down to the French seaside in winter. Because of more free time and enthusiasm for the most suitable and best treatments many of the middle class travelled from Vienna and from other big cities to Karlsbad, Marienbad and Teplitze.

Members of the Hungarian upper and middle class often spent the summer in their villas in the Buda Hills surrounding the capital. Alternatively, they travelled to the Tatra Mountains, the Adriatic or Lake Balaton for stays of various duration. Whoever could went 'abroad', which generally meant Austria or Bohemia.

In all parts of the Monarchy the middle class remained hierarchically divided. In Hungary the distance between divisions, mainly within the growing civil service, intensified with the use of titles, which emphasised one's rank and pay scale. The titles of social rank began with *Tekintetes Úr* (authority), and moved up to *Nagyságos Úr* (greatness), to *Méltóságos Úr* (dignity), to *Kegyelmes Úr* and, on rare occasions, *excellenciás* (Excellency). Most of these titles could be translated as some form of 'Your Excellency' or 'Right Honorable.' The 'úr,' equivalent to 'Herr' in German, basically meant 'mister,' but with an air of hierarchical respect. Its use simply emphasised the divide between the so-called gentleman and those below him.

The life and activities of this diverse middle class is often what we think of when we recall the Dual Monarchy. Much of the literature and scholarship on fin de siècle Vienna and Budapest examine middle-class themes like the music of Johann Strauss in Vienna, coffeehouses, fashion and even tourism. This 'happy world' was bourgeois, and at times even members of the noble class and social climbers from the lower classes were participants in this middle-class world.

One cannot think of Viennese culture without the Vienna coffeehouse, yet coffeehouse culture was not unique to Vienna, nor did it originate there. It could, and still can, be found in other urban centres of Central and Eastern Europe, as well as in other cities such as Paris and Berlin. And Vienna was not the first. Budapest had actually acquired the Turkish habit of coffee drinking a century before the Viennese or even the Parisiennes. The Austrians procured a taste for coffee in the late 17th century as local merchants began brewing and selling the beans of the retreating Turks. By the late 19th century, the Viennese had grown accustomed to various forms of coffee, especially with sugar and milk. Altogether, the coffeehouse in the late 19th century epitomised the new class – a bourgeois class – that began to wield more and more influence in urban centres such as Vienna.

Coffeehouses became a home away from home for artists, intellectuals, and writers. Members of the 'Young Vienna' circle (Hermann Bahr, Hugo von Hofmannsthal, Stefan Zweig and Karl Kraus) made Vienna's Café Griensteidl famous in the late 19th

Above: *Café Central in Budapest.*

century. Café Griensteidl had first opened in 1847, and when it closed in 1897, Café Central took on the 'leading coffeehouse' role in Vienna, and Café Central became an essential meeting place for many writers, intellectuals, chess players and Marxists (like

Coffeehouse Life in Vienna and Budapest

Café Central opened in Ferstel Palace on Herrengasse, Viennan in 1860 and is still in operation today. Towards the end of the 19th century it became one of the city's leading coffee houses and the most important meeting place for writers, intellectuals and Marxists, such as Otto Bauer, Victor Adler and even revolutionary Leon Trotsky. Because of the chess matches played there, it was also referred to as the 'chess school'. Other places, for example, the Museum Café, attracted artists and musicians such as Oskar Kokoschka, Egon Schiele, Ferenc Lehár and Alban Berg. There were many famous coffee houses in Budapest, including Korona, Török Császár, Szökőkút Café, Fehér Hajó and Hét Választófejedelem. New York Café, designed by the architect Alajos Hauszmann (who was working on the renovation of the royal palace around this time), opened in 1894, and Andrássy Road, which had just been built, was also lined with cafés: Japán, Művész, Opera, Dreschler and Abbázia. Some of them were frequented by writers, poets and actors, while painters and journalists had their own favourite respective venues.

Otto Bauer, Victor Adler and even the future revolutionary Leon Trotsky). Other establishments such as Café Museum appealed to artists and musicians, including Oskar Kokoschka, Egon Schiele, Franz Lehár and Alban Berg.

Just like in Vienna, coffeehouses were popular, middle-class establishments in Budapest, where they even played an influential role in national politics. The 1848 Hungarian revolution began in Café Pilvax in Pest on 15 March 1848. One of the main roles of the nearly 600 coffeehouses around 1900 was to provide space for middle-class men's clubs and second homes for writers and artists. Nevertheless, many of them also served the function of a restaurant, providing full-course meals any time of the day, some of them 365 days a year. One could spend hours in a coffeehouse, sipping one cup of coffee, reading newspapers, both local and foreign, and even receiving and sending postal messages – a kind of early internet café. Many editors had their own tables in coffeehouses, where they met with authors and collected articles. Actors and actresses often gathered in cafés after performances. For all the various groupings within the middle class, coffeehouses were the place to be.

Already in the early 19th century, there were famous coffeehouses in Budapest, such as the Crown, the Turkish Emperor, the Coffee Fountain, the White Ship, the Seven Elector Princes. Most of these, however, were replaced with more elaborate ones later in the century. Café New York, designed by Alajos Hauszmann, the architect working on the reconstruction of the royal palace at the time, opened in 1894, and a string of coffeehouses lined the newly restyled Andrássy út: the Japan, the Hall of Arts, the Opera, the Dreschler and the Abbazia. Some served writers and artists, others painters and yet others journalists.

Middle-class coffeehouse culture flourished in tandem with the growing presence and importance of the press. (In theory there was freedom of the press in Austria–Hungary, but various laws curtailed some of these liberties.) The era around 1900 has been called the golden age of newspapers partly owing to the increase in literacy and population. Newspapers had already, in the early 19th century, played an important part in political life, many of them portraying events with a liberal slant, but the late 19th century witnessed the introduction of cheap penny newspapers in many places. *Esti Ujság* first appeared on the Budapest boulevards in 1896, the same year when

The Golden Age of the Press

As the role and readership of papers increased the selection also became larger. Street vendors were allowed to sell newspapers, i.e. 'boulevard' papers, which tried to boost circulation with sensational stories and pictures. For example, Esti Újság *(Evening Newspaper), first published in 1896, exploited the opportunity afforded by street vendors in Budapest.*

One of the papers that resisted this temptation was the Neu Freie Presse, *a liberal, centrist paper that supported the government. The Notes from the Editor that appeared here were read by many. It was the dream of every ambitious writer to be published in its pages. The illustration shows a special edition of the paper published following the assassination of the heir to the throne in Sarajevo.*

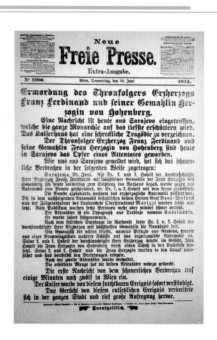

the hawking of newspapers, mostly by young boys, was legalised. These new 'boulevard newspapers,' whose successors can be found today in many supermarkets in Central Europe as well as throughout the world, appealed to the reader by printing sensational stories and images.

Around the time these newer style newspapers, as well as picture weeklies, were introduced, the general quality of many serious newspapers declined. And in addition to the reduction in quality, newspapers in general had become provincial in nature. Many were ethnocentric and focused on local and national politics. They printed little foreign news. An exception to this rule was the Viennese *Neue Freie Presse*, a liberal, centralist paper that stood close to the government. In many places in the world, it was considered a great newspaper, whose editorial views were often read and taken seriously and within the bourgeois world, it was the dream of every aspiring writer to be published in the feuilleton of the *Neue Freie Presse*. The calibre of the press in general varied, however, in different regions of the Monarchy. According to Arthur J. May, there was a basic difference between Viennese and Budapest newspapers: 'Budapest's press was much more animated, less restrained in expression than that of Vienna. It represented and propagated Magyar national interests to the detriment of the minorities and was less concerned with considerations of monarchical solidarity.' Prague also had its major papers, especially *Čas* (the *Times*), founded in 1886 as a weekly, and published after 1900 as a daily. Edited by T.G. Masaryk, it mixed liberalism with new socially progressive forces.

According to Andrew Janos, newspapers in Hungary had a distinctly bourgeois flavour: they catered to the tastes of the urban properties classes. Yet the socialists – mainly the leaders of the working class and the proletariat itself – also read and published newspapers. In Budapest in the early 20th century there were 24 socialist newspapers out of the hundreds of daily newspapers and periodicals. In Vienna, since 1889, the social democrats also had their famous weekly, the *Arbeiter Zeitung*. (It only became a daily in 1895.) Yet there were also newspapers that went beyond class boundaries and preached a national or ethnic agenda. In Hungary, for example, almost all the nationalities had their own newspapers.

The coffeehouse, the increase in reading material and the bourgeois life that they represented succeeded because of the abundance of leisure time. The new middle class, as well as some members of the noble class, mainly professional and business people, possessed a great deal of free time, allowing some to spend several hours a day in a coffeehouse, sometimes conducting business, but other times simply observing, reading, and interacting. This increase in leisure hours brought numerous changes. In the Dual Monarchy 'tourism' had become the new magical word. Vacations were generally taken in the summer; it was rare, but not unheard of, that someone journeyed to the

Above: *It was in the Steinergasser (Petőfi) coffee house by the Danube that the public were informed of the Pest Skating Society's establishment. This society obtained the permission of the city council to set aside a small part of the lake in the Városliget (City Park) as a public skating rink.*

Since skating was a splendid form of social entertainment the initiative was a great success. When the above report appeared in Vasárnapi Újság *in 1904 the Neo-Baroque skating hall, designed by Imre Francsek and inaugurated in 1895, was already standing. It is still in use today.*

French Riviera in the winter. More leisure time as well as continual searches for the best form of therapy sent many middle class individuals from Vienna and other urban centres to Karlsbad, Marienbad, or Teplitz. Hungarian tourists journeyed to summer homes in the Buda hills, to vacation destinations in the Tatra Mountains, the Adriatic coast and Lake Balaton. Those who could, went 'abroad,' which typically meant Austria or Bohemia, specifically the spas of Karlsbad, Marienbad, Ischl, Gastein, the Semmering, etc.

In addition to coffeehouses most urban centres also had numerous taverns, since liquor was commonplace in urban and rural cultures throughout the region. The poor quality of water often meant that some form of alcohol was the main drink. In the countryside it was common for peasants to drink a watered-down wine, a kind of 'Trink Wein.' In cities and towns drinking often led to problems associated with alcoholism, but not everywhere. In Budapest, for example, drinking problems were not as common as in other parts of Europe. For the middle class, especially Jewish families, sobriety was central. Wine was common especially in Hungary and the German-speaking provinces around Vienna. Beer was drunk throughout the Monarchy, with major breweries in Vienna, Budapest and Pilsen. In Hungary, rum was also a typical drink, since it was a cheap byproduct of the sugar refineries.

The growth of the middle class culture mainly in the urban centres of the Monarchy also affected dress. In most cities of Europe by the late 19th century, the modern world of the bourgeoisie marginalised and displaced regional culture. French fashion found its way to even smaller centres, towns, and villages. These changes often caused alarm, such as in the province of Carinthia, where many feared that traditional local dress would disappear. Ordinarily men's dress changed first, and the standard male attire of trousers and shirt was a sign of the new dominant bourgeois culture. Women more slowly gave up their folk dress for new fashions. Shoes, for example, had basically replaced boots, except for poorer women.

Below: One of Budapest's middle class streets in a photo by György Klösz. The owner usually lived in the flat with a balcony on the first floor, or this was the most expensively rented out flat in the building.

Lower Classes: Industrial Workers

The continued importance of the noble class and the growing influence of the middle class did not create a better life for the lower classes. Of course, there are arguments that in Austria–Hungary, as well as in Europe in general, the economic, social, and political advances, created by the upper and middle classes, led to some betterment in the standard of living for everyone. But the everyday life of the burgeoning working class left a lot to be desired.

Today the world of the working class in late 19th-century Europe seems shocking. All industrial workers and even the artisan class faced bad working conditions, low pay, uncertain futures, bad housing, as well as a basic struggle to feed oneself and stay healthy. The worst of these problems was usually housing. In places such as Vienna, Cracow and Graz workers paid a quarter to a third of their income on rent, compared to an eighth or tenth in London. Most working-class families rented apartments; it was rare for someone to own his home. In Graz, in 1900, four-fifths of small housing had no running water. In 1910, Vienna only 7 per cent of residential buildings had bathrooms and toilets. In addition, only 22 per cent of them were indoors; most toilets were in the courtyard to be shared with all residents of the building. Conditions were not better in the workplace. Only 20 out of 530 factories in Budapest had facilities for washing hands. Safety was no one's concern.

Much of the working class lived in buildings shared with members of the lower middle class. The layout of most of these apartment houses was similar everywhere in Central Europe. They were often rectangular or quadrangular, with an inner courtyard. Stairways were usually very wide, except for the separate dark and narrow staircase for the servants of the middle class. The style in Vienna was to have closed staircases and to have many staircases; whereas in Budapest, in order to squeeze as many people and apartments as possible into a building, open staircases and open-corridor patterns were common, thereby allowing access to parts of the building inaccessible from the staircase. This difference shows that the bourgeois desire to separate itself from the working class, which the closed staircase allowed, was not always satisfied in Budapest. In a description of the differences between various types of apartments in Budapest built between 1865 and 1914 John Lukacs points out that the better ones, that is the larger ones, were on the first or second floors above the ground floor, and their doors opened onto the stair landing. Farther up were the cheap apartments, with their doors facing the courtyard. These types of 'mixed-resident Budapest tenement buildings' were typical in many parts of the city.

The layout of a standard apartment in Budapest consisted of a narrow entrance hall, with a closet and lavatory on one side and the kitchen on the other. Many apartments, especially those of the middle class, had a room off the kitchen for the domestic servant. Living rooms were often large, with a view to the street. Children regularly slept in the same room as the parents. Having separate quarters for the children usually distinguished a lower-middle class family from an upper-middle class one. Most middle-class families had at least one live-in maid, lower class families had none.

Lower-class living conditions were quite different from those of the middle class. It was not uncommon for the 400,000 members of the working-class in Budapest that four or more people lived in one room. In 1869, the average room in Budapest housed 3.2 persons. In 1900 this had improved to 2.6 persons per room. In Vienna conditions were just as bad. In 1910 the average number of persons in a Viennese apartment was 4.4. It also occurred that people would rent out bed space – not a room, just the use of a bed. Two-thirds of these 'bed-tenants' were men.

The working hours of the proletariat were long. Galician textile workers put in 17

Above: *One of the typical elements of folk architecture was the veranda, which was articulated by a row of covered columns that ran the entire length of the house. Photo by Mór Erdélyi.*

hours a day in the summer and between 14 and 15 in the winter. In Budapest, before 1914, 12 hours a day were common, sometimes people worked as many as 16 hours. Viennese workers in the late 19th century worked 7 days and 70 hours a week.

Lower Classes: Peasants

Late 19th- and early 20th-century life in Austria–Hungary, as it was described in the scholarship of fin de siècle Vienna, Budapest and Prague, for example, is often remembered for its bourgeois character, but the majority of the population in both halves of the Dual Monarchy until 1914 was rural, mainly peasants. Both halves of Austria–Hungary were essentially agrarian. Rural life was local with an emphasis on traditions and maintaining the status quo. This meant that daily life in the rural Habsburg Monarchy was varied, depending on one's location and customs. Yet even village life began to change in the late 19th century. As mentioned earlier, many rural youth left the village for either the new world or an urban setting. Sometimes they returned. This interaction as well as the innovations of modernism being introduced into their rural environment began to change the peasant's world everywhere in the Monarchy.

Educational policies, those of both Vienna and Budapest, brought more schools and standardised educational programmes to all people. In Galicia, which had had a fairly bad track record, by 1900 two-thirds of the children of appropriate age were attending school. The expanding bureaucracy often brought new members of the intelligentsia to rural villages, adding a local administrator to the common duo of priest and teacher. These individuals and motivated reformers also brought new ideas to the rural world. Especially in Cisleithania, but throughout the Monarchy, new forms of associational life were created, such as singing societies, agrarian circles, and peasant credit societies, frequently led by educated or more cosmopolitan individuals.

What was available to peasants also changed. Many rural communities used to live off what they produced; village stores might have carried liquor and salt. By the late 19th century, stores began to carry clothing, rice, white flour, paraffin, oranges and various other products that peasants had never seen before. It also became more common for peasants to travel to regional markets. This often brought rural peoples into contact with new ideas, as well as different languages and customs, since the entire Monarchy was multinational. Some of the most famous multinational markets were the Swabian (Hungarian German) markets in Budapest.

Austria–Hungary survived for more than 50 years, until it succumbed to the circumstances at the end of World War I. Its life was not an easy one; like most European states at the time it struggled to modernise in a socially and economically changing environment. Neither half of the Monarchy was 'backward,' as some historical literature may emphasise, rather both halves faced constant tension between the centre and the periphery, between Vienna and Prague or between Budapest and its nationalities. The conflicts and the changes were not in the interest of everyone, especially the peasants, the working class, and many of the nationalities. The lives they had in 1867 had been radically remade by 1918. The history of the Habsburg Monarchy was complicated and full of tension as its political and economic leaders worked to make both halves of the Monarchy modern.

Right: *Courtyard of a suburban house, Budapest.*

Péter Hanák

The Garden and the Workshop:

Reflections on the fin de siècle Culture in Vienna and Budapest

Vienna as the hotbed of European culture, the maturing metropolis of Budapest close behind, cultural florescence thriving throughout the Austro-Hungarian Monarchy – these were some of the subjects of concern to cultural historians over the past quarter century. Historians have repeatedly posed the question, 'How could such a flower garden bloom on the depleted soil of a worn-out and eroding empire?' Impressionism, Sezession, Jugendstil, psychoanalysis, the New School of Music – were they merely the *fleurs du mal*, the 'flowers of decomposition', of the Monarchy? Was this culture inspired by the 'slight rapture of death', or was the whole structure void of a foundation and its glitter nothing more than a mirage? Such reflections by modern historians are postscripts, of course. Contemporaries, if they saw or experienced the deficiencies or sensed the decline at all, had no foreknowledge of the inexorable collapse. Stefan Zweig, the Austrian novelist, wrote in his memoir that the period before the First World War was the 'golden age of security'. Everything in the thousand-year-old Monarchy was made for eternity, 'and the State itself was the foremost guarantor for this durability'. Security in one's life and one's life's course, the durability of objects and institutions, were taken as self-evident by the people of this time.

Above: *Gold pendant decorated with enamel, rubies and moonstone from about 1900, made in Vienna.*

Of course a writer need not be a prophet, especially in Austria a good quarter century after the decline of the era of peace. The retrospections of Zweig and many other contemporaries will not invalidate the premonitions among impregnable writers and intellectuals, premonitions that we present-day historians are so eager to expose. What the Monarchy's, and specifically Vienna's, intuitive, perhaps even neurotic, intellectual prophets sensed was a malaise on a societal scale and a growing feeling of foreboding. The outside world became ever more frightening, the liberal rational outlook grew ever fainter, and centuries-old European values became shallow. Vienna's vibrant culture experienced what Carl Schorske fittingly called the 'crisis and dissolution of the liberal Ego'. In looking at fin de siècle Vienna and present-day interpretations of it, one readily accepts the notion that this wonderful culture fed on the chronic failures of the Austrian bourgeoisie; the middle class was impelled to retreat into the private sphere, into the seclusion of Gardens.

The notion is certainly valid for Vienna; but what about Budapest, Prague, or Cracow, 'the provinces'? Here also the decline of liberalism and the signs of upheaval were evident. Impressionable artists could sense the anxiety, and decadence infiltrated the public mind. In Budapest the spark of liberalism flared up once more, most prominently in the 1890s. With the new century political radicalism caught fire – as it did, for example, in France. The phenomenon might be called a late reaction, a feverish 'catching-up complex' of a backward agrarian country, an argument with ready evidence to support it. When Hugo von Hofmannsthal and his literary group Junges Wien appeared in Vienna, Budapest had only one politically loyal and diffident literary journal, *A Hét* (The Week); when in Vienna, Klimt and his friends

Left: *Gustav Klimt (1862–1918) painted two portraits of Adele Bloch-Bauer. This painting (1907) marked number I and partly decorated in gold and silver, can now be seen in Neue Galerie in New York. After purchasing the work Ronald Lauder said, 'This is our Mona Lisa'.*

were provocative and bold enough to
launch their *Ver Sacrum* and erect the
brilliant Sezession building, in Hungary
a group of young painters withdrew to
Nagybánya in the far corner of the
country to grasp open air and the
fleeting image in provincial reclusion.

Between Vienna and Budapest
there was a delay of a decade or
two; yet to use this circumstance to
explain the essence of the differences
between the two would be a gross
oversimplification. There were similar
signs of what has been called 'the
decadence of the Monarchy' in the two
neighbouring strongholds of Munich
and Berlin as well, and even beyond
the German borders it is evident
that Sezession, symbolism, the search
for novel forms to express the
intelligentsia's new sentiment, the crisis
of tradition and cultural upheaval were
phenomena not confined to the
Monarchy or to Central Europe. They
affected Europe overall, a fact that
underlines the argument that the turn-
of-the-century cultural boom was by no
means an outgrowth of the decaying
Monarchy. The boom was not the result
of failure, retreat, or confused identity
on the part of the Austrian bourgeoisie.
In fact, no single factor or tendency can
account for the complex historic
phenomena of a whole era. There must
always be several factors that happen to
coincide at a given time, and they defy
hierarchical classification.

The Garden: An Illusion-and-Reality Play

In 1890 a group of writers, led
by author and critic Hermann Bahr
and poet and playwright Hugo von
Hofmannsthal, gathered in Vienna to
form Das Junge Wien. The same
year in Budapest the journal *A Hét*
(The Week, but initially planned to be
named 'Young Hungary') was launched
as the herald of a new literary age.
What these young people in both

capitals wanted was a modern literature. Their definition of 'modern', however, was not quite the same.

In Vienna modern meant submersion into an inner reality, the psyche, and reality was the world created in a work of art. 'Man either researches the anatomy of his own psyche or he dreams. Reflection or fantasy, mirror or dream image,' wrote the young Hugo von Hofmannsthal. To be modern was to listen to the grass grow and the tremors of the soul, an instinctive, somnambulant surrender to any expression of beauty. Hysteria, neurosis and dreams were favoured subjects, not to say symptoms, of the erudite elite well before Freud. Das Junge Wien started out as an outright antinaturalist literary movement, which was a strange paradox, because in Viennese culture, with hardly a trace of naturalism, there was nothing there to defeat. This 'gathering of a generation', was motivated by social and political influences rather than literary ones, even though their ideals and criteria were purely aesthetic.

What the young writers in Budapest considered 'modern', it was, more than anything else, to do away with the outdated popular-national art of epigones and replace it with trends prevalent in the west of Europe. In other words, modernity was realism and naturalism – though at the end of the century Symbolism and the Sezession also seeped into Budapest. For a more concrete sense of the differences between the two cultures one must look at their experiences, the subjects and styles they dealt with most often.

The intimate home and figurative setting of the Viennese youth was the Garden.

The Garden meant either what it is by primary definition, a closed-off piece of preserved nature or, metaphorically, a place of solitude and retreat; or as with Rilke, the antithesis to the bleak concrete landscape of the chaotic metropolis. So the Garden was not just a refuge for body and soul but was the vehicle for aesthetics, the unity of man as a product of nature and the work of art as a product of man.

The Garden and solitude, solitude and the narcissistic self; these are ready metaphors. More involved is the relationship between the Garden and the theatre, which was the other decisive experience of the young Viennese in their cultural renewal. To them the

Hans Makart (1840–1884)

'No other master in the 19th century exerted as profound and great an influence on the development of art in Vienna as this young man from Salzburg,' said Albert Ilg, praising Hans Makart. And indeed, paintings such as Catherine Cornaro in Venice *(1873),* The Entry of Charles V into Antwerp *(1877), and* Cleopatra *(1875) – the latter of these showing eastern influence – earned Makart worldwide fame. His style, characterised by brilliant colours and a love for splendour, influenced an entire generation of painters. His paintings often decorated the banqueting halls and ceilings of Viennese palaces. His achievement in applied arts and in the so-called 'industry of opulence' was also of abiding value: Makart hats, Makart nosegays and Makart roses were among the characteristic pieces of fashion in Vienna at the turn of the 19th and 20th centuries.*

The subject matter of his art, which was imbued with monumentality and classicism, was equally dominated by historical events and mythology (e.g. Nessus Abducts Deianeia*, 1874), but his portraits of women (e.g.* The Portrait of Madame Rosa Riess*) are also well known. His atelier, decorated with musical instruments, and bedecked with flowers and jewellery, was not only the 'birthplace' of his paintings but also functioned as a salon where prominent artists could meet their audience, and played an important role in social life in Austria.*

Garden was often a stage, a theatrical setting. What comes to mind most prominently is Hugo von Hofmannsthal's prologue to Arthur Schnitzler's cyclic drama *Anatol*.

Eine Laube statt der Bühne,
Sommersonne statt der Lampen, Also spielen wir Theatre, Spielen unsereeignenStlicke …
A bower, not the stage,
The summer sun, not lights, Thus we play theatre, Act our own plays …

Many saw in this Garden-theatre, this arbour play, a Rococo motif: a nostalgia for the 18th century. Of course, Baroque theatre did have a strong tradition in Vienna, but the fin de siècle Welttheatre was Baroque only in its respect for tradition; its content had nothing to do with morality plays or pastorals. It was, rather, a moment snatched out of the cycle of life and death.

Fin de siècle theatre in Vienna was not a gallant Rococo play but a tragic life experience. In life we take on roles, we feign, 'put on an act', and only on the stage do

Below: *This characteristic Secessionist building, which opened in 1891, was designed by Josef Olbrich, who was Otto Wagner's student.*

we act out the tragicomedy of our lives, thus showing our true selves. An interpretation such as this of the relationship between stage and reality may have been inspired by Kierkegaard or Nietzsche: we must live life as a piece of art because art is true reality. If that is so, then illusion and reality are not opposites but mutual substitutes, two states of one and the same reality; the concept runs through many of Schnitzler's dramas.

Closely related to the subjects of Garden and theatre is a third notion, that there is a continuity of, and relation between, life and death, a continuity that is symbolised by dreams, or Psyche, and love, Eros.

As we know, dreams play a central role in Viennese art. They inspired Freud, just as he in turn inspired art when he uncovered the depth of the psyche.

The ambiguous, transitional interpretation of dreams appeared in Gustav Klimt's great works of the Sezession, most likely inspired by psychoanalysis. One of his symbolic murals commissioned by the University of Vienna (*Medizin*, 1901) shows Hygeia in the foreground holding up the symbols of healing, the snake and the chalice with the water of the Lethe; behind her are floating figures, half awake and half in slumber, nascent or dying. Even more expressive, even in its title, is the painting *Death and Life* (1916), where Death stands apart, robed in a splendid cape with a pattern of crosses, and directs the circulation of sleeping beings, nascent, resting and dying.

Yet Klimt, and other Viennese artists of the Sezession, also saw dreams in another way. Dreaming, or closed eyelids conveying surrender and transfiguration, expressed the timelessness of sexual ecstasy. The mutual influence of dreams and reality is already discernible in Klimt's earliest picture on the subject (*Love*, 1895), and became a more and more frequently recurring motif in his erotic pictures (*Danae, Judith-Salome*, the kiss motif in his *Beethoven* frieze, and so on). We might explain this accent on sensuality with the Sezession's idolisation of beauty, or the erotic atmosphere of the Viennese art world, or even take it as a kind of war of liberation against prudish academicism, which tried to take the erotic even out of mythological nudity. But there is more behind such eroticism: something mystic, metaphysical and philosophic.

It is sexual ecstasy, the timeless moment, new life conceived and the lovers, their task fulfilled, meeting symbolically in death. In the Sezession death there was nothing horrifying, neither hostile nor glorifying, not a superhuman principle. It was life's partner and escort, admonishing when all went well, and embracing at the time of tribulation and suffering. A wonderful example of this view is one of Egon Schiele's masterpieces, *Death and the Maiden* (1915/1916), in which Death is an old Franciscan friar softly embracing the Girl, whose life is as worn as her dress.

Perceiving death as an organic part of existence and treating it as something aesthetic were central ideas in the Austrian empire. Such writers as the young Rainer Maria Rilke (1875–1926) wrote about this.:

Lass mich nicht sterben, eh ich weiss
Wie sich der Tod zu dir verhalt!

Above: *A nostalgic yearning for rural life and mischievous flirtation can both be seen in Simon Hollósy's* Corn Husking *(1885).*

Anton Bruckner (1824–1896)

Practically contemporaneous with the birth of the Dual Monarchy, Anton Bruckner arrived in Vienna in 1868, to take up a teaching post in the Vienna conservatoire. Son of a primary school teacher in Ansfeld, former organist at the cathedral of Linz, he had difficulty finding his feet in the teeming and alarming splendour of the capital of the empire. Though he lived, taught and composed here until his death, for nearly 30 years, he never found a way out of his social isolation, or his solitude as a man and an artist.

The era resounded with the fray between the factions of the 'new Germans' and the 'conservatives'. Against Liszt and Wagner, the standard-bearers of the renewal of musical language, Vienna (naturally) represented the first defender of tradition. In such an atmosphere it is noteworthy that Bruckner (who incidentally was a Wagner lover) managed to gain increasing recognition with his symphonies. The eternal riddle of Bruckner literature is how the composer's acknowledged 'modest simplicity', his old-fashioned appearance and naive behaviour can be reconciled with the incredible scale of his works, with their monumental proportions, eccentricities and defiance. The contrast between Bruckner's character and his oeuvre is likely the trace of a more general Zeitgeist: behind the overblown symphonic language lies an almost desperate gesture of the era – at once to retain and to surpass the legacy of the past.

Starting with Symphony no. 2 *in 1872, Bruckner produced orchestral works every one or two years, as if to schedule, while also pursuing a respectable teaching career. As mentioned earlier, he taught harmony and counterpoint, first at the Conservatoire, then from 1875 at the philosophy faculty of the university.*

Above: Anton Bruckner

Gustav Mahler (1860–1911)

That the spirit of the peculiar art of the Ninth Symphony, *composed over nine years yet left unfinished, was sustained was in part thanks to Gustav Mahler, who was briefly in personal contact with the maestro, and who later felt his art to be most akin to that of Bruckner. Mahler's career and music were no less contradictory than his elder colleague's. His guiding principle –* Tradition ist Schlamperei *(tradition is slovenliness) – which characterised primarily his career as conductor and director, in the moderately progressive intellectual air of Austro-Hungary at the dawn of modernism, was bold in the extreme. It is hardly surprising that when Mahler was appointed to the helm of the Vienna Imperial Opera, the critic of the* Vienna Fremdenblatt, *Ludwig Speidel, displayed concern over the looming criticism and sniping: 'Not only is Herr Mahler an excellent conductor, he is a first-rate director, and even privy to the secrets of theatre management … Herr Mahler will certainly work as artistic leaven, if, that is, he is allowed to work at all,' he wrote.*

He was, quite rightly, regarded as the best conductor in Austro-Hungary. He had already proved his abilities as director of the Budapest opera (1888–1891), and the premiere of Mascagni's Cavalleria rusticana, *on 26th December 1890, was talked of long afterwards. But his world fame and the peak of his conducting career were without doubt due to the 10 years spent as head of the Vienna Opera (1897–1907). While his 'new spirit' productions of* Tristan, Fidelio, Don Giovanni *and* Rigoletto *won great acclaim, Mahler's own works, composed mainly in the summers in Maiernigg next to Lake Wörth, including such masterpieces as the* Second, Third *and* Fifth Symphonies *and a good few orchestral songs enjoyed more modest popularity. Members of the young upcoming generation of musicians, including Schoenberg, Zemlinsky and Bruno Walter, however, looked with admiration on the works of Mahler, whose oeuvre, precisely through the rise of this young generation, slowly became reinterpreted as the end of an era: the era of Romantic music.*

Left: Gustav Mahler

Ist er der Widerspruch der Welt? Ist er ihr Heil?

Ist er ein Teil von dir, des Lebens Teil?

Do not let me die before I know

How Death behaves with you!

Is he the contradiction of the world? Is he its good,

Is he a part of you, a part of life?

Very similar is the perception of the young Hofmannsthal. In his first drama, *Der Tor und der Tod* (*Death and the Fool*, 1913) the protagonist, Claudio, his life squandered, is led by the hand by a gentle fiddler who personifies his death.

The beauty of dying, such a refined, perhaps decadent, pleasure, is also what hinders Anatol in Schnitzler's *Agonie* (*Agony*) from breaking off with his lover. In the Viennese Sezession, the aesthetic treatment of death directly gave rise to regarding death as something erotic.

That death was not just aesthetic but also erotic and associated with love, or to put it differently, that Eros and Thanatos were alternates, has long been discovered and written about in literature. The Salome theme had a revival at the turn of the century, in Beardsley's stirringly erotic drawings or Wilde's forceful play, which in turn inspired Richard Strauss's musical drama (conceived in Vienna but premiered in Dresden because of its provocative, erotic treatment of death), and *Tristan and Isolde* was extremely popular. Less known are Schnitzler's variations on the love-and-death theme in short stories and dramas, his danse macabre of love in his *Reigen* (*Hands Around*, Dover Publications, 1995), or the ecstatic agony that was Professor Bernhardi's source of conflict.

Above: *The portrait of Alma Mahler in a hat was taken in Madame D'Ora's photographic studio.*

Solitude, Garden, illusion and reality, the play of life and death, are all evident in the works of the rebellious young writers and painters of the fin de siècle. However, the Viennese Sezession forked out into another direction as well. It was the Wiener WerkstJitte, the renowned studio of applied arts of the Viennese Sezession, which while abnegating eclectic art did not retreat from public life, and while working a garden also erected a real and famous workshop.

No doubt there was a sort of ambivalence to this sort of abnegation without retreat. A foremost representative of the Garden culture, Hofmannsthal was quite deliberate when he claimed that its refined aesthetics and ornamentation brought to light a well-defined social stratification in Vienna that had been present since the baroque. To break

Left: *The writer Hermann Bahr in Emil Orlik's coloured print. Bahr was the organiser and propagator of new Austrian literature, and the leading voice of the modernists.*

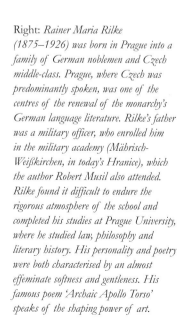

Above: *Arthur Schnitzler's school-leaving photograph was taken by József Székely.*

Right: *Rainer Maria Rilke (1875–1926) was born in Prague into a family of German noblemen and Czech middle-class. Prague, where Czech was predominantly spoken, was one of the centres of the renewal of the monarchy's German language literature. Rilke's father was a military officer, who enrolled him in the military academy (Mährisch-Weißkirchen, in today's Hranice), which the author Robert Musil also attended. Rilke found it difficult to endure the rigorous atmosphere of the school and completed his studies at Prague University, where he studied law, philosophy and literary history. His personality and poetry were both characterised by an almost effeminate softness and gentleness. His famous poem 'Archaic Apollo Torso' speaks of the shaping power of art.*

entirely with tradition was to be rejected, to sustain it rigidly was impossible. Beauty in art and knowledge must be shared with the people, yet it is questionable and uncertain whether the people wish it. Several of Hofmannsthal's short stories and dramas testify to his social conscience and also to his fear. His retreat was motivated not so much by what the Roman philosopher Horace called *odi profanum vulgus* but rather the intellectual attitude of *timeo vulgus* (that is, not 'I loathe the uninitiated masses' but 'I fear the masses').

'Look,' Hofmannsthal wrote in 1900, 'if I pronounce: I and you, chaos breaks out. So leave me be, let me read my dictionary.' Two years later he formulated his famous Chandos letter, a document on the impossibility of human communication.

Branching out of Junges Wien and the fin de siècle artists of the Sezession was another, socially more open and active, group, hallmarked by Hermann Bahr and the art of Josef Hoffmann. In the introductory words of their magazine, *Ver Sacrum*, in 1898, they declared war against 'Byzantinism and all bad taste'. This young generation was out to take on art that addressed its own age and people. 'We know no difference between "high art" and "mass art" or art for the rich and art for the poor'. And should the simple folk fail to understand the culture that was to become public property then it must be instructed on how to gain a firm knowledge, to understand and get involved, 'so that you shall rule over the spirits! That

The greatest cabinet-maker: Michael Thonet

Michael Thonet (1796–1871) set himself up as a cabinet-maker and building joiner in 1819 in Boppard on the Rhine. He relocated to Vienna on the invitation of Chancellor Metternich. He experimented with bending wood from the beginning of his career: first he tried to boil and glue wood, then he patented his steam bending method.

In this process wood was steamed, placed in a bender and then compressed in a press. Thonet's innovations not only included the design and bending methods of his furniture but also the organisation of work. In 1857, he had his first furniture factory built in Moravia, far from the cities and near to birch woods, the main raw material of his furniture. This was followed by a further eight factories by 1900. The furniture produced in these factories was not glued but joined by screws, and was thus suitable

for baling (14 chairs were packaged in a bale of about one cubic metre) and transported by sea. By the 1860s Thonet's bent birch wood furniture products had become an essential feature of the coffeehouses in the Monarchy, and were popular worldwide. By 1930, 50 million pieces of the legendary Thonet chair had been sold.

At the turn of the century prominent architects and applied artists, such as Josef Hoffmann and Otto Wagner, worked with the Thonet brothers' company.

The chair (middle left) was made after 1905. It is a variant of Otto Wagner's design, originally made for the Sparkasse in Vienna. The bent birch cane-seated resting and armchair (left) from about 1885 is an example of the highly decorative style of the Secession.

Right: *Hermann Bahr, Richard Beer-Hofmann, Hugo von Hofmannsthal and Arthur Schnitzler posing in an instant photograph taken in the Prater.*

shall be our mission.' Hermann Bahr called on his fellow artists to create something entirely new: 'You must accomplish something that has never before existed, you must create Austrian art ... I long to live among such objects that are a part of Viennese art ... Envelop our people in Austrian beauty!'

The initial slogan of the Viennese Sezession had been a militant '*Der Zeit ihre Kunst, der Kunst ihre Freiheit*!' (Art to the Age, Liberty to Art!). It was passionately social and extroverted, with a determination to make life better. It knew that the artist 'has to stand with both feet in the thick of life.'

It may appear as a mistake, a self-contradiction on my part, to label as an esoteric 'Garden culture', a trend that is so consciously aware of its mission, but paradoxical as it may seem, the label fits. Rarely were intention and execution so disparate as with the rebellious generation of the Sezession. Their ornamentation was charming, impressing even the average person in the street, yet their choice of form, their philosophy and subconscious symbolism remained alien. The contradiction lies much deeper than could be gauged by the person in the street, however. The Sezession was detached and therefore in a bad mood, full of existential anxieties. This was not something that could be expressed by decorative, stylised beauty, any more than a cripple can find a cure in beauty or art.

Nor did the household objects the Wiener Werkstatte created really reach the person in the street. The tenet that everything the group created must be fully handcrafted drove up the prices beyond his means. The Sezession's aim was to deliver humankind through beauty. They offered clearly laid-out, hygienically polished houses, handcrafted wallpaper and furniture, door knobs and dishes, in short, industrial art. But in the end only the wealthy and only people with refined tastes and a sense for art were able to move into such houses, because only a select few could afford these paintings, jewels, silks and tapestries. The Viennese Sezession failed to lift the barrier between high and mass culture, in making art a public treasure and, even its most typical workshop, the Wiener Werkstatte, failed to break out of the Garden. Rather it remained confined to the greenhouse, a peculiar Garden culture workshop of the cultural elite. That became its downfall.

Above: *Egon Schiele's water-colour,* Embrace, *1915.*

Typecasting always holds the risk that from the overwhelming mass of data, one selects the ones that best fit one's intellectual disposition and preconceptions. Typecasting is arbitrary; it shows things to be either simpler or more important than they really are. What I treated as typical in the intellectual cast of fin de siècle Vienna was its aesthetic focus, even though there were also (aside from the light, operatic genres) the popular, socially committed dramas of this period in Germany, and pamphlets and fiction dealing with the Austrian's confused sense of identity.

Nor have I mentioned as typical Karl Kraus, the relentless and acrimonious critic of the Monarchy's political system and the society and literature of his time. I omitted him not only because he was a self-declared outsider (who said that Vienna's population of 2,030,834 consisted of 2,030,833 inhabitants and Karl Kraus) nor because in spite of all his sympathies he refused to join the Social Democratic party (who took offense and called him an ivory-tower aesthete). The reason I did not mention him lies in his own explanation for his self-isolation. 'If my choice is only the lesser of two evils,' he replied to a critic, 'I prefer to choose neither.' Kraus also lashed out at the young artists of the Sezession, at their flight into the Garden world of illusion, and he predicted the catastrophe that was to befall the Monarchy and subsequently humankind.

Out of all the parallel and contradicting tendencies I took Junges Wien as typical because it best represented the unity of tradition and the break with it, that ability to strike a balance that is an attribute of the Austrian intellect. But is there such a thing as the Austrian intellect? And if there is, how can it be defined? To Thomas Mann it balanced lack and excess of form; to Rudolf Kassner it was the gauge that, wedged between life and death, holds both together. Hermann Bahr characterised the Austrian intellect by its inability to choose between antipodes, so that by avoiding saying no to anything it strikes a balance between extremes. Everything is true and at the same time interchangeable. At the point of utmost happiness come tears; in greatest suffering is a trace of happiness; in life and art, happiness and pain, illusion and reality blend.

It must have been exactly this modern reinterpretation of the relationship between illusion and reality that was the specific and lasting achievement of fin de siècle Vienna. It set forth not only the illusiveness of the real world and the realness of the illusory world but also the relative relationship between illusion and reality. The thought must have come from Ernst Mach, whom the young rebels took it from, as did the sober physicist Einstein. But with them all, Mach included, the thought sprang from, and was nurtured by, the Monarchy itself.

Above: *Freud's apartment, where he also had his medical practice, now houses a museum.*

The Workshop: The Attraction between Life and Public Life

As seen from Vienna, the Monarchy was inspirational and nurturing. In Budapest the old world's expiration was perceived and depicted differently. Here the young

Opposite: *Otto Wagner, Vienna, Linke Wienzeile 38.*

generation, a newly maturing age group, grew up, lived and worked not in gardens and villas but, for the most part, in editorial offices and cafes. The question arises whether the cultures of the two capitals may be compared at all. Can we put Garden and Workshop in the same balance? What can we hope to gain from searching for exotic flowers in a bustling editorial office or by trying to discover the Viennese's experiences in the background of the people in Budapest? Or if we take the Budapest Workshop, with its own works and its belief in a Utopia, how could we possibly compare it with the aesthetics of the Viennese, who renounced Utopia altogether? The answer is that we can gain something from the comparison, namely, an understanding of the differences in social commitment and orientation between the two cultures.

Cultural renewal in Budapest was initiated by the young staff of *A Hét*. All were in their twenties, apart from editor Jozsef Kiss who was in his late forties. *A Hét* reveals hardly a trace of fin de siècle ennui and melancholy. The paper was fresh, full of ideas and open to everything. Its aim was to refine middle-class tastes and to instill the value of freedom; its articles dealt with social problems and inequities. It latched on to anything to do with public life at home and abroad. As the philosopher Bernat Alexander put it, 'For decades literature to us was something much greater than a source of aesthetic pleasure … Our writers served aesthetics with one hand only, with the other they took on … the defense of the national spirit. Our literature was to us not our entertainment but served as our temple.'

Life and public life merged in this philosophy on art, where life was relevant to the artist only insofar as it was an integral part of public life.

Above: *Kálmán Mikszáth (1847–1910) made his mark as a writer, publicist, newspaper editor and parliamentary representative. In his first truly successful collection of short stories, he portrayed the typical characters living in his native land, Northern and Upper Hungary with love and irony. By the 1880s, Mikszáth had become one of the most popular writers in Hungary alongside Jókai. His short stories and novels, often containing sarcasm and social criticism, are among the most reliable pieces of documentation on Hungary at the time of the Monarchy.*

The central theme of the new Hungarian culture was the country's backwardness, which this generation may have thought more severe than it really was. They decried the country as medieval and beset with social injustice. Their sensitivity found expression not only in journalism but also in fiction and writings on art theory. In the solitary, mystic painter, László Mednyánszky, they saw someone who 'revealed to us the world of suffering, exposed the wounds of life, proclaimed for us the doctrine of relief.'

Of course, poverty upset young writers everywhere, even in Vienna. As the young poet Sándor Bródy wrote about Budapest, 'And amidst the almost listless prosperity of the happy city came to mind again and again the poverty of the metropolis'. It was not uncommon for young writers like Bródy to be in love and willing to face death for the sake of their ladies, or perhaps to write an aesthetic 'thanatology' (a study of death among human beings). But it is surely a Budapest specialty that the kiss of the muse inspired a volume on poverty. 'How could I have chosen not to write it if she, too, wished it?' Bródy was to argue later.

The young people of Budapest were enthusiastic about the Sezession, though perhaps less for its style than for the revolutionary spirit that came out of it. 'My Sezession is the struggle of progress against narrow-mindedness,' wrote Ady. 'The Sezession is not a style but a liberty, the artist's revolt against art which is not created by him but which governs him,' wrote an admirer about Ödön Lechner, the pioneer of the Sezession in Hungary. He saw Lechner's greatness in his being a truly 'heroic freedom fighter who helps tear down barriers and overthrow tyrants.'

In this sense the young painters who followed their master, Simon Hollosy, to Nagybánya were freedom fighters also. Far from the bustle of the capital and public life they nevertheless propagated a bourgeois culture in painting that opposed the traditional trend with its aristocratic/national/historical themes and its rigid academism. In this sense the Vígszínház Theatre that opened in 1896 was also innovative. It was established as an alternative to the inveterate National Theatre, and looked out to Europe; it popularised Ibsen, Chekhov, the German social dramas and the fashionable French plays, and at the same time established a veritable workshop for modern acting. A decade later the avant-garde company Thalia was established for the express purpose of propagating progressive ideas. It came to symbolise the coming together of radical intelligentsia and socialist workers.

The solitary heroes, life's drop-outs, were given a place in Hungarian literature and on the stage, provided they were the bearers of the real historical and social drama. 'Our Fate is that of the albatross thrown on the dry shore, helplessly stumbling in the

The national–historical romantic novel

The most popular Hungarian writer in the period of the Monarchy was the great storyteller Mór Jókai (1825–1904), who was inspired by Victor Hugo and Walter Scott. He had 202 books published, in his lifetime, and the first publication of his oeuvre, encompassing the period from 1894 to 1898, consisted of 100 volumes. His works covered almost every major event in Hungarian history, from the Turkish period to the end of the 20th century. Jókai's approach to Hungarian history is clearly expressed in his own definition, which appeared in his first anthology of short stories entitled Pictures of Fight, *after the failure of the War of Independence of 1848–1849.*

'Let's write mythology. Let's describe the events of the year truly and faithfully, including all that happened, every wonderful, superhuman splendid thing we saw and experienced and to which we were witnesses'. Mythology changes the traditional genre framework of the adventure novel and the social novel and Jókai consciously related the most superb novels that appeared in quick succession following the Compromise to the epic genre: The Baron's Sons *(1869),* Black Diamonds *(1870) and* The Golden Man *(1872).*

The narrative style represented by Jókai's national-romantic works found many followers among the younger generation. Among these adherents was Géza Gárdonyi (1863–1922), whose novel entitled Stars of Eger *(1901), mediated the same noble, heroic–patriotic ethos. The idealisation of Hungarian nobility presented in his historical novels was paralleled with the idyllic picture of the world of the peasants. His short stories portraying the harmony, honesty and purity of the world of peasants and rural life were published in the volume entitled* My Village *(1898).*

Hungarian Musicians on the World Stage: Goldmark and Dohnányi

Above: Károly Goldmark

'With all due modesty perhaps you will forgive me the small satisfaction of stating: I am the only Austrian composer (Brahms and Volkmann cannot be counted as such) whose works can be found on every German and non-German concert programme,' wrote Károly Goldmark (1830–1915), the best-known composer of Hungarian origin of the late 19th century, in a letter of 1873. Keszthely-born Goldmark, whose importance in Hungarian music history has faded alongside Erkel, Bartók and Kodály, sought the assistance of a powerful Viennese music critic with a view to producing his temporarily 'boycotted' opera, The Queen of Sheba. *The opera was finally premiered in March 1875 thanks to the forceful intervention of Franz Liszt and Johannes Brahms, and due to its great success made the reputable 'Austrian' composer's name known far and wide. During his long life, the composer (who from 1870 until his death in 1915 travelled between Gmunden in Upper Austria and Vienna) was eye-witness to many changes in history and the arts. But he could not always keep up with the unexpected and frequent turns of fashion. He said: 'As I couldn't lead, and I didn't want to go with others, I preferred to progress alone.' Since he produced good, balanced work in almost every genre all along this individual path, by the end of his life he enjoyed a good reputation in Vienna and throughout the empire. This is well signalled by* the fact that in 1897, when Gustav Mahler was applying for the post of director of the opera, he went to Goldmark for support.

In the same year the Pressburg-born 20-year-old Ernő Dohnányi (1877–1960) won what was known as the King's Prize for his First Symphony *and* Zrínyi Overture. *A young student at the Academy of Music, who like Bartók, Kodály and Leó Weiner completed his studies in composition with Hans Koessler (1853–1926), he was a particularly talented performer: with his performance of Beethoven's* Fourth Piano Concerto *he conquered the hearts of first Vienna, then London and with it the whole of Britain. In 1900, after touring America, and premiering his* op. 1 C minor Piano Quintet *and his* op. 5 Piano Concerto, *he was spoken of as the greatest Hungarian pianist and composer since Liszt. Not so back home. In Hungary, both public and critics were fiercely divided over Dohnányi. Many thought his King's Prize was unwarranted and considered his piano quintet to be a mere imitation of Brahms'.*

No wonder then, that negative opinion drove the young artist to the venues of his successes: Vienna and then Berlin. The works of Dohnányi the composer are indeed much rather embedded in the centuries-old tradition of German music. In terms of composition he was conservative, and never ventured beyond the tonal idiom. But with his perfect and strict forms, his clarity of part-writing, he carried out important work: he

Above: Ernő Dohnányi

tried to transplant European musical language into Hungarian musical culture. Between 1905 and 1915 he lived and worked in Berlin, but after war broke out he returned to Hungary. From 1919 to 1944 he was the president-conductor of the Budapest Philharmonic Society, and from 1934 the director-in-chief of the Music Academy. He died in New York aged 83.

Opposite: In the *Album of the Exhibition of Hungarian Musical Composers*, published for the 1885 National Exhibition, editor István Bartalus collected compositions by 24 Hungarian musicians.

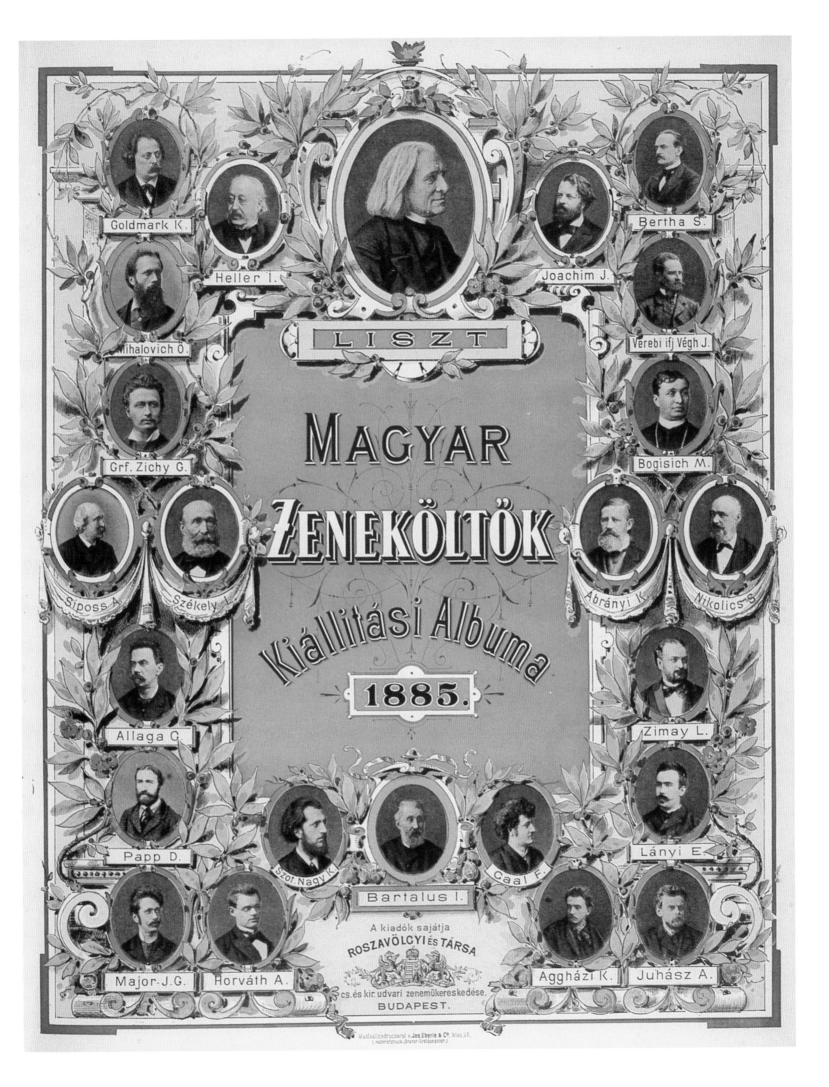

LISZT

MAGYAR ZENEKÖLTŐK Kiállitási Albuma 1885.

A kiadók sajátja
RÓSZAVÖLGYI ÉS TÁRSA
cs. és kir. udvari zeneműkereskedése.
BUDAPEST.

Goldmark K. — Heller I. — Bertha S. — Joachim J. — Mihalovich Ö. — Verebi ifj Végh J. — Grf. Zichy G. — Bogisich M. — Siposs A. — Székely I. — Abrányi K. — Nikolics S. — Allaga C. — Zimay L. — Papp D. — Szot. Nagy K. — Bartalus I. — Gaal F. — Lányi E. — Major J.G. — Horváth A. — Aggházi K. — Juhász A.

Right: *The Academy of Music in Ferenc Liszt Square, Budapest, is the largest concert hall in Hungary and is able to accommodate an audience of over 1,200 people. It also has the best acoustic qualities in Hungary.*

The Academy, opened in 1907, was designed by the winners of the 1902 competition, Kálmán Giergl and Flóris Korb. They designed several other famous buildings in Budapest but this remains their principal work.

Right: *The walls of the vestibule are decorated with colourful and ornate mosaic tiles, and the plaque placed above the well expresses acknowledgements to the king and the leading politicians of that time.*

Opposite: *A majestic seated full-length statue of Ferenc Liszt adorns the powerful facade.*

Late Romantic Fine Art

The elevation, harmony and pathos that appeared in literature in the novels of Jókai and Gárdonyi, in music in Erkel's operas, could be seen in painting in the historical tableaux and portraits of Viktor Madarász, Bertalan Székely and Gyula Benczúr. Themes pertaining to national history enjoyed enormous popularity. The historical paintings of Viktor Madarász, who fought in the 1848–1849 War of Independence, show the allegories of the war and the retribution that followed it. His main work, László Hunyadi on a Bier *(1859), alludes to the tragedy of this retribution through the depiction of the past.*

Gyula Benczúr was a painter with outstanding technical skill. He achieved enormous success with both his tableaux and portrait paintings. He painted the portraits of Sissi, Count Gyula Andrássy and Kálmán Mikszáth.

The public spaces of a rapidly developing Budapest were ornamented with statues in the historical style. The most significant of the impressive monuments at the turn of the century was Albert Schickedanz and György Zala's Millenium Monument *(1895–1929). The work of art which was created for the millennium celebration of the Magyar Conquest served to symbolise the eastern origins of the Hungarians and their joining the Christian fold, as well as the superiority of the people that constitute the nation and the validity of the Compromise: thus, the Archangel Gabriel holds the*

Bertalan Székely's *The Women of Eger*, 1867

Viktor Madarász's *László Hunyadi on a Bier*, 1859

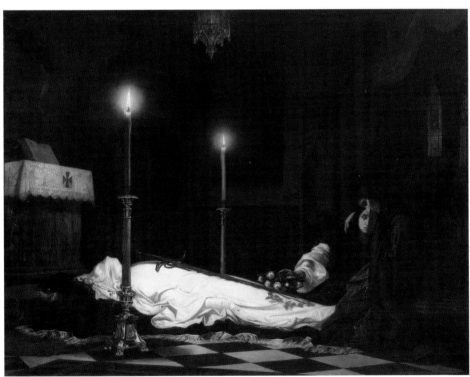

Holy Crown above the war leaders of the Conquest, while on the colonnade, half of the statues of the kings are from the House of Árpád and Anjou and the other half are of Habsburg rulers.

Alajos Stróbl's design of the Kossuth Mausoleum *(1901–1909) is an example of great use of symbols. In an interview the artist said: 'This is a charging, enraged lion, the nation and the genius running alongside it that has freed itself from its chains, while chasing the snake of intrigue. The lion is trussed up with a chain, but the end of the chain is held by the genius. He holds a torch in his hand, from which gas will burn on every All Saints Day.'*

sand, to the great amusement of the shore-dwellers.' But on the Hungarian stage mysticism was hardly a factor, and there were no mystery dramas. Also missing were agonies of private concern. Only the nation was entitled to a 'wonderful death'; common individuals could not put their trite death before the public, the country. 'Death is ordinary, it stinks, a thing without any poesy at all,' wrote Ignotus, one of the notables of the young generation.

The Hungarian cultural elite set only its ideals and not its life before the public, and showed tangible reality in an easy-to-understand, naturalistic form. Death from love was

Above: *Simon Hollósy's sketch,* Rákóczi March*, 1899*

frequently written about in the newspapers, pamphlets, and sometimes in fiction, but this was not the kind of death the Sezession spoke of. It was the usual romantic version, like a Biedermeier oil canvas. One young *A Hét* writer, Dezső Szomory, neither a romantic patriot nor at home in the Biedermeier, presented a touching drama about romantic love. A sick husband gets out of bed on his wedding anniversary to buy a gift for his beloved wife, thus causing his death, which in turn drives his equally loving wife mad.

In the workshop of *A Hét* lyrics, daydreaming and dreams were the tools at hand. The basic experience in Zoltán Ambrus's moving short story is an agonising dream; a boy comes under the spell of a beautiful but wicked fairy, and though he wishes to flee in terror he cannot. Later in his life the fairy of his dream pops up repeatedly, in the guise of a friend or a lover. We are almost swayed to believe that this is the death symbol of the Sezession, but at the end of the piece we find just the opposite. Death brings the writer out of his sweet dreams about dying and awakens him to bleak reality: when he was young death had wanted to bind him, in his old age and with death approaching it is love that leaves him by the wayside.

In comparing the cultures of fin de siècle Vienna and Budapest, negative parallels present themselves more readily than positive ones. In Budapest the culture was very public, as we have seen. Men of intellect did not appear on their private arbor-stages but in the forum, and did not reveal a private reality but lived the trials and tribulations of public life, which they turned into their personal problems. The trend became even more pronounced and more gripping in the first decade of the 20th century. That is especially true in one significant sense, namely, that in the literary consciousness of the young generation backwardness was now perceived as a self-evident fact. It was even bestowed a metaphoric name, taken from the poet Endre Ady's symbol of the Hungarian 'wasteland' with its smell of death, a grave of souls. The symbol is there also in Mihály Babits's *Fekete orszag* (Black Country), where everything to the marrow of

Left: *Béla Czóbel's* Sitting Man, *1906*

Nagybánya

In the summer of 1896 Simon Hollósy (1857–1918), the successful director of the free school in Munich, made an excursion with his artist colleagues and students to the picturesque, beautiful mining town of Nagybánya in eastern Hungary. Thanks to the environs of the town and the excellent young teachers, these occasional visits became the basis of another free school and a movement. Excursions were made every summer for 6 years. National diversity was a characteristic feature of the Nagybánya and Munich schools, the students of which were Hungarian, German, Polish, Romanian, Russian and Swiss.

The artists in the Nagybánya colony were initially influenced by the French Jules Bastien-Lepage, who enveloped the forms in his paintings with a nacreous glimmering and depicted genre scenes with refined naturalism. However, within a short time, the riotous colours of the nature around Nagybánya inspired the artists to paint cheerful plein air pictures. Because of his artistic approach, as well as for personal reasons, Hollósy was not able to reconcile with these changes and left Nagybánya, but the artists' colony continued.

The first period of painting in Nagybánya is mainly associated with István Réti, Béla Iványi-Grünwald and Károly Ferenczy (1862–1917). Ferenczy was the first artist in Nagybánya who gave an account of his artistic attempts aimed at using 'stage-design composition' in landscape painting ('placing forms into nature'). In 1903 the most successful pictures at his exhibition were the most characteristic works of the Nagybánya colony: Evening in March *(1902),* Summer Morning *(1902),* Summer *(1902),* Female Painter *(1903) and* October *(1903).*

Left: Károly Ferenczy's *Archaeology*, 1896

Right: *Károly Ferenczy's* Sunny Morning, *1905*

Above: *Béla Iványi Grünwald's* Outing in Spring, *1903*

Above: *József Rippl-Rónai's* Small Town Room, *1906*

Left: *József Rippl-Rónai's* Woman with a Bird Cage, *1892*

the bones is black; or more directly in his *Szimbolu-mok* (Symbols), where the speck of the country that is home lies abandoned and lightless: 'Fortune's great current dropped you halfway and you stand motionless, like an idle lake'.

The same picture appears in Dezső Kosztolányi's poems about the Hungarian Great Plain, where in the motionless, ancient land everything sleeps, 'dreams still hover here, sluggish dreams', and 'even the earth dreams of Asia'.

Above: *The Hungarian writer and playwright Dezső Szomory*

'Socially we live in prehistoric times,' Ady wrote in an article. This society had not come of age; it was uneducated, superstitious, and sick. 'In this country only aristocrats, priests, and asses can exist. And those who want to accommodate them.' 'Oppressed, backward, and beggarly, that's what we are ... Our people perishes because fate wants to destroy it.' But fate has its names: class society, class state, gendarmes. Oszkár Jászi, the leading figure among the young radicals, saw the problem similarly, in the system of the great estates, in the power of the landlords over the villages, in the towns and industrialisation that had not come of age.

The sense of backwardness and of perishing had a double source: the structure of society with all its remnants of feudalism weighing it down; and the strong sense of national identity felt by the Hungarian intellectual elite. So their slogan was not, as in Vienna, 'Liberty to Art!' Instead it was 'Liberty to the people!' meaning they did not want to redeem man through pure art rather they wished to mobilise the people with art for the war for the liberation of society. In Vienna modern political science was replaced by a subjective and relativistic philosophy. In Budapest it was founded on a positivistic sociology.

Literature and the newly evolving drama ran along the same lines as science and journalism. In the powerful play by Sándor Bródy entitled *A Tanitono (The Teacher)*, the heroine takes on a mission in hope of gaining social reform. Flora, pretty and educated, leaves the capital to teach in a godforsaken village. When questioned about her views she flings them at the petty village lords, 'I am a socialist ... on emotional grounds. I've created my own prayer, the same as I've created my own political creed, individually. Decent rich people must not be harmed. To poets ... we must erect palaces. And the concept of fatherland is beautiful, don't anyone dare touch it ... My dream: I'd like a big, an enormously big school that all peasant children would attend. I love peasant children. Did you ever see an ugly one? One is prettier than the next.'

'What is Magyar lies in the reforms,' wrote Ady around this time. To continue Ady's quote, 'Oppressed, backward and beggarly, that's what we are. But this is not the worst of our woes ... The people of Gog and Magog were shut away behind iron gates, but ... at least they could pound on the iron gates. Our people cannot do that. Their arms have been chopped off and they cannot pound even the gates of hell, only tumble into its grave as cripples, with bodies putrefied'. Out of such a tragic national condition and individual reclusion must come disillusionment, a longing to escape, the loss of a sense of identity. It did. In the early 20th century almost every great artist felt compelled to retreat, and faced a crisis of this sort. It was a time 'when autumn, winter, spring, and summer all came together.'

The Workshop's Double Identity: Life on the Run and a Shared Fate

In the one and a half decades after the turn of the century, the generation that made the journals *Huszadik század* (Twentieth Century) and *Nyugat* (West) – and perhaps all major Hungarian progressives – worked wonders. Here, where Asia was the product of the soil and of dreams, the time had come when they were catching up with Europe. Europe was there in the subject matter, the way they perceived things, in their depth of thinking – in short, in society's way of responding to the challenges and problems of becoming bourgeois. And much more than that, it was in their power of expression, their aesthetic treatment, their modern approach to the language of music, painting, and writing. Without self-glorification, the generation was able to 'elicit letter, line, colour and belief' in the adherents they recruited, though with varying success. They did it first of all by rebelling against the cliche that artistic expression had become, against imagination turned bland, against puffed-up platitudes and the deterioration of the language. In a single decade they caught up with, brought home, and instituted what there was to European culture. Intellectual rebirth was by no means directly and unambiguously in line with positivist rationality.

In approaching the ideas, the intellectual content, of these years it becomes evident that subjects of concern to Symbolism and the Sezession in Europe years earlier were dealt with in Hungary only in the decade preceding the war. Clearly the main theme here also was loneliness, chilling solitude, the severing of the communal transmission lines between communication, understanding – and along with that and from the same roots, the desire to escape, either into the self, the soul, the tower, or the Garden if you will, the harmony of the Garden before the Fall and the adoration of beauty. Solitude, a lack of understanding, anxiety, the wish to escape – these might be seen as a legacy of

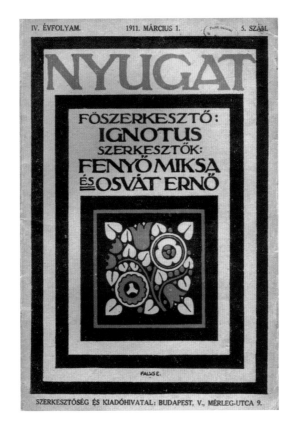

Above and left: *From its launch in 1908 up until 1929 the chief editor of Nyugat (West) was Ignotus (Hugó Veigelsberg). The new periodical was financed by the wealthy Lajos Hatvany, who was an ambitious writer himself.*

Romanticism or a bohemian eccentricity, if only in the meantime there had not evolved a stratum from the urban intellectuals that, having lost its footing and become marginal, sustained this type of thinking. Creative solitude was making its way into the depths of the soul: Mihály Babits, Endre Ady, Dezső Kosztolányi, Frigyes Karinthy – all arrived at psychoanalysis, the recognition and acceptance of ambivalence as the modern form of existence. Resolve was sought in art, there was reverence for beauty. Out of this grew the *Nyugat* generation's euphoria about language, their belief in the magic of the word; and this gave rise to the thesis of György Lukács and his circle that artwork is the primary reflection of reality. Now it became a constituent of literary taste to express amorous desires outright, whether that meant confessing to

Above: *The young Endre Ady.*

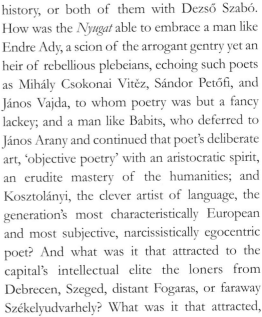

Right: *The cover of Ady's volume of poetry* Who Saw Me?, *published in 1914.*

masochistic and autoerotic narcissism or the portrayal of sensuality in the nude.

With the decades-long delay of these subjects, their counterpoint came almost automatically. Ugliness, sin, perishing and death were expressed and made aesthetic. To Ady, Babits, and especially Kosztolányi, Gyula Juhász and Árpád Tóth, the prime mover of existence was a fear of death coupled with a desire for it.

Literature and art suddenly became colourful and polyphonic. In Babits's words, 'the old idea shall wear a thousand coats, and the old form shall reappear as the suit of the new idea'.

Such was the renaissance of the capital and in part of the country at the beginning of the 20th century.

People with quite different views and from different subcultures came together in this young generation. Temperament, tradition and taste drew a chasm between, for example, Endre Ady and the young Mihály Babits and Dezső Kosztolányi, as they did between Zsigmond Móricz and Frigyes Karinthy and Milán Füst. Or taking the broader circle, it seems strange in retrospect how Oszkár Jászi and György Lukács could have been of one mind if only for a fleeting moment in history, or both of them with Dezső Szabó. How was the *Nyugat* able to embrace a man like Endre Ady, a scion of the arrogant gentry yet an heir of rebellious plebeians, echoing such poets as Mihály Csokonai Vitéz, Sándor Petőfi, and János Vajda, to whom poetry was but a fancy lackey; and a man like Babits, who deferred to János Arany and continued that poet's deliberate art, 'objective poetry' with an aristocratic spirit, an erudite mastery of the humanities; and Kosztolányi, the clever artist of language, the generation's most characteristically European and most subjective, narcissistically egocentric poet? And what was it that attracted to the capital's intellectual elite the loners from Debrecen, Szeged, distant Fogaras, or faraway Székelyudvarhely? What was it that attracted, and what repelled them? Perhaps the promise of Europe and modernity; and then the spiritual emptiness of their environment that became animated only when it came to uttering curses.

I think we may accept a 'yes', the answer that has been consecrated by posterity.

Ady's relentless political anger was incited by those 'Pumpkinseed Johnnies' who questioned his Magyarness and sought his downfall. They also kindled his poetic fire: 'How I should wish to hate myself. But God! they hate me too: I must not, cannot cease.'

Babits's later memoirs speak of the same theme. 'I was openly rebelling even then … I didn't drink, didn't hunt, and didn't talk politics, which in itself was considered revolutionary in Hungary at that time, where even poetry was tolerated and permitted only for politics' sake. They began to regard me as unpatriotic, which I was proud of, considering its horrendously wild, base mouthpieces.' Not the desire for, nor the idea of, social truth but a compulsion for it was what drove these tower-recluses back from Paris and Rome and into the forum. And something else: the fatherland, the Magyar nation, that lay hidden in and under the ground, somewhere below the present.

How often, and perhaps most pressingly in the critical year of 1905, did Ady write about having to become free of 'this hideous, murderous filth … I am leaving and that is that.' And he stayed on.

It was impossible to flee for someone who had relinquished the traditional framework and had preserved his popular and national identity even at the cost of losing his political home. Just when he was most impatient to leave, Ady asked in his programmatic poem whether one may cry at the foot of Carpathians. Babits, even under the blue skies of Italy, was tortured by the memories of his 'woeful land'. No matter how much he wished to rest idly, he was compelled to run and search. When he saw how obscure delusions were lulling his country to sleep he turned to Ady. Without denying all the differences between them, 'But we had one mother: Hungary. Still we're of one blood, we two, Though opposites, together one; My struggle is the continuance of yours.'

In search of the truth and in concern for the Magyar nation, otherwise reclusive poets like Árpád Tóth and Gyula Juhász were driven to the Workshop, the public forum, and even Kosztolányi, a man of European horizons, was also forced to raise his voice. To the latter, however, it was of no consequence where he was; at seeing the unstirring Hungarian Great Plain in full bloom he was driven to cry out, 'You send me to revolt now, to brawl, A drunken Magyar in the tavern of the world!'

Instead of withdrawing from the national community, the generation that made *Huszadik század* and *Nyugat* solved its identity problems by modelling a new national idea. Without exception they demanded that it be anti-feudal, self-examining, critical and resting on the people. At this point I must clarify a question of semantics. The terms 'national', 'popular' and 'the people' covered different things for the radicals and socialists of the early 20th century than for their Russian *narodniki* contemporaries or the popular writers of the 1930s in Hungary, and had

Above: *Mihály Babits, Gyula Juhász and Dezső Kosztolányi on a trip to Szeged.*

nothing to do with the German Volk and *volkisch* between the two world wars. To them 'the people' simply meant workers who made their living by the sweat of their brow, the poor peasants, servants and day-wage men, or the 'fourth estate' if you will, who spoke out in concert but without identifying with the bourgeoisie against domination by the aristocrats and bishops.

The Budapest Avant Garde: A Synthesis of Hungary and Humanity

In following a logical train of thought I have broken the chronology and stepped over an important demarcation line. Both in politics and in culture the quarter century before the war was cut in two by the crisis of 1905–1906. In the middle of the first

Above: *Margit Kaffka*

decade of this century there were new signs and events indicating that time was swerving off its track. There were the first Russian revolution and in its wake the great upsurge of social movements, the birth of the entente block and the speeding up of the immediate preparation for war. At the same time, in only a few years new trends were making themselves known in art, with Picasso, Braque, Léger and Cubism, the German circle Die Briicke, Kandinsky's group Der blaue Reiter, Marinetti's manifesto and Futurism, and later Russian Constructivism; and in literature Apollinaire, Proust Gide, and others all pointed to the coming of a new age.

In Hungary the date is marked by the printing of Endre Ady's volume of poetry entitled *U/ versek* (New Poems) in 1906, the launching of the literary journal *Nyugat*, and the breaking away of the group of eight painters who formed Nyolcak in 1908. The time-span here was not as narrow, but the change went consistently and embraced different branches of art, languages, and forms of expression, and entirely different artistic personalities even within one group. I have spoken of the social and national links and the new ideals that tied them together. There were a few more connecting threads within the fabric of art, however, which, though related to the ones I already mentioned, were less obvious.

One such link was language, the renewal of the literary language of the 19th century, meaning both its modernisation and its archaization. Again *Nyugat* was the germinator.

Ady's linguistic innovations at the end of the 1910s came as a revelation when he discovered *kuruc* (peasant) poetry, which lent itself to renewed passions for the fate of the *kuruc* rebels. Taking up arms for 'fatherland and liberty', repeatedly betrayed and forced into hiding, the *kuruc* served as the popular antithesis to hollow patriotism. This was more than mere political or historical opposition. In his verse form, language and rhythm, and even his poetic imagery, Ady reached back to 16th- and 17th-century Hungary, buried by the language reform movement at the turn of the 18th to the 19th, and the journalistic language of the late 19th century.

This poem was followed by leaner and more bitter ones during the war, but the language and form were there. There was a

Above: *Mihály Babits and Endre Ady reading the Bible.*

peculiar, chilling mixture of an archaic, biblical tone and the modernised, reformed language. Mihály Babits also reached back to 17th-century language, though he was more deliberate and crafty, while his fellow poets Dezső Kosztolányi, Milán Füst, Árpád Tóth, and Gyula Juhász refined the reformed language with the temperament of the deliberate, 20th-century man of intellect in mind.

The same motivation that spurred the launching of *Nyugat* gave rise to a search for identity in music. Béla Bartók and Zoltán Kodály turned away from well-liked gypsy music and the composed 'folk songs,' in demand on the stage and in the cafes, in search of the early source of the music. To offset the gentry taste for a tearfully jolly 'Magyar' sing-along they found something that was even older than the verbunkos recruiting songs, embraced by the romantics, in the villages of Hungarians, Slovaks and

Romanians. True folk music was pentatonic music that the tribes had brought with them from the East, with its own rhythm, melodic line, and store of songs. The folk-music arrangements by Bartók, Kodály, and Leo Weiner, Bartók's etudes for the piano, but also Dezső Malonyai's folk-art collection and the use of motifs from folk art in the architecture of Ödön Lechner and his followers as well as Béla Lájta, and the integration of the structural and decorative elements of Székely peasant houses into modern architecture, all became the ingredients and propagators of the new national idea.

Finding the 'pure source' were only one part of the cultural synthesis. Another part, of cultural historical significance, supplemented and balanced the former. The folk music these composers set before the public was the modern musical expression that dissolved the tonality of the Sezession of the 20th century, of Symbolism, of the avant garde that dug below the surface of artistic form. Take the Nyolcak, for example, who claimed to believe in nature, but without copying the approach of old schools they were carefully selective in adapting nature to their constructivist pictures inspired by the European avant garde. Or the best-known examples, Bartók's *Allegro Barbaro* or *Blue Beard's Castle*, with their folk motifs and rhythms, but which, in addition, changed the whole of late-Romantic musical harmony and tonality.

The writers who rallied around *Nyugat* were alike in more than just their desire to renew linguistic form or their search for a synthesis. Take the favourite subjects of the turn-of-the-century modernists:

Above: *The cover of the first edition of The School-Mistress.*

Solitude. A motif that runs through the generation's poems and prose, it is a universal feeling, but with an Eastern and Central European flavour, or perhaps particular reference to a small people. First of all, complete solitude or withdrawal was not possible to Hungarian writers for the simple reason that they had no villas and gardens, estates or fortunes; they could not even withdraw from the editors' offices. Second, if they did get away now and then, they were never able to be entirely alone, their loneliness could never be totally existential, because they were always grounded in the land and the people, pulled back by their urge to accept the common fate. And, finally, even if one or the other writer did get away for brief moments it never became a qualitatively new state of being, but lead to destruction, voluntary death, or the madhouse.

Sin. Since Baudealaire elevated a motif of modernism into a literary subject, sin has become something acsthetic and accepted. The motif was not alien to Hungarian poets, either. But in its unconventional sense what did it mean to Endre Ady? More than anything, idleness, backwardness glorified, the sick century. But from a historical perspective, even common individual sins are elevated to become national sins: 'If my sins sometimes pull me down, If I fall into the wallow of my blood, Is it not the torpor of the ancient wine Of revenge that kills me, unexplained, Of an old, great sin and grievance?'

Babits set inaction, 'unsinfulness' without virtue, against the sin of creating, innovation, discovering. This is not Baudelaire's sin in his aesthetics of decay, nor

Dostoevsky's ethics where goodness redeems sin, but again very much a public sense. The same goes for a related term, decadence. As György Rába put it, in Babits's vocabulary decadence was synonymous with 'the unaccustomed, the original, what's more, the complexity of the soul.'

Death. This third motif lends itself especially readily for comparison. Western Symbolism and fin de siècle Vienna's affinity for death were not foreign to the Budapest Workshop. Next to a public death of national rank, a private death now gained justification in art. Dezső Kosztolányi was especially close to the modern concept of death, to Freud's Thanatos thesis or Rilke's death experience. Most of Kosztolányi's early poems revolve around death. Death and suicide, if only as a chilling game, are hauntingly present in the small child's complaints, and even more so in his later, schizophrenic dialogues: 'Often it is as if a coffin clutched me, I am covered by a cool shroud And know that this is the head On which hence a grave cap must be.'

The fear of death and the longing for it are feelings that run through Endre Ady's volumes, as well. The spell of perishing, the affinity for death, the readiness for self-destruction and the erotics of death are all preferred subjects for him. Granted, the death motif was a fashion of the time, a fin de siècle mood, and initially perhaps a morbid game and pose. Ady himself later said so, 'I have amused myself quite enough With Death.'

The great persecutor, the 'Unknown', as Kosztolányi's 'great unknown Lord', is mysterious, not to be comprehended by the rational mind.

It is perhaps not contrived to associate with this train of thought Babits's *Esti kerdes* (Evening Question) with the well-known lines: 'Why does the grass grow, only to wither? Why does it wither, only to grow again?'

This is the most specifically existential question of the early 1900s; we come across it with Rilke, Hofmannsthal, and dressed in a unique pictorial symbolism with Klimt. It comes up again with Kokoschka, Kafka and Brecht, the avant garde's agonisers.

István Várady wrote about the volume of selected short stories by his contemporary Gyula Krúdy (above right) as follows: 'The Szindbád stories (above) ... collected in a volume create the impression of some kind of sad and very delicate music ... like a single part in a musical composition, clear, simple and melancholy and beautiful in its monophony.'

Vision and Ecstasy: The Deceptions of the Mind

Not all creative intellectuals may be assigned to the workshops, however. For the sake of integrity the itinerants as well as those who stayed at home must not be omitted. In the cultural ferment of this time there were also those in Budapest who dropped out of community and public life. Their outlook on life was like the Sezession's; they wished to escape from a reality they perceived as dismal and threatening, coupled with the bitterness of not belonging. Their mouthpieces were not from the assimilated wealthy bourgeoisie and intelligentsia but the sensitive, impoverished gentry and petty nobility who were going through an identity crisis much like the 'freely fluttering' bourgeois intelligentsia to the west. Their withdrawal from the shoddy gentry present was as voluntary and deliberate as the retreat of the Viennese from their well-to-do bourgeois existence. In spite of having lost much of their property and being forced to take up office work, these families surely would have had enough left to get their most hopeful young into the county hall or secure them a protected status. But the young chose to walk into editors' offices, from there into cafes and theatres, and from there into art, a dream world of their own creation.

Gyula Krúdy (1878–1933) and Lajos Gulácsy (1882–1932)

Of the artists of the Sezession I wish to present two notable personalities, the writer Gyula Krúdy and the painter Lajos Gulácsy. Both came from impoverished gentry families and inherited neither wealth nor rank, only tradition, passion and outward gestures. There was nothing extraordinary about Krúdy's early career; from a provincial newspaper he went to work for a paper in Budapest, in short, the Workshop. In the

bohemian setting it was an accepted way of life to stay up and make merry till the early hours. But soon it became evident that in reality he joined neither the radical reformers nor the keepers of tradition, because he was not a part of the present. Deep down inside Krúdy was an outsider, just as his dreamy and erotic characters were. He lived in a dream world transposed to the past, or rather a world of dreams created by the waking imagination, of visions.

Above: *Tivadar Csontváry Kosztka's (1853–1919)* Railway Station in Cairo, *1904.*

He brought *Sindbad the Sailor of The Arabian Nights* to Hungary where, left without oceans, he roamed the small country and 'the dead seas of the past', the small towns suspended in the night; he came upon women longing with love, friendly pubs and inns and the sweet scents of memories. The present was to him merely a backdrop, a surface from which gradually rose the ever more luring and realistic layers of a sunken past, as rapture comes to an opium smoker. The dream existence needs no interpretation because it is the natural world, compared to which waking demands relief from endless neuroses. This is not the exact Hungarian copy of the Viennese play of illusion and reality. With Krúdy, vision and ecstasy stood opposed to everyday sights, the external to impressions, the internalised self-love for loneliness in the outside world, which were connected only by a thin thread of self-irony.

Such characters straying on the beyond of society could be created, as Ady remarked, only by a man whose own place in society was unclear, who 'incessantly oscillates between being day-wage man and God'. Not just the present was suspended but also the vision of the future. And as there was no longer a clear image of the future, life was perceived not as backward but as ephemeral. Consequently, Krúdy's struggle was not with the Hungarian Wasteland but with a death without dreams. That the two were connected somewhere in the deep, imperceptible to common sobriety, was to be sensed when it came to affronts and duels or in the aftermath of what Ady called 'the hours of great euphoria,' and only in the greatest clash, the revolution in the fall of 1918, was the connection unmistakably apparent.

Krúdy's closest spiritual counterpart in the early 1900s was Lajos Gulácsy. Without any antecedent in Hungary, Gulácsy began to paint in the style of Dante Gabriel Rossetti (who died in 1882, the same year Gulácsy was born) and the Pre-Raphaelites. He brought home the trademark style and subjects of the Western European Sezession, the Garden, solitude, escape, the aesthetic treatment of eroticism, fine lines and mysteriousness. Sharp-eyed art experts did not fail to note the new phenomenon, his lyricism, his 'sacred languor', his 'wilted colours of autumn', yet they associated him with Symbolism. Very few understood him, and fellow painters rejected him.

Like Krúdy, Gulácsy did not belong anywhere, not to any workshop, and for his part he did not go to pubs or participate in the nightlife. He was no smalltown Sindbad but a living wanderer in, and lover of, far-away Italian and French landscapes and times still extant after their decline. He longed to go away, to escape from the strange present, from irrational anxieties and interrogation, into love that never was, into Dante's Italy and Florence of the quattrocento, the gardens of sorcerers where sad, languid, and sensuous lovers meet and

Below: *Lajos Gulácsy's (1882–1932) Snow Falls in Nakonxipan (One-Day Snow), about 1910.*

are there for him to meet. The adoration of beauty, sensuality, art saturating life – these were clearly feelings and ideals of the Sezession. Use of decorative elements in his paintings was modest, his symbols were simple and unambiguous. There was no devastating love or erotic death; dreams were not the transition between being and not being, consciousness and unconsciousness, but a quietly pensive, sometimes visionary state where imagination was free to create, dissolve, and reconstitute time.

Gulácsy's painting depicted a visionary reality, if a little poetically and grotesquely, but to a greater extent and more enduringly than any other artist's. His figures are for the most part imaginary, yet part of our reality. Clowns and fools, or fools dressed like clowns, old women in Rococo fashion, on the peripheries of the times and of life, hunchbacks and the disfigured, the mad and eccentric, but pensive without exception – just like Hofmannsthal's young girls, intoxicated by dreams, who so readily understand death.

To single out one picture to illustrate what I have said, it is Gulácsy's *Az Opiumszivo alma* (*The Opium Smoker's Dream*), a panel painting he did during the First World War. On top, blowing bubbles, are the heads of a clown, a Negro woman, and others. In the centre an attractive young lady, a Rococo figure, reclines in an armchair; her feet are fins entwined in seaweed, and one arm reaches into a lake out of which grow aquatic flowers. Every detail – the heads, the flowers, the jewels – all are real, but overall the picture is illusory, possibly truly an opium vision. What holds it together is its mood, and it is very suggestive, intuitable, perhaps comprehensible.

Gulácsy was himself an eccentric, a fantasist, who succumbed to mental illness at a young age. As a painter he was to the end deliberate in being one of the modern and progressive, radical reformers.

Krúdy and Gulácsy bring to mind another visionary painter, Tivadar Csontváry, and a writer little known in his time and since, Géza Csáth. The latter's short stories, diaries and some of his plays reveal the same aesthetic and erotic treatment of death as that of the Viennese. Csáth still remembered the Garden, knew the magician's garden with all its strange and unreal flowers, its secrets and tales. He also knew the death of the magician, who smoked opium so much that even the most unselfish and erotic love could not help him. Csáth was a heavy morphine addict who knew well the euphoria and suffering of poison and loneliness. Csontváry and Gulácsy died in mental institutions; Csáth, after killing his wife, committed suicide.

The Austrian Avant Garde: Absurdity Attained

The Viennese Garden was not able to provide security for long for the seekers of solitude. To use Carl Schorske's description, the Garden 'exploded'. The apt metaphor comes from Oscar Kokoschka's childhood prank; after being shown the gate of an exclusive garden, he actually set off an explosion there. The artistic explosion came more than 10 years later at the 1908 Kunstschau, when Kokoschka broke out of the Garden of Sezession, just as did Arnold Schönberg in music, Adolf Loos in architecture and Robert Musil in literature.

The Austrian avant garde that came into being in the first decade of the 20th century definitely rejected the narcissistic adoration of beauty. Most of this generation

Above: *After graduating from military boarding school, which also appears in his first novel, Robert Musil (1880–1942) earned a degree as an engineer at the technical university in Brno. He worked as a clerk for a rather extended period of his life, first at the Ministry of Defence and then at the Ministry of Foreign Affairs. In the meantime, he also wrote articles and books with a strongly critical vein about the Monarchy. His first novel, entitled* The Confusions of Young Törless *(1908), inspired by the experiences of his youth was published, but he could not finish* The Man without Qualities, *a novel about the state of the Monarchy, or Kakania, which he intended to be the chief work of his life. The first volume was published in 1930 and the second in 1933, and based on these it can be certainly included among the great works of the 20th century.*

was born in the 1880s, when one crisis topped another. To the avant garde it was already obvious what Hofmannsthal and his friends had been forced to learn through bitter experience, that 'everything disintegrated into parts, and the parts again disintegrated, and nothing wanted to fit into its concept', and that the possibility for intelligent communication was lost. It is true that the great artists of the Sezession did not hibernate in the Garden, as demonstrated in the above quote from what is known as *Ein Brief des Lord Chandos* (*The Lord Chandos Letter*, 1902). When their own insecurity and bad disposition became a concern to society at large and coincided with doubts about the endurance of the Monarchy, Junge Wien, now on the threshold of adulthood, also became aware of the symptoms of decay. The change is perhaps implied in Hofmannsthal's drama of 1905, *Das gerettete Venedig* (*Venice Saved*), and Arthur Schnitzler's novel of 1907, *Der Weg ins Freie* (*The Road into the Open*, University of California Press, 1991), when it became clear that it was not

Schoenberg and the Second Viennese School

In Vienna on 31 March 1913 in the Großer Musikvereinssaal preparations were underway for a special concert. In addition to the Chamber Symphony op. 9 *for fifteen instruments by Arnold Schoenberg (1874–1951), also on the programme were new orchestral works by Anton von Webern (1883–1943) and Alban Berg (1885–1935) (*Six Pieces for Orchestra op. 6, *and* Five Songs on Picture Postcard Texts *by Peter Altenberg* op. 4 *respectively) alongside Mahler's* Kindertotenlieder. *The event degenerated into one of the most memorable and also the most telling scandals of music history: 'Once more stormy and rude language, blows and arrogance took place. Herr von Webern shouted from his box that the whole band should be driven out, and immediately from the audience came the answer that disciples of this unpopular trend in music should be locked up in the Steinhof (the madhouse). The fury and shouting in the hall showed no sign of abating. Nor was it surprising when a gentleman in the audience, with great eagerness and nimble as a monkey climbed over the parquet to clout the object of his ire ...' Perhaps equally telling is the fact that the concert did not even get as far as Mahler's songs — the Viennese public, famous for its strident opinions and its stubborn insistence on the 'customary' would not tolerate the forthright rejection of the centuries-old rules of musical taste. Of course, nobody then could yet have known that the works and their creators that finally were not played that night were the harbingers of a new direction in music. The culture of Austria–Hungary did not open up to Schoenberg and his followers. The few who enthused about New Music were able only at privately organised concerts from 1918 to savour the idea that there was an antidote to tradition, in its death throes even as it continued to proclaim its own triumph.*

Above: Arnold Schönberg

Below: Alban Berg

art that infiltrated life, but that life was making its way into art.

The avant garde was more sensitive than the preceding movement to the disintegration of the whole, of concepts, institutions, the system of values, and to the relative value of illusion and reality, of what was possible and what was not – in short, to the absurdity of the world. To the avant garde of the early 1900s, anxiety and threat came no longer from nationalistic or socialistic mass revolts, which were gradually turning into institutionalised movements and becoming part of the 'establishment'. Their feeling of helplessness came rather from the establishment itself, the inscrutable power.

A second, crucial difference was that, for the avant garde, illusion and reality were not set on any stage but in villages, towns and above all in the dominant, imaginary Castle, the fictitious Court of Law that pronounced judgment on the autonomous individual; and the Prison, whether that meant the school, the barracks, or the middle-class home. 'I seem to be going home,' Kafka once said to his young friend Janouch, 'but I am crawling into the prison established for me.' It was all the more difficult to endure because it resembled the traditional middle-class home, which made it impossible to break out of. 'Everything sails under false banners, not one word covers the truth.' The decisive experience in avant-garde literature and art was not voluntary solitude but incarceration and claustrophobia. Breaking out, escaping, flying were their frequent themes.

Closely related to this is a third difference between the two groups, and that is their concept of what is aesthetic. The Austrian avant garde rejected the Sezession's idea of beauty, and what their expressionist aesthetics termed as art was the representation of psychological reality, desires, fears, and suffering. The aesthetic treatment of death was now eclipsed by representing the relationship between death and erotics in the dark tones of brutality and aggression. Decorative beauty and aesthetic suffering that had been the Garden now gave way to distortion, mythic perversion, and the absurdity of attainment.

In an absurd world the identity crisis became complete; there were themes of a loss of the self and a homelessness eminating from the pictures of Egon Schiele and Oscar Kokoschka, and from the music of Arnold Schönberg and his followers. The young Torless, Robert Musil's 'Hamlet', had the distressing experience that as he watched

Above: *Oskar Kokoschka's* Veronica's Veil *(1911)*

Franz Kafka (1883–1924)

Franz Kafka, a German-speaking Jew, lived in Prague in the last years of the Empire. He obtained a doctorate in law (1906) and worked in Prague as an insurance official until 1917, when he had to leave his office job because of laryngeal tuberculosis.

Several important figures of 20th-century German literature were born and lived in Prague. Franz Werfel, Rainer Maria Rilke, Kafka's friend Max Brod, and besides them a generation of talented writers and poets formed the peculiar literary circle that took shape in a Czech environment. Into this circle came the young Kafka, and though the larger public may not have noticed him, the writers, including Werfel himself, recognised the talent in their living contemporary.

The model for his novels was the official machinery of the end of the monarchy; he borrowed his motives from the impersonal bureaucracy alienated from its original function, though his works, due to their metaphoric-parabolic nature have become haunting images not just of a state of society, but of a kind of universal state of existence. A decisive element of Kafka's style is that he combines detailed realistic descriptions with bizarre, surreal events, presenting the unreal as realistic as seen by his protagonists. (for instance Metamorphosis – Die Verwandlung*). On his deathbed he asked his friend, Max Brod, to burn his unpublished and partially fragmentary manuscripts. Brod did not carry out the wish, and from the mid-twenties a series of Kafka's works was published, including some which have since become world-famous masterpieces, such as* The Trial *(Der Prozess), or* The Castle *(Das Schloss).*

Adolf Loos (1870–1933)

Adolf Loos was born in Brno in 1870. As an architect, interior designer and furniture designer he was one of the most prominent figures of Viennese and European Modernity.

Like other young radicals, such as Karl Kraus, Peter Altenberg, Arnold Schönberg and Oskar Kokoschka, he devoted his art to the rebellion against traditionalism. His architectural masterpieces and theoretical essays form an organic unit, representing a unique worldview that places emphasis on the close relationship between architecture and the broad concept of culture. Loos believed that conspicuous elements, ornaments and the overflowing praise of tradition damage art and people's everyday lives. His ambition was to primarily appeal to 'people with a modern disposition', who he thought were able to clearly recognise the vanity of mythicising art.

His manifesto-like essay 'Ornament and Crime' (1908) was an often quoted source for his progressive contemporaries. In his architectural projects Loos strove to apply the concepts of conciseness and maturity, mottos he himself formulated in his essay. Two of his buildings, the Goldman House (1910) on Michaelerplatz, today known as the Loos House (pictured), and the Steiner House (1910), can still be viewed in Vienna.

The Happy Years of Peace – the Population of the Monarchy at Rest
Operettas – Orpheums – Cabarets

In December 1881 Vienna was shaken by a catastrophe: during a performance the Ringtheatre burned to the ground and many people lost their lives. The event led to the public in the capital losing interest in theatre going for several years and during this period the only person who could tempt people back to the theatre was Johann Strauss (1825–1899) with his waltzes and operettas. The composer's works interwoven with light songs, dancing interludes, humour and love stories had enjoyed great success and the Strauss name became one of the labels for light music throughout the empire. As a result of

Above: Girard in Gipsy Baron

the phenomenal success – unimaginable by the standards of today – of Fledermaus *(1874) first in Vienna and then in Pest eight years later, and that of* Gypsy Baron *(1885), adapted from Mór Jókai's novel entitled* Saffi, *hundreds of works flooded the market and the operetta became the most important stage genre.*

The birth of Hungarian operetta can be primarily attributed to József Konti (1852–1905): based on the play script of recognised playwright Gergely Csiky his work entitled The Lively Devil *(1886) with Lujza Blaha in the leading role was not only received very favourably by the press and its audiences but also by Johannes Brahms, who was visiting Budapest at that time.*

Above: Lujza Blaha, the star

Another composer, Pongrác Kacsóh (1873–1923) made his debut with John the Valiant, *popular even today, and it was at this venue that a work by Ferenc Lehár (1870–1948),* The Merry Widow *was put on the stage. For 50 years during the period of the Monarchy and ever since the operetta has not lost its popularity.*

Cabaret first appeared in Vienna in the 18th century, becoming a genre of entertainment in the middle of the 19th century. A series of music halls opened their doors as the popularity of the singer-comedian-actors increased. By 1907, when Fledermaus *had begun to make its round of the theatres, Viennese cabaret was already known for its range of writers (Peter Altenberg, Ludwig Thoma, Egon Friedell) and actors striving for world fame, e.g. Alexander Girardi (1850–1918), also known for his special hats. For a long time only German-language variety acts could be seen in the Hungarian capital but recognising the latent opportunities in the genre, increasing numbers of well-known Hungarian writers and performers collaborated in performances at newly opened places. Jenő Heltai, Ferenc Molnár, Ferenc Herceg and Zsigmond Móricz appeared in cabarets which often contained social criticism and political commentary, while the songs in the performances were often composed by the already celebrated figures of the Hungarian operetta, Imre Kálmán and Béla Zerkovitz.*

Hungarian cabaret was especially indebted to Endre Nagy (1877–1938), who as a master of ceremonies brilliantly combined humour, 'high' literature and journalism, while as a writer his name is linked to The Cabaret Novel *(1913) and numerous satirical musical comedies, which were a favourite with audiences at the turn of the century (*The Genius, The Prime Minister*).*

Below: The Parisiana Bar, designed by Béla Lájta, today's *Új Színház* (New Theatre)

objects, people, and himself he felt ultimate incomprehension coupled with a vague sense of affinity for them. And when for a moment something seemed comprehensible after all, he could not entirely put it into words or shape it into thoughts because between his own feelings and his innermost self there 'ran an inobliterable demarcation line'. The incomprehensibility of the outside world grew inside him into a sense of terror on learning of the theft by one of his schoolmates, the feminine Basini, and he almost involuntarily became an accomplice to the sadist tortures carried out in the 'dark chamber.' If all this, all these underground games, are admissible, 'then anything is possible' – even that 'from the bright world he once thought to be the only one there was a gate leading to another, musty, gushing, passionate, naked, exterminating world.' But what is more terrifying than stepping over the threshold from the regulated and transparent, bright world into a world of darkness, blood and filth and debauchery, is that the two spheres are very close, and 'their secretly touching border we might cross at any moment.'

The war, whose coming the majority of intellectuals in Budapest thought absurd right up to that ominous night in late July, proved to those who were able to see clearly how in our age absurdity can easily turn into reality. Again it was Endre Ady who was the first and most perceptive in recognising this. 'I am very much afraid,' he wrote to Oszkár Jászi not much after the outbreak of the war, 'that I won't be able to bear for long what must come … The horrors are inexhaustibly inventive, man is more disgusting and more hopelessly pitiful than anyone ever imagined.'

And then a postscript, on the destruction of the Magyar nation and humankind, a bitter consolation in the argument 'now all is very well because it can get no worse,' and a resigned, 'now the Devil shall lead us'.

Above: *Alois Jirásek*

What remained of the one-time revolutionary belief was only a wish to protect what there was. It was less a creed than a defensive reflex to remain a seed under the snow, so that humankind and the Magyar nation, rejected by an absurd world, would have the potential to continue on. Again at the nadir of absurdity there was attained the deferent acceptance of the sacred reason behind subsistence.

In Conclusion

In their self-concepts, attachments, the subjects they treated and their forms of expression, Vienna and Budapest at the fin de siècle were very different. As they were nearing collapse their intellectual peaks came so close as almost to converge. They had a quarter century of magnificent efflorescence behind them. Describing and interpreting nevertheless fall short of explaining it. I have not arrived at a full and coherent answer to the question I posed in the introduction, what were the reasons behind this extraordinary cultural boom in Central Europe? In my conclusion the answer is still not there – because I wish to avoid quick and easy explanations.

The Slavic Art of the Monarchy
Alois Jirásek (1851–1930)

A late master of the historical novel, who to the end of his days worked as a history teacher, developing the oeuvre of

Above: *The Rudolfinum is an important venue of music life in Prague.*

František Palacky, he wrote a series of historical novels according to the historical view of 19th-century historicism and academicism, in which Czech history developed in three key eras. In his most famous work, the trilogy *Mezi proudy* (*Between the Currents*, 1891), *Proti všem* (*Against All the World*, 1894) and *Bratrstvo* (*Brotherhood*, 1900–09), Jirásek discusses the era of Hussitism. This era is seen as the apotheosis of Czech national consciousness, but the century following defeat in the Battle of White Mountain, the darkest period of Czech history; the title of his novel evoking the time of the counter-reformation, *Temno* (*Darkness*, 1915), has become synonymous with this tragic period in Czech history. The Czech reformation (*obrezni*), beginning at the end of the 18th century, is again viewed positively (as portrayed in Jirásek's five-volume series of novels, *F. L. Věk*, 1890–1907), since for him this time is again the beginning of the struggle in which the Czech nation, bearing European values, is able to implement an anti-Habsburg and anti-Catholic turn in events, achieving complete independence. In 1917, on the last day of the Empire, Jirásek set down the Czech writers' Declaration of Independence. He became enormously popular through his novels, and his birthday was celebrated by the masses even during his lifetime.

Above: *Bedřich Smetana*

Left: *The first page of the New World Symphony.*

The Dawn of Czech National Music

In the multi-ethnic empire, various national schools of composition developed in the 1860s. Of these, the Czech was without doubt the most important, not counting the Austrian and the Hungarian.

Right: *Leoš Janáček
and his young wife.*

Bedřich Smetana (1824–1884)

Bedřich Smetana stands out from among the first internationally noted Czech composers: it is only a slight exaggeration to say that single-handedly he laid the foundations of Czech national musical culture. Smetana contributed to the flourishing of Czech musical life with outstanding works such as the historical operas *Dalibor* (1865–1867) and *Libusa* (1881; written for the ceremonial opening of the Czech National Theatre), or the six-movement symphonic cycle *Mávlast*, still hugely popular today. His appointment as conductor of the Prague opera in 1866 also brought changes. During the eight years that he was director, he limited the influence of Italian opera. Due to his fiery patriotism he preferred new Czech works. He did not conceive the new national art as a paraphrase of folk music; rather, he wanted to make current musical innovations part of his country's music. This approach, attacked by many of his contemporaries, is still a topic of debate decades later: will a new national music be created from folk music roots, through drawing from the past or by looking to nations that have created inspirational music?

Antonín Dvořák (1841–1904)

Smetana was never particularly interested in popularising his works abroad. It was therefore left to Antonín Dvořák to promote Czech art music internationally. Although much time elapsed before he found a path into the concert halls of Europe, Dvořák's *Slavonic Dances*, composed in 1878, brought the desired breakthrough: his music caught the public's attention in Hamburg, Berlin and then in London and New York.

In 1880, on the threshold of world fame Dvořák requested his publisher in Germany to print the titles of his compositions and the libretti of his dramatic works in Czech as well as German. In 1892, Dvořák's growing international fame brought him to North America, where Jeannette Thurber, founder of the National Conservatory of Music, offered

Above: *Hasek (in the photograph he is lying in front, supporting himself with his elbow) with his friends on an outing.*

him a post as artistic director and teacher of composition. Over the three years that he spent in America he composed two works, perhaps to this day his most popular; the *Symphony in E minor*, 'From the New World' *op. 95* and the *String Quartet in F major*, 'The American', *op. 96*.

Leoš Janáček (1854–1928)

Although his own work points in the direction of the New Music of the 20th century, as conductor of the Brno Philharmonic Society, Leoš Janáček did much to popularise the two best-known figures of Czech 19th-century music. Janáček burst into the European music scene with his opera *Jenůfa* (1904). What he achieved for Czech national music can perhaps only be compared to the efforts of Béla Bartók and Zoltán Kodály: collaborating with the philologist and folklore researcher František Bartoš, he collected and published over 2,000 Moravian folksongs. He willingly used the songs in his own instrumental and orchestral pieces.

In the work of Janáček's younger colleague, Alois Hába (1893–1973), the encounter between folk music and the language of modern art music is even sharper. Even as a child, Hába sang and played the violin in his father's folk ensemble, and his mother, who had a reputation as an excellent folk singer, taught him many Moravian songs, which at times contained intervals smaller than the semitones known in art music. During his career, which culminated after the collapse of the Dual Monarchy, these so-called micro-intervals played an important role in Hába's music, just as his studies with Franz Schrecker and a visit to Schoenberg's famous Viennese Privataufführung (private performances held from 1918) exercised a great influence on him. In his most important composition, the opera *Die Mutter*, he found his own voice in a synthesis of these various influences.

Alfons Mucha (1860–1939)

One of the most popular masters of art nouveau, Mucha was not only a painter and graphic artist, but also worked in sculpture, jewellery, interior design and the applied arts. His particular talent flourished in decorative graphics (posters, panel paintings, illustrations, and such). Of Moravian origin, Mucha lived in Paris from 1888. He only achieved a breakthrough with his art in 1895, when he made his first lithograph poster for the acclaimed actor Sarah Bernhardt (1844–1923) and the Théâtre de la Renaissance.

In the wake of the consequent success, Bernhardt signed a six-year exclusive contract with Mucha to create lithographs for her plays. (*La dame aux camélias*, 1896; *Lorenzaccio*, 1896; *La samaritaine*, 1897; *Médea*, 1898; *Hamlet*, 1898; *Tosca*, 1899.) From 1901, Mucha also designed scenery and costumes for the theatre.

Around this time the Champenois printers in Paris began to manufacture 'decorative panels'. On an assembly line, they produced Mucha pictures printed on thick paper or silk, which they then sold framed.

Between 1904 and 1910, Mucha lived in the United States. Interestingly it was only there, in 1908, that he first heard Smetana's *Moldva* performed by the Boston Philharmonic, and, influenced by this, decided to turn all his energy to the service of Slav history and culture. In 1910, he returned to Prague, and began a series of 20 vast historical canvases, entitled *The Slav Epic*, which he finished in 1928.

Pavol Országh-Hviezdoslav (1849–1921)

Pavol Országh-Hviezdoslav was the son of a Hungarian nobleman on his father's side and a Slovakian poet on his mother's. In common with other Slovakian poets, he was bilingual, speaking and writing in both Hungarian and Slovakian.

Országh-Hviezdoslav first studied at the Hungarian secondary school in Késmárk and then later in Miskolc. There, under the influence of Sándor Petőfi's and János Arany's

Above: *The placard of the Sokol exhibition.*

Left: Salammbô *was*
inspired by the French novelist
Gustav Flaubert's novel of
the same title, 1896.

Above: *Vojtek Stasik's portrait of Pavol Orszagh-Hviezdoslav.*

work, he started writing poems in Hungarian. He wrote his first poem in Slovakian in 1868, first under the name of Jozef Zbranský, then, from 1877 onwards, he used the pen name of Hviezdoslav (which can be translated loosely as 'the glory of the stars').

Országh-Hviezdoslav's epic poems, which romanticised the Slovakian village, quickly became very popular among Slovakian intellectuals. After translating *The Tragedy of Man* by Imre Madách into Slovakian, he was elected as a member of the Kisfaludy Society. When Endre Ady's acclaimed poem *Song of the Hungarian Jacobins* was published in 1910, he wrote an ode to Ady, primarily because he admired Ady's opposition to the official ideology regarding minority policy.

Apart from short stories, depicting Upper Hungary's gentry, his work as a literary translator is also significant: Országh-Hviezdoslav translated Hungarian, Polish, Russian, German and English literature into Slovakian, with expertise. However, the most significant part of his oeuvre is his poetry: he wrote more than 15 volumes of poems, and it was due to the influence of his work that metrical poetry became widespread in Slovakian poetry. Perhaps his most important cycle is the string of anti-war poems entitled *Bloody Sonnets* (*Krvavé sonety*), written during World War I (1914–1918).

Miroslav Krleža (1893–1981)

The internationally acclaimed writer and representative of Croatian national literature, Miroslav Krleža, was born in Zagreb (in present-day Croatia). He studied at the Cadet School in Pécs (1908–1911) and then at the Ludovika Military Academy of Budapest. Thus, he spent his youth immersed in the world of pre-war Hungarian culture.

In accordance with the general tendencies of the Austro-Hungarian Empire, the national culture that was formed by Krleža was not based on the myth of the 'morally unspoiled village', or on national-folk roots. Instead, it was built along the anti-canonical, anti-traditional sounds of Parisian and Budapest modernity. From an aesthetic point of view, the writers and poets of the literary periodical *Nyugat* (West), had a strong effect on him, while from an ideological aspect, the Galilei circle, including Oszkár Jászi, influenced his art.

The aforementioned Endre Ady, wrote two poems *Song of the Hungarian Jacobins* and *Confession of the Danube*, which urged the union of Slavic and Hungarian intellectuals. It was extremely popular among those inhabitants of the Austro-Hungarian Empire striving for their own national identity.

At the beginning of his career, he tried to find his own voice by writing poems. His first work in prose, *Croatian Rhapsody*, published in 1918, is a strange mixture of short story, drama, poetry and prophecy, and thus a document of how different literary genres meld together in Krleža's art in the interest of expressing the message.

Above: *Miroslav Krleža.*

Ivan Cankar (1875–1918)

Born into a Slovenian family of craftsmen, Ivan Cankar completed school in Ljubliana and then moved to Vienna, the empirical capital of intellectual ferment at the time. In this German linguistic environment, he became a living classic of Slovenian literature; Cankar's literary works were almost without exception written in Slovenian, whereas a considerable part of his journalism was German. His social-democratic leanings can also be traced back to his Vienna experiences: he became a member of the social democratic party (and in 1907 stood as a candidate). However, after his speech urging southern Slav unity he was imprisoned, and after his release he eschewed active involvement in politics.

Every copy of his first book, *Erotika* (1899), which created Slovenian symbolism, was bought up by the Bishop of Ljubljana, and publicly burnt. Through this unfortunate incident, Cankar became known in Carniola. He won considerable acclaim with his main work, a small novel entitled *The Servant Jernej and his Right* (*Hlapec Jernej in njegova pravica*) in which he reworked Mihály Kohlhaas's story in a Slovenian folk-language environment. In 1910, he left Vienna and moved back to Ljubljana. There he died in December 1918, in what was now an independent Slav State. Shortly after his death he was seen as one of the greatest figures of modern Slovenian literature.

Ivan Jakovics Franko (1856–1916)

Several outstanding figures of the Slav national movement spent a few years of their youth in Budapest or Vienna. Thus, the Ukrainian Ivan Franko, author of the large-scale poem *Moses* (*Moisei*, 1905), on the leader who served his people, obtained a doctorate in the Austrian capital after studying at the University of Lemberg (Lviv, Lwów). As a member of a student society, he came into contact with workers' groups and revolutionary émigrés, and in 1877 he was arrested. When he was released he wrote what is perhaps his most famous poem *Stone Breakers* (*Kumenari*), which earned him the title 'the stone breaker of Ukrainian literature'.

On his return home he became the leader of the Galician workers' movement. Due to his open support of the principles of socialism and national independence, he was denied a post at Lemberg University, so he made a living from journalism; like the Slovenian Ivan Cankar, he wrote many articles in German. However, all of his literary works were written in Ukrainian. He created works of lasting value in every genre. The central theme of his works is peasant poverty. He was also important as a translator, putting Goethe's *Faust* and Jókai's *The Golden Man* into Ukrainian.

Stanisław Wyspiański (1869–1907)

Born in Cracow, the capital of Galicia, Stanisław Wyspiański was one of the most outstanding artists of his time. In 1890, he travelled to the artistic centres of Europe on an art scholarship, visiting Paris several times between 1890 and 1894. From 1898 onwards he worked as the artistic manager of *Życie* (*Life*), the weekly publication of Cracow's modernists. Although he made his living from painting, he also designed furniture and other objects of applied art. He was also the creator of modern Polish drama. From 1905, he was a professor at the Cracow

Above: *The cover of the first edition of* The Servant Jernej and his Right.

Below: *The statue of Ivan Franko in front of the entrance of Lvov University.*

Academy of Fine Arts. With his works of art, and more especially his designs for stained-glass windows, he created the Cracowian variant of art nouveau. However, only the stained-glass windows designed for the Franciscans in Cracow were ever completed. His other designs (made for the Wawel and Lemberg cathedrals) were abandoned. In order to house these unrealised projects the city of Cracow erected a special modern building in 2005 in the city centre, based on the plans of the architect Krzysztof Ingarden.

Only the last 10 years of his short life were spent writing drama. In his work he successfully blended the tendencies of modernism with Polish folk traditions and symbolism. In order to achieve an operatic effect Wyspiański took special care to write his dramas in rhyme in order to integrate musicality into his works. Fellow poets, such as Rydel, also wrote plays in rhyme and the modern classical writers, including Mickiewicz and Słowacik were famous for their verse plays, too. In his 37 dramas he often borrowed themes from classical antiquity as well as the important events of Polish history. In 1901, the Cracow premiere of his most critically acclaimed and popular play, *The Wedding* (*Wesele*), was one of the greatest successes in the history of Polish theatre. The film version of the play was directed by the famous Polish film director Andrzej Wajda in 1973.

Above: *Cracow, the capital of Galicia, was part of the Austro-Hungarian Monarchy from 1846 to 1918. The city was a diverse centre for culture and the arts, as well as for education. Due to the national pride of its citizens, it was called 'Polish Athens', and for good reason too. The picture shows an uniquely designed block of flats in the city centre.*

Above: *Stanislaw Wyspianski's Self-Portrait*

FRANZ'JOSEPH'I

Left: *This picture was painted in the early 1900s by Wilhelm List, one of the founding members and first exhibitors of the Viennese Secession. By the ruler's right hand is the Hungarian crown with the Austrian crown on his left. The painting can now be seen in the ceremonial hall of the main building of the Austrian Post Office and Savings Bank (Österrreichische Postsparkasse) in Vienna.*

Csaba Fazekas

The Super-ego of the Empire: Church and State

The most lasting changes that took place in the relationship between the Church and the State were brought about in the reign of Joseph II (1780–1790). Joseph began with the premise that society as a whole had common interests, and therefore concluded that he had to initiate comprehensive ecclesiastical policies. This primarily meant a revision of the role played by the Catholic Church as well as a declaration of religious tolerance towards non-Catholic Christian denominations. This defined the life of the Empire's religious institutions until 1918.

After 1790 a legal basis was formed in Hungary and Transylvania granting freedom of religion to the Lutheran, Reformed, Greek Orthodox and Unitarian Churches, albeit with more restricted rights than those enjoyed by the Catholic Church. At the same time, the state reserved the right to appoint the bishops of the Catholic Church.

As a result of the increasing liberalism of the first half of the 19th century, a struggle was waged in both the eastern and western halves of the Empire to restrict the privileges of the Catholic Church and achieve equality between all denominations, much of which was indeed ensured by the constitutions of 1848. The suppression of the Hungarian Revolution and War of Independence of 1848–1849 created a fundamentally new situation. In the 1850s, absolutism became popular again. This resulted in a questioning of the conduct of many of the Hungarian bishops during the Revolution, which forced many of them to step down from their positions. At the same time, another group of leading churchmen retained their politically conservative opinions. At the beginning of this period, the Church was unhappy with the

Above: *The construction of Saint Stephen's Basilica in Budapest, designed by the architect József Hild, was begun in 1851. Because of construction delays and Hild's death the church was finally built in the Neo-Renaissance style according to Miklós Ybl's design.*

measures introduced by Franz Joseph to curtail Joseph II's policies (which were known as Josephinism) and in 1855 this process led to the concordatum signed between the Holy See and the Habsburg Empire. The state fully embraced the standpoint of the Catholic Church in the area of marriage law and furthermore ensured the predominantly Catholic nature of education. The objective of Archbishop Rauscher of Vienna was for the political unity of the Empire to be coupled with religious unity. However, the Hungarian episcopate was not able to fully enjoy the numerous advantages granted to them by the concordatum, since the agreement did not take into account the independence of the Hungarian Catholic Church. At the same time, the ecclesiastical

Percentage of denominations in the Austro-Hungarian Monarchy at the time of the 1880 census

	Catholics Total	From all Catholics		Greek Orthodox	Lutheran	Calvinist	Unitarian	Israelite	other
		Roman Catholic	Greek Catholic*						
AUSTRIA									
Lower Austria	93.96	93.86	0.10	0.09	1.49	0.22	–	4.08	0.16
Upper Austria	97.63	97.62	0.01	0.01	2.13	0.02	–	0.13	0.08
Salzburg	99.46	99.45	0.01	0.00	0.42	0.04	–	0.07	0.01
Styria	99.06	99.06	0.00	0.02	0.72	0.04	–	0.15	0.01
Carinthia	94.93	94.93	0.00	0.01	5.01	0.01	–	0.04	0.00
Krajna	99.80	99.76	0.04	0.07	0.08	0.03	–	0.02	0.00
Coastal region	98.29	98.27	0.02	0.50	0.23	0.11	–	0.79	0.08
Tyrol and Vorarlberg	99.69	99.68	0.01	0.01	0.18	0.06	–	0.06	0.00
Bohemia	96.04	96.02	0.02	0.01	1.01	1.14	–	1.70	0.10
Moravia	95.23	95.18	0.05	0.03	1.05	1.63	–	2.05	0.01
Silesia	84.48	84.48	0.00	0.00	13.960	0.02	–	1.52	0.02
Galicia	87.72	45.43	42.290	0.05	0.62	0.06	–	11.520	0.03
Bukovina	14.35	11.14	3.21	70.87	2.32	0.17	–	11.790	0.50
Dalmatia	83.38	83.35	0.03	16.540	0.01	0.01	–	0.06	0.00
Total	91.35	79.86	11.490	2.23	1.31	0.49	–	4.54	0.08
Population	20,229,825	17,645,648	2,544,177	493,542	289,005	110,525		1,005,394	15,953
COUNTRIES OF THE KINGDOM OF HUNGARY									
Hungary	58.07	47.22	10.850	14.110	8.07	14.740	0.40	4.55	0.06
out of this Transylvania	40.36	12.68	27.680	31.870	9.59	14.050	2.64	1.44	0.20
Fiume (and environs)	98.38	98.24	0.14	0.19	0.44	0.49	–	0.43	0.07
Croatian/Slavonia	71.71	71.15	0.56	26.300	0.81	0.45	0.00	0.71	0.02
Total	59.77	50.18	9.59	15.560	7.18	12.990	0.37	4.08	0.05
Population	9,350,183	7,849,692	1,500,491	2,434,890	1,122,849	2,031,803	55,792	638,314	8,271
AUSTRO-HUNGARIAN MONARCHY	78.28	67.58	10.700	7.75	3.74	5.67	0.15	4.35	0.06
Population	29,580,008	25,495,340	4,044,668	2,928,432	1,411,854	2,142,328	55,792	1,643,708	24,224

*Including data about Armenian Catholics (3,223 in Austria, 2,854 in Hungary; 6,077 persons in total).

Source: Statistisches *Handbuch der Österreichisch-Ungarischen Monarchie*. Neue Folge. Vienna, 1888. pp. 6–7.

The above table illustrates that in Austria (Cisleithania) – with one or two marked exceptions – the Catholic Church was clearly dominant, while there was a diverse range of denominations in the Kingdom of Hungary. The old Austrian hereditary provinces (Upper Austria, Salzburg, Styria, Carinthia, Krajna and Tyrole) were almost homogenously Catholic, but Bohemia and Moravia also had a high proportion of Catholics at some 95 per cent. There were significant minorities of Lutheran Germans in Silesia and Greek Orthodox Serbs in Dalmatia. Galicia was the only independent province in which there was no absolute majority of one denomination. This was because of a significant number of the Rusyn-speaking Catholics, with a similar proportion to those following the Latin liturgy. It is worthy of note that some 70 per cent of Bukovina's population was Greek Orthodox. Both Galicia and Bukovina had a significant proportion of Jews.

policy of absolutism regarded the strengthening of the Catholic Church's influence in Hungary as important, and this approach was initially expressed by the re-establishment of the Hungarian Jesuit order in 1853. From the end of the 1850s the letter and spirit of the concordat were increasingly less adhered to in Vienna.

The development of the relationship between State and Church in the two halves of the Empire

Below: *Europe's biggest synagogue is in Budapest. It was built in the Romantic style, between 1854 and 1859, and was designed by Ludwig Förster with the collaboration of Frigyes Feszl. There are over 3,000 seating places in the three-aisled hall church.*

Directly following the Compromise of 1867 the most important issues of ecclesiastical policy concentrated on two problems: on the one hand, how the State would deal with the legacy of the concordatum (to be more precise, how they would put an end to it while at the same time keeping the Church's interests in mind), and on the other hand, to what extent the State would be capable of realising reforms in ecclesiastical policy, and the division of State and Church demanded by a society undergoing modernisation. After 1867 the revival of the liberal heritage determined ecclesiastical policy in both halves of the Empire. It was true throughout the entire history of the Monarchy that although the Compromise created the opportunities of equality before the law in principle for all denominations, certain privileges harking back to feudalism were still retained by the Catholic Church. The State exercised its right of patronage towards the Catholic Church and of supervision towards the rest of the religious denominations. The Catholic Church received financial support from the State budget but was able to supplement this with income derived from its position as the most important landowner in the Empire, while other established churches were only able to supplement their respective incomes from the State with what could be collected from their parishioners.

The focal point of the most important reforms in ecclesiastical policy was the 1870s in Austria (Cisleithania) and the 1890s in Hungary. Austrian liberals had been preparing for social reforms as early as the first half of the 1860s and on the eve of the Compromise the dissolution of the concordatum became the symbol of constitutionality for them. Their aspirations were demonstrated by the Austrian Basic Law, passed at the end of 1867, which ensured among its fundamental rights of the individual a declaration of complete freedom of religion and conscience, including the right to the free practise of religions not formally recognised by law. However, the revived Hungarian generation of 1848 and those liberals who had returned from emigration were far

Above: *The Graz Cathedral between the buildings of the old town.*

more concerned that the validity of the civil laws of 1848 should be recognised, which inevitably included issues in regard to the relationship between State and Church. The concordatum issue, which was seen as a sensitive issue in Austria, was not even raised in Hungary, since in the Hungarian interpretation the concordatum was signed in a period when the constitutional independence of the country did not exist.

In the summer and autumn of 1867, the concordatum issue tested the strength of the liberals preparing for government. The relevant draft bills had been drawn up, and it was no coincidence that 25 prelates submitted a joint supplication demanding that Franz Joseph uphold the integrity of the concordatum, which was especially emphasised by Pope Pius IX (*see painting, top right*). At the beginning of 1868, Eduard Herbst, the Minister of Justice in Karl Ausburg's cabinet, submitted three draft bills relating to the basic pillars of the concordatum. In cases where the Church opposed the conclusion of marriage, civil marriage was offered as an alternative, while marriage trial cases were taken out of the hands of Church courts. The 'imperial public education act' upheld the practice of compulsory religious education and the observation of the religious fundamentals of moral upbringing, but at the same time it stipulated eight years of compulsory education independent of any religious denomination, and in addition laid down the State's most important supervisory rights in issues of education policy. These acts, which had a markedly liberal tone, were sanctified by the ruler on the 25 May 1868.

At the end of the 1860s, József Eötvös, the Minister of Religion and Public Education in Hungary's Andrássy cabinet, sought before all else to base future reforms in ecclesiastical policy on the provision of autonomy for the Catholic Church. The reason for this was that the Hungarian episcopate would only support the government if its interpretation of the reintroduced ecclesiastical act of 1848 did not promote secularisation and endanger the monopoly the Catholic Church had over educational policy. While Eötvös regarded an autonomous Catholic Church as a joint self-governing organ of the priesthood and believers, the prelacy of the Catholic Church, led by the Bishop of Esztergom János Simor (*see painting, left*), saw it as a self-defensive initiative aimed at avoiding the possibility of State intervention. The 1868 public education act made it possible to establish schools independent of religious denomination as well as inter-denominational primary level schools, all of which was regarded by the Catholic Church as an attack upon the monopoly it had enjoyed in school affairs. A storm of a similar scale was stirred up by the issue of mixed marriages and in a wider sense by the general regulation of marriage law, both of which became the starting point for debates that ensued about ecclesiastical policy. The relevant passage of the act on 'the reciprocity of established Christian religious denominations' declared that in future children born out of a mixed marriage would follow the religion of their parents

Above: *Prince primate János Simor, who crowned Franz Joseph King of Hungary on 8 June 1867, had been awarded the Grand Cross of the Order of Saint Stephen two days earlier. His portrait, which is now preserved in the Esztergom Christian Museum, was painted by Sándor Liezen Mayer in 1886.*

according to gender. In contrast, the Catholic Church wished to maintain the practice whereby its priests would only bless mixed marriages if the Protestant partner in the marriage declared that their offspring would be baptised in the Catholic faith. Although these recognizances had lost their State validity, the Catholic Church wished to continue employing them, even though in legal terms they ended up christening children that were registered by law as a different religion.

By a twist of fate, in the summer of 1870 the conservative-leaning Austrian government, led by Count Potocki, facilitated the termination of the concordatum. This created a new situation, opening the road towards further reform in ecclesiastical policy; however, this was then hindered by the liberals being ousted from governmental office as a result of their defeat in the election of 1870 as well as by the coming to power of the conservative leaning Hohenwart cabinet that put aside the relevant draft bills. The Hungarian government was in a far more uncomfortable position at the time of the Vatican council: at a time of uncertainty, when the main objective of the government was to stabilise the system created by the compromise of 1867, the Andrássy government had no desire to open up new fronts, for example with the Catholic Church, but at the same time it had clearly stated that council decisions contrary to Hungary's traditions and interests would be rejected. In the end, the Hungarian episcopate – similarly to the Central-European bishops – did not participate in the final vote. One consequence of the conflict involving the placetum in Hungary was that during the period of 1874–1875 a comprehensive draft bill to regulate the relationship between Church and State was drawn up upon the demands of the liberals in the Hungarian parliament.

In Vienna, the aspirations of liberals who believed in the separation of Church and State accelerated in the first half of the 1870s. The Constitutional Party pressed for 'bills on ecclesiastical policy replete with real and true spirit, and real reform', and primarily for mandatory civil marriage to be codified into law. In the parliamentary debates on the proposals numerous representatives of the Constitutional Party made demands that went beyond the government's proposal (e.g. that civil registration of births be made compulsory), calling for the settlement of the situation of the old Catholic parishes that had rejected papal infallibility and for the State supervision of religious denominations to be guaranteed. The Catholic Church interpreted every change as an attack against their Church and Christianity (according to Archbishop Rauscher the government's plans 'carry on them the peculiar mark of distrust and mercilessness'), and the Pope renewed his protest. In the spirit of returning to the tradition of Josephinism, the cabinet argued that the reforms were not directed against the Catholic Church and that their aim was rather to realise a model of State–Church relationship that was in line with a modern society. The situation of the old Catholics was finally settled, and the achievements of the school act were ensured in this spirit. The acts on ecclesiastical policy introduced in the mid-1870s fundamentally defined the ecclesiastical policy in Cisleithania until the end of the Monarchy, and no radical reform took place after this point. No further results could be expected from 1879, when the conservative Taaffe cabinet was formed. Yet, the liberals did not suffer a defeat, since during the development of a fundamentally State–Church (absolutist) system, they were able to place the relationship between State and Church in Austria onto a new foundation. The two spheres were separated to such a degree that there could no longer be any doubt that the State was secular in nature. The Church's influence became increasingly focussed on its own internal affairs, and it was allowed to assume its role in the public sphere only within the existing framework provided. Back in 1871 Franz Joseph had clearly stated that he was aware of Stremayr's proposals; however, he was not willing to go beyond them.

In Hungary, the governments which followed that of Gyula Andrássy devoted less attention to ecclesiastical policy due to the uncertainty that existed in internal affairs (they did not wish to burden public life with new conflicts), and in a paradoxical way the same can be said of Kálmán Tisza's long period in office as prime minister (between 1875 and 1890). The process of separation between Church and State continued mostly in the area of educational policy, especially in regard to the secondary school act of 1883. In 1881 a proposal was prepared to allow marriage between Christians and Jews, although

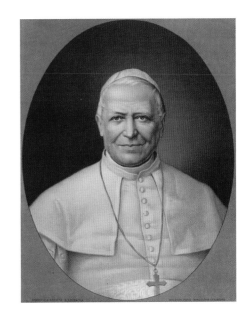

Above: *During his long papacy (1846–1878) Pius IX was unable to change the thinking or behaviour of the Catholic Church to make it conform with the needs of the period.*

Below: *The conservative Joseph Othmar von Rauscher, the bishop of Saint Stephen's Cathedral (Stephansdom) in Vienna, conducted the wedding ceremony of Elizabeth and Franz Joseph in 1854.*

Tisza wanted to postpone this because of the anti-semitic sentiments that were aroused by the 'blood trial' of Tiszaeszlár both in internal and external politics. This was the trial in which Jewish koshers were accused of murdering a 12-year-old girl to use her blood in a ritual sacrifice. Nevertheless, the proposal failed in the Upper House of Parliament due to the opposition of the episcopate.

In Cislaitania, during the period of the Taaffe government the Church and the conservative-clerical political forces that were allied with it made several attempts to trim earlier reforms. In the course of these efforts their most significant success was in 1883, when they achieved the revision of the school act. The new act not only declared that communities would have recourse to their own scope of authority in deciding whether to introduce six or eight years of elementary education, but also that pupils' religious affiliation should be taken into consideration and that religious education in schools should only be directed by Catholics. The period of the Taaffe government is also marked by attempts to improve the financial lot of the clergy through both minor and more significant measures. For example, the annexation of Bosnia and Herzegovina was followed by the introduction of an act in 1912, which granted State recognition of the Islamic faith.

The Hungarian government had long procrastinated in dealing with the problems inherent in ecclesiastical policy but in the end they were no longer able to avoid the issue; in fact, after a while they did not even wish to. The government urged the regulation of the most important issues of marriage law as the number of mixed marriages continually increased. Furthermore, it wanted to address the problem of the heterogeneous regulation in regard to canon law of established Christian denominations. The 1868 act of reciprocity provided only a partial solution to issues that emerged in the Monarchy with a population of many nationalities and denominations living together. Another problem was that the legal basis for the separation of Church and State was seriously lacking. However, what for the liberals was a trifling matter was an extremely shocking one for the Catholic Church. One of the passages of the penal code of 1879 sanctioned the acceptance of individuals aged under 18 into a non-Catholic denomination. The Minister of Culture, Ágoston Trefort, published a decree that made it obligatory for pastors who baptised children 'away from the Catholic Church' to forward the certificates of baptism to the legally competent parish. The Catholic Church opposed the very mention of this decree and rather sought to trim away at the legal basis of the measures introduced by the act of 1868. In 1890, the decree prohibiting the baptism of children 'away from the Catholic Church' was renewed by a text that took religious interests into consideration more than ever before; yet, the response of the Catholic Church was one of rejection and a stormy campaign ensued from the pulpits as well as in the press.

Above: *Sándor Wekerle on his village estate with his wife. As prime minister, Wekerle was committed to bringing about ecclesiastical reform.*

The government even tried to find a path that would lead to agreement with Rome; however, in his response to the government's initiatives Pope Leo XIII made clear his insistence that the act of 1868 'trampling upon the rights of the Church' should be abolished. The government was forced to take a certain approach because the papal letter resulted in mass opposition from the Church, and internal political tension was created by the punishment of priests who carried out baptism away from the Catholic Church. There remained no other recourse than to again turn to the alternative of State birth certificates and the related issue of civil marriages. The conservative religious political forces were confident that having succeeded in postponing the drawing up of ecclesiastical policy acts through compromises they would also be able to block it for good. In 1891 Simor was succeeded in his seat of archbishop by Kolos Vaszary, who at the outset showed himself to be more open to compromise. However, by this time the government did not want a half solution, and thus put forward proposals on civil marriage and State birth certificates. In the meantime, the post of prime minister was occupied by Sándor Wekerle (1892–1895), who was committed to bringing in ecclesiastical policy reform. For the Catholic Church the stakes were enormous: to preserve what was left of the State–Church heritage and to prevent the rules of law required by a developing middle-class society from being introduced.

In the autumn of 1893, in his encyclical letter beginning Constanti Hungarorum devoted entirely to Hungary, the Pope expressly exhorted the Catholic Church and its adherents to follow the path of opposition. However, shortly after this (following the draft bills proposing equal rights before the law for Israelite denominations, the introduction of State registration of births and the free practise of religion) the bill on mandatory civil marriage was prepared. This time Franz Joseph – in line with Cisleithanian practice – did his utmost to keep liberal demands to a minimum. At the same time, an interesting situation arose in the Hungarian parliament: the acts on ecclesiastical policy that the liberal opposition had long demanded were now advanced by the government side; thus presenting the liberals with a dilemma whether they should support the government or reject their own initiatives.

The parliamentary debate had to be suspended following the death of the 92-year-old Lajos Kossuth (*see box below*). The Catholic Church did not officially participate in the mourning and went so far as to prohibit bell ringing in connection with the event. After a

'At Kossuth's funeral everybody was there who counted the least bit in Hungary … Hundreds and hundreds of thousands occupied the streets because it had been declared in advance by what route Kossuth's body would be conveyed to the cemetery,' reported Gyula Krúdy in his piece entitled The Dead Kossuth in Pest.

Above: *Dezső Bánffy, who was unpopular in liberal circles, also found himself in conflict with the representatives of the radical line of the Church. In April 1895 the new papal legate, Agliardi, arrived in Hungary and called for people to fight the anti-ecclesiastical laws. He even declared a crusade against modern legislation. Bánffy's protests led to diplomatic complications and the resignation of the joint minister for foreign affairs.*

lengthy parliamentary tug-of-war the liberals finally won with a narrow majority, while Wekerle even gained the sanctification of the Emperor by threatening to resign. The acts on civil marriage and the State registration of births took away the monopoly long enjoyed by the Catholic Church, creating equality before the law for all denominations and providing the conditions for the actual realisation of a secular state. The act on the religion of children revived the provision of 1868 (i.e. that a child adopts the religion of his/her parent of the same sex) and also provided the opportunity for parents to freely decide prior to getting married which denomination, if it happened to be one other than their own, they wished their children to be baptised into. However, this agreement had to be sanctioned before State and not Church officials. Wekerle was succeeded in his post by Dezső Bánffy and it was during his prime ministership that the Israelite religion was declared as established, and the act sanctifying the freedom of religious practise was passed, which crowned the success of ecclesiastical reform. The act declared that everybody was free to follow any kind of religious conviction, within of course the limitations set by public order and morality. It provided complete freedom in the area of choosing one's religion and indeed, in keeping with Austrian legislative practice, it also declared the opportunity to remain outside of any denomination. From the aspect of State, ecclesiastical law denominations fell into one of three groups: established denominations, groups recognised by law and groups not recognised by law. The established denominations were granted a wide range of licences, such as being entitled to a share of the public budget and the maintenance of their institutions. It was a clear indication of the legislator's intention that at the time of the act being passed the category of 'recognised by law' was still blank, since the possibility was left open for new religious movements that were willing to adapt themselves to society in a legal way. For example, in 1905 the Baptist Church was declared as legally recognised by ministerial decree, and later in 1916 Islam attained the same kind of status on the basis of this legal authorisation.

At the turn of the century the attention of the Catholic Church in Austria was increasingly directed at the revival of religious life in the face of a religious crisis, which occurred in parallel with the development of Christian socialism. Also playing a role in the revival of religious life was George Schönerer's pan-Germanic movement, which initiated the *Los vom Rom Bewegung* (Away from Rome Movement; meaning a step away from the Catholic Church) which primarily promoted the idea of converting to Protestantism. During the early 1900s, the movement caused a deep division within the Catholic Church in some provinces (Czechia, Lower Austria and Styria) with the number of converts to the Protestant faith numbering tens of thousands. The Catholic Church did its utmost to rise to the challenge, primarily by the revival of religious associations. They

Right: *This portrait of Lajos Haynald, now preserved in the Hungarian National Gallery, is one of the few that Mihály Munkácsy painted of pontiffs. The painting, like many of Munkácsy's others, has darkened over the years. A copy made in 1893 by Jozef Hanula is now in the treasury of the archbishopric of Kalocsa.*

received significant help from the city of Vienna through its mayor, Karl Lueger.

In Hungary, one of the repercussions of the ecclesiastical policy acts worthy of note was that political Catholicism, which had to this point been latent, now underwent a process of organisation at lightening speed, developing from mere movements into parties with their main political objective naturally being to revoke the acts on ecclesiastical policy. Although later governments also insisted on keeping the ecclesiastical policy system unchanged, they did respect the Catholic Church's demands in regard to more minor issues, demonstrating that they were not oppressive anti-Church governments. In 1898 an act was passed granting a supplement to a state salary for non-Catholic clergymen, which in 1909 was extended to the Catholic lower clergy. The most important event in regard to ecclesiastical policy was the setting up of the Greek Catholic Episcopate in the town of Hajdúdorog in 1912. The members of the episcopate were – in the words of the German

Left: *Cardinal Friedrich Schwarzenberg, the archbishop of Prague, painted by František Fienišek. The painting is preserved in the bishop's palace in Prague. Schwarzenberg was an advocate of state secondary and primary schools taking on a spiritual leaning.*

Chief Consul in Budapest – 'more like patriots than Roman prelates'. In other words, they concentrated on activities connected to public life and did not strive for the revival of the Catholic Church in the midst of a period of social transformation. They primarily wished to repel the challenges posed by liberalism through political means, as well as through concluding agreements with the government. The Catholic general assembly became the venue of the main forum for the awakening and consolidation of religious consciousness, while the first assembly to work for a truly societal movement and revival of the Church took place in 1900.

Even the Catholic Church, which played a dominant role in ecclesiastical processes, was burdened with problems relating to nationalities. It could be said that the Catholic Church had exclusive influence in Croatia, which enjoyed wide-ranging independence. This was further consolidated by the fundamental role Catholicism had played in strengthening Croatian national consciousness. The impact of the Croatian Catholic Church in public life and politics increased as a result

Above: *In 1912, Vienna organised the 23rd Eucharistic World Congress, which was also regarded as a demonstration of Austria's commitment to Catholicism.*

of the system that developed with the Compromise and also because it counterbalanced the national and religious aspirations of the Serbs, who accounted for approximately one quarter of the population, and in addition facilitated the realisation of political objectives in regard to the union with Dalmatia. The aspirations of the Catholic Church in Czechia can be described with similar characteristics in regard to Austria. It usually supported the respective governments, although, despite their German origins, they were not always insensitive to the cause of Czech national independence (in the case of bishops Schwarzenberg and Schönborn). The nationality issue was especially acute for the Catholic Church in Hungary. In the years following the Compromise individual bishops did try to develop parishes of different nationalities, although later such aspirations were shunted into the background. Assimilation within the Church was far more moderate, with, for example, Kolos Vaszary supporting the Slovak-speaking priests while the bishop of Pécs supported the German and Croatian speaking ones. Within the Catholic school system the number of schools for each nationality remained a pertinent issue. The role played by the Church and the priesthood was especially important in the Slovak nationality movement, for example through the activities of the parish priest Andrej Hlinka, who represented a position of self-defence.

The Ruthenians (Transcarpathian Ukrainians) of Hungary were almost exclusively of the Greek Catholic faith and their religious organisation was comprised of the episcopate of Munkács and Eperjes. Their bishops proclaimed peace between all nationalities. Similarly to other nationalities, it was the religious associations that provided the background for the Ruthenians to practise their linguistic cultural rights. Alongside the vigorous assimilation of the Ruthenian Greek Catholic priesthood, a typical and also important process of the period was the often successful Schism Movement, the objective of which was to convert Greek Catholics to the Greek Orthodox Church, an endeavour which to a large extent was supported by Russians (and American immigrants). Approximately one third of Romanians belonged to the Greek Catholic Church and they sought to express their strong national aspirations within the Monarchy. In 1868, the independent Romanian Greek Catholic hierarchy was recognised by Hungarian legislation, along with its equal rights in the civil and political areas and the self-government of its diocese. It was in 1900 that it expressed a renewed forthright declaration calling for independence from the Bishop of Esztergom. A visible indication of a strengthening of the nationality movement within Roman Greek Catholic circles was in 1893, when one of their priests, Vasiliu Lucaciu, was found guilty as one of the chief defendants in the Memorandum trial.

The other large group of Romanian nationality at the turn of the century comprised of some 1.7 million adherents of the Greek Orthodox Church. In the middle of the 19th century and during the years of absolutism, Andrei Saguna, the bishop and later archbishop of Nagyszeben who became known for his policy of dedicated loyalty to the emperor, played a major role in the Romanian national movement. Following the Compromise The Greek Orthodox Church protested bitterly against coming under the jurisdiction of the Hungarian government through Hungary's union with Transylvania, although in 1868 the Hungarian legislature affirmed the independence of the main Greek Orthodox diocese in Nagyszeben. With its 90-member local government, one third of which was from the Church, it enjoyed wide-ranging authority in religious and school affairs. Priests from the Greek Orthodox Church were the first to play a major role in the Romanian national movement; however, their role was increasingly taken over by secular members. Another reason why their position was weakened was that the Hungarian government regularly tried to block financial aid received by the Church from Romania. Some one million Serbs lived in the Kingdom of Hungary but there were significant numbers of them living in Croatia and Dalmatia too. The Greek Orthodox Church was traditionally an institution of Serb culture and the Serb nationality movement, and under the leadership of Bishop Josip Rajačić it had made an alliance

Above: *During the 1870s the motor behind the reforms in ecclesiastical policy was the ministry of culture led by Karl von Stremayr (pictured above). Laws passed in May 1874 enforced minimal liberal demands, the substance of which provided the State with the right to interfere in every ecclesiastical matter that did not strictly belong to the Church's internal scope of authority.*

with the Austrian absolutist government (similarly to the Romanians) against the Hungarians' Struggle for Independence in 1848–1849. After the Compromise, the Hungarian legislation recognised the Serb local government, which operated under the authority of the Serb Congress, the basis of which was popular representation rather than feudal, and in 1875 this recognition was again endorsed by the ruler. Their funds and educational affairs were managed by a body operating under the direction of a bishop. In the years following the Compromise the Serbs were the most active nationality; however, after the vigorous intervention of the Hungarian government they restricted their activities to the framework of national-religious local government, and gradually relocated their political activities from the southern Hungarian counties to Croatia. In the 1890s the Serbs strove harder to co-operate with the government in Hungary in order to act as a countermeasure against secular Serb nationalist and separatist aspirations, in which an important element was the fact that the emperor took into consideration the Hungarian government's recommendation when he confirmed the elected patriarch in office. The Serb prelates were capable of extended co-operation with coalition as well as later governments; however, even they demonstrated their antipathy when the local government of the Serb Church was suspended, the role played by secular members in decision-making was terminated, and a government commissioner was appointed to handle the financial funds of the Church.

The Calvinists living in the Monarchy mostly lived in Hungary and when there was a census they professed themselves to be Hungarian nationals. The Hungarian Calvinists accepted the system created by the Compromise and on the whole were the beneficiaries of the enacted ecclesiastical policy laws providing for the equality of denominations before the law and reducing the privileges enjoyed by the Catholic Church. Problems only arose, however, when for example the poorer Calvinist communities were unable to procure the school equipment that the 1868 public education act prescribed, and they therefore had to convert into State- or local government institutions. However, during the years of dualism a far greater problem arose. Although the attention of their leadership was focused on the struggles of public life, the process of laicisation appeared unavoidable. It gradually became obvious that the Calvinist ecclesiastical model had characteristics which put them in a disadvantaged position compared to other denominations. The internal life of the Calvinist Church was also rendered more difficult by the fruitless debates between adherents of religious liberalism and 'Orthodox Calvinism'. The attitude taken by the liberal thinkers was more in line with the requirements of the period and therefore they were more accepting of the need to transform the traditional system of religious institutions. In contrast, the 'Orthodox' members of the Calvinist Church were rigid and uncompromising in regard to the preservation of tradition. This paralysed the missionary impetus of the Church, which would otherwise have had the opportunity to bring new members into the faith as a result of the new acts providing the freedom to convert to any denomination and to choose one's religion.

Above: *The Greek Catholic Cathedral, Ungvár.*

In 1881 a countrywide synod was held in Debrecen, which fundamentally restructured Church organisation. Although it recorded that the Church would keep its bottom-up structure it nevertheless regulated the setting up of presbyteries. It declared that a central governing body, called the general convent, would preside over the five dioceses and that the general synod would be the main legislative body. The most important changes introduced by the synod only manifested themselves later, but the conditions for the so-called home mission movement were created. Significant numbers of Lutherans lived not only in Hungary but also in the province of Silesia, which was dominated by a German-speaking population. About 35 to 40 per cent of Lutherans living in the Hungarian Kingdom declared themselves to be native Slovak, while another almost one third were of Hungarian or German nationality. The Lutheran population

traditionally lived in urban areas, except the Slovak speaking Lutherans who lived primarily in Upper Hungary and south-eastern Hungary. The cultural centres of the Lutheran Church (Budapest, Pozsony or Bratislava, Eperjes, Sopron, Lőcse, Selmecbánya, Brasov) were ethnically diverse; however, there was a marked increase in the number of Hungarians during the years of dualism. The Lutheran deaneries of northern Hungary protested against the modification of dioceses introduced in 1893, which gave preference to ethnic interests over other issues. (They were afraid that the nation in majority would want to turn the Slovak Lutherans into 'Hungarian Calvinists'.)

The life of the Lutheran Church demonstrated many similarities with that of the Reformed Church. 'Liberals' and 'Orthodox' Lutherans were involved in theological debates, one of the consequences of which was the revival of the missionary movement

Above and right: The numbers of Jews varied from province to province, but it was higher in urban centres. This synagogue, in Budapest's Rumbach Sebestyén Stree, was designed by 27-year-old Otto Wagner. The building was constructed from 1870–1873 and although it did not fit in architecturally with the residential buildings in its immediate vicinity, nobody would think that it is actually an octogonal synagogue. 'Coloured light comes into the inner space from the octagonal raised roof through the lantern and the large, round lateral windows accentuate the sacred character of the building', wrote Wagner researcher Otto Antonai Graf.

after the turn of the century. The Lutheran Church organisation was the same as the Reformed one in many respects with an important difference being that Transylvanian Saxons did not have a separate diocese but instead formed their national Church, independent of the Hungarian Church organisation. Among other things, the Saxon Lutheran Church, which was regarded as the most important institution of Saxon national and cultural autonomy, did not welcome the 1867 union of Transylvania and Hungary. Until the end of the Monarchy, it was also regarded as the most important institution propagating Saxon national and cultural autonomy. Although they eventually found their place in the system created by the Compromise, they always had

Right: An 18th-century tombstone with Hebrew inscription in a cemetery in Northern Hungary.

their small conflicts with the Hungarian State. In Hungary it was the legislative synod of Budapest in 1891–1892 that created a unified structure of Lutheran Church organisation. The main central organ became the general synod, and the elected bodies – similarly to those of the Reformed Church – were organised on a parity system, which meant that half of the members were ecclesiastical and half of them non-ecclesiastical.

Although only active in Transylvania, the Unitarian Church, which was regarded as having equal status with other churches and accepted by law, was rather significant in regard to the number of its followers. While its seat was in Kolozsvár (Cluj) and its members consisted almost exclusively of the Hungarian nationality the Unitarian Church remained a community preserving its own Protestant ideology and at the same time one that continued to leave behind lasting achievements in the spheres of intellectual and spiritual life until the very end of the period. It was only from the turn of the century that more vigorous attempts were made to establish Unitarian congregations in Budapest and in other towns.

The Israelites played a key part in the embourgoisement process of the era, since their acceptance (problem areas of assimilation and emancipation) determined the state of society and political modernisation in general. The number of Israelites varied greatly in the various provinces of the monarchy. The Jewry concentrated in cities and towns was as follows: in 1910, almost one-quarter of the urban population was Jewish; there were greater numbers in Krakow and Lemberg, while it was around 8 per cent in Vienna and Prague. In Cislaitania the ecclesiastic acts passed in 1868 linked the declaration of Jewry's individual equality before the law with the declaration of the equality of denominations, among other things, whereas in Hungary the former was announced after the Compromise and the latter only in 1895.

Above: *Immanuel Lőw, who was a botanical scientist, Judaist, Orientalist and folklorist, was born in Szeged in 1854. He completed his university and theological studies in Berlin. From 1878 he was the chief rabbi for the Jewish community in Szeged. He played an important role in compiling the catalogue of the Somogy Library, and he regularly enriched the collection with donations of books. On the occasion of the 150-year anniversary of his birth the town of Szeged erected a statue to him in the National Pantheon on Dóm Square. He died in 1944, during the Second World War, in the Budapest ghetto.*

Modernisation and the legal act of asserting the equality of Jews also affected the internal life of Israelite parishes. Debates about the various possibilities and restrictions in regard to cultivating religious traditions as well as about the degree and ways of assimilation to a majority society continuously took place in the religious communities. In Hungary these debates even led to a formal separation within the Israelite community, something without parallel anywhere else in Europe. The objective at the first general assembly (congress) of the Israelites that convened in 1868–1869 was to set up a nationwide representation for the parishes; however, the conservative members did not approve of this – thus founding the Orthodox Israelite parishes – while the majority established the Neolog (congressional) parishes. Those that did not accept the point of view of either side qualified themselves as status quo ante. The situation that resulted from this separation was acknowledged by the Hungarian parliament in 1871, which also encouraged the proliferation of different interpretations of certain Jewish religious tenets (liturgy, attire, use of tombstones, etc.). The parishes that were active in Czechia and Austria usually belonged to the modernist wing, while the ones in Galicia, Bukovina and northeast Hungary insisted on the strict upholding of traditions. Assimilation in regard to language use and identity accelerated in the Neolog communities, which manifested itself in the increased use of German in Austrian communities and in the Hungarian language in Hungarian communities. The emancipation of the Israelites, i.e. the way they utilised the opportunities offered by a modern liberal state, could be truly regarded as a success story. This was indirectly indicated by the emergence of modern political anti-semitism, which in return affected the Jews. It is no coincidence, therefore, that the Monarchy became the birthplace of Zionism, one of the major intellectual-political Jewish movements. The previously mentioned 'blood trial' of Tiszaeszlár was an instructive example of how far the acceptance of assimilation by non-Jews could go, as was the general anti-semitism of Austrian Christian socialists and of the conservative movements in Hungary.

At the turn of the century newly emerged religious movements started to spread at a faster pace in the Monarchy. In the western part of the Empire Old Catholics were present in great numbers. Some other congregations of interest included the Herrnhut, Mennonite and Lippovan communities, which advocated rigorous moral principles and represented a radical trend of Reformation. In Hungary the Nazarene movement was similar to these; Baptists attracted an especially high number of believers, and the first Adventist, Methodist, and Jehovist preachers appeared on the scene. The historical Christian churches urged that strict measures be used against these small religions, and some Catholic and Protestant theologians warned that the success of these 'sectarian' preachers also reflected the general criticism expressed towards the activities and moral standing of the old established churches.

Above: *Kálmán Tisza's slogan with regard to ecclesiastical policy was 'quieta non movere' ('let sleeping dogs lie'). He was able to secure the cooperation of the Church's prelates for his economic and social policy reforms, which he regarded as more important than ecclesiastical policy.*

Parties and Associations

The political structure of the Austro-Hungarian Monarchy was basically paradoxical. On the one hand, the traditional political ideologies, primarily liberalism and conservatism, were 'operated' by the objective of obtaining power in the government, which was in line with the tendencies of modern political development. On the other hand, however, the formation and activities of parties were not governed by a commitment to some ideology but by how parties interpreted the public law system that came into being after the Compromise (the relationship between the two parts of the empire after the Compromise of 1867 is called the public law system). Parallel party structures developed but politics was not determined by constantly shifting powers since any party political turn would have posed a potential threat to the maintenance of the system that came into being in 1867. The party structures were fundamentally determined by the legislation in Vienna and in Budapest, and in addition to the parties' relationship with the system that appeared after the Compromise two factors also exerted great influence: one was the 'conventional' movements organised along specific values and the other one was the national movements which initiated the establishment of independent parties. These influences could be equally felt in both parts of the Monarchy. The Compromise of 1867 was realised by the liberal generation of the first half of the century. In addition to traditionally understood liberal values, both sides considered it important to maintain the unity of the Empire, as well as the central role it played in Central Europe. It can be generally stated that all governments that came to power typically began their activities by initiating liberal economic- and social political reforms, and only then did they start emphasising the importance of preserving the Empire's unity and the role it fulfilled. Prior to Taaffe's coming to power, Vienna was dominated by the liberal Constitutional Party. Their social base had become narrow by the 1880s, they were forced to give up a significant number of their positions, and their return to power was practically made impossible when Taaffe's electoral reform was introduced. (By decreasing the property qualification in voting the conservatism of anticapitalists, clerical traditions and Slavic nationals gained significantly more importance.) Numerous parliamentary clubs and associations appeared (the Progressive Party, the United Left, the Young Liberals, etc.) in addition to the Constitutional Party, partly formed from members who had left the latter. While undergoing constant change, these new organisations tried to enforce their own interests. From this time onwards, the elements of conservativism began to dominate, even though the conservative and liberal trends did not clearly separate. Taaffe was only able to form a stable coalition – the objective of which was to avoid government crises – by entering into agreements with the old conservatives and the Slav federalist (primarily Czech and Polish) elite. It is no surprise that this formation was named the 'iron ring'. Taaffe's 15 years as prime minister can be characterised by the concessions made to the Czechs and Slovenes as well as by a conservative social policy. The electoral reform of 1906 had a crucial role in the crystallisation of the party structure in Cislaitania. Due to the general suffrage (although applicable only to men), certain social groups (the agrarian party, radicals, etc.) were now represented in the party system. Furthermore, the 'compromises' with the various nationalities offered the alternative of a conservative orientated yet functional party system. The governments in Vienna and the imperial council underwent many crises; however, the system of dualism was preserved throughout the existence of the Monarchy, although it cost them a great number of special deals. The fact that the liberals lost ground after the turn of the century can be linked to the emergence of German nationalism and the manifestation of political Catholicism in the form of a popular party. The headway made by the radical right wing parties only accelerated this process.

In Hungary, after the Compromise, the party that gathered round Ferenc Deák was not strong enough to efficiently counter those opposing the public law system. Having left behind his earlier oppositionary sentiments Kálmán Tisza established the Liberal Party in 1875 and managed to realise the kind of stabilisation that Taaffe achieved in the other part of the Monarchy. Tisza's strong government, which enjoyed the firm support of parliament, made it possible for the numerous acts on modernisation as well as economic development to take place in the 1870s–1880s, while it integrated the conservatives who wished to preserve the Compromise. The Independence Party, which formed the opposition, often stood on the same liberal platform as the government. By the 1890s it had become obvious in both parts of the empire that the original system provided by the Compromise was outdated. The strong foundation of the party system on public law is illustrated by the fact that after the defeat of the Liberal Party in 1905 (and the ensuing transitional government crisis) Sándor Wekerle became the prime minister of a cabinet dominated by the Independence Party. In 1910, conservative tendencies prevailed in the Party of National Work, a reorganised version of the former liberal government, which manifested in the form of a growing intolerance towards national minorities.

Political movements organised around special social programmes played an important role in the Monarchy. The varieties of political Catholicism can be counted among these. Catholic social and political associations were organised in Cislaitania right after the Compromise. The strengthening of Christian social and conservative Christian movements can be linked to the policy of Pope Leo XIII's, called *ralliement* policy (accepting some aspects of the emerging middle-class society and modernisation), while the final impetus to these developments was given by his encyclical *Rerum Novarum* (1891). Catholic political organisation in Cislaitania was rather of a social nature, which meant that it set out to repair social injustices based on the social mission of Christianity. However, political Catholicism in Hungary focused more on public affairs, and the emergence of the movement was triggered by aspirations to counter the reforms of ecclesiastical policy in the 1890s. It was Karl Lueger, who turned the Christian Social Association into a strong political party in 1889. He coupled social Christianity with a conservative, anti-democratic and anti-semitic programme, which was met with the wide-ranging support of the lower middle class. The Christian socialists in Austria achieved their greatest success in 1897, when the leader of their party was elected mayor. After the turn of the century they formed a significant faction of the imperial council; what is more, their conservative aspirations were welcomed by the heir to the throne, Franz Ferdinand. Lueger and his party gave priority to loyalty to the Habsburgs over pan-Germanic sentiment. In Hungary, the Catholic People's Party emerged in 1895, under the patronage of Nándor Zichy. Early disagreements within the party soon came to an end and it was agreed that Catholic politics could only take a conservative direction, and be loyal to the dynasty. They expressed their allegiance to the system provided by the Compromise, which led to their participation in government between 1906 and 1910. The Hungarian Christian socialists first formed an association and then, in 1907, established a nationwide party with Sándor Giesswein as the main organiser. It is important to note that while Lueger's party enjoyed popularity in Vienna in the early 1900s, the Christian socialists in Hungary, who tried to take the 'sound and cleansing spirit of Christianity' to the Budapest city hall, were unable to break out of their isolation. Christian social trade unions achieved successes primarily in the industrial regions of Cislaitania, and the movement's central committee was established in 1909. In Hungary, the first such trade union had been established earlier, in 1898, in Győr; however, it did not manage to play a significant role in the area.

From among the parties of the labour movement it was only the social democrats who operated in both parts of the empire. They established their party in Austria and in Hungary in 1888 and in 1890, respectively, with Viktor Adler, Karl Renner and Otto Bauer playing a significant role in the former, and Pál Engelmann in the latter. Besides the issues of representing workers' interests and their struggle for the right to vote, both parties had to address the issue pertaining to nationalities. The solution proposed by the 1899 Brno Congress was a programme of granting equal rights to nationalities living in the Monarchy, while the social democratic party programme in Hungary outlined a far more moderate solution. At the same time, it must be noted that social democrats in Hungary did not play a substantial part in parliamentary politics up to the end of the Monarchy but their counterparts in Austria did from the turn of the century. Due to the different social structure in the eastern part of the Monarchy, parties such as the Peasant Party, the Independent Socialist Party, etc., the objective of which was to organise agricultural workers, were accorded at least as much importance as the social democrats.

When trying to represent their interests, agrarians encountered limits imposed by the prevailing economic policy, the objective of which was to facilitate industrialisation; as a

Above: *Josip Juraj Strossmayer (1815–1905) was the bishop of Dakovo (Djakovar). He was the founder of the Croatian National Museum, the Croatian Academy and the University of Zagreb and supported these institutions with his donations.*

reaction, they demanded the protection of traditional agriculture and for restrictions to be introduced in regard to the free buying and selling of land. Political anti-semitism was also hotly discussed, and while it was linked primarily to Christian social and pan-Germanic parties in Austria, an independent anti-semitic party was nevertheless formed in Hungary. In areas with a population composed of various nationalities, parties were established on an ethnic foundation in addition to the great parties based on 'countrywide' politics. The two most important trends in Czechia were the Old Czechs, favouring absolute co-operation with Vienna, and the Young Czechs, who wanted to achieve greater autonomy within the Monarchy. In parallel with these two political trends, an independent party structure with national demands as well as a social programme gradually developed. For example, the Czech-Slavic Social Democratic Workers' Party later became the strongest party of the Second International. The Agrarian Party, embracing agricultural interests, and the Czech Progressive Party, attracting the middle-class intelligentsia, emerged around this time. At the time of the Compromise, the Croatian Constitutional (Unionist) Party came to power in Croatia, in accordance with the interests of Vienna and Pest–Buda. One of the leaders of the opposition National Party was Bishop Josip Juraj Strossmayer (*see painting on page 168*), who played a major role in the adherents of the autonomist movement accepting the model provided by the Compromise.

The fundamental issue in Croatian politics was determined by the public law position of their own country, and this also applied in the cases of Czechia and Hungary. The formation of a party that caused the greatest stir was that of the Croatian Party of Rights led by Ante Starčević. Until 1903, the Independent Serbian Party had sympathised with the leadership led by the 'ban' (viceroy) and had taken Hungarian interests into consideration, but they then decided to form a coalition with the Croatians. The Croatian Social Democratic Party was founded in 1894, followed by the Peasants' Party, which, along with the spreading of cultural associations, was a clear indication that the party structure based on public law was being eroded. Miletić, the mayor of Novi Sad, founded the most influential organisation among the Serbs in Hungary, the Serbian National Liberal Party. It was able to gain its positions primarily through exerting influence on congressional elections and wished to achieve the expansion of local government rights in the Hungarian parliament. Of at least the same importance was Omladina, the social association of young Serbian intellectuals, which spread its operations abroad. Romanians in Transylvania and Hungary started working on establishing a form of political representation straight after the Compromise when they founded the Romanian National Party. Their 1881 programme demanded that the injustices committed against Romanians and the damage (from their perspective) resulting from the Transylvanian Union be repaired. In addition to the party, which expressed serious demands under the presidency

Below: The charity, burial, benevolent and firemen's societies, which formed in the early 19th century, carried out diverse social tasks following the Compromise. The events they organised fundamentally contributed to the creation of public spaces which defined the everyday life of citizens and the way they thought.

Above: *Franz Joseph took pains to ensure that he was not just regarded as the Austrian emperor but also as the Hungarian king. In this interesting photomontage the royal couple are dressed in Hungarian attire.*

of Ioan Ratiu, an association organised by radical youth, Liga Culturala, played an important role. Among the Slovaks it was also a cultural association called Matica Slovenska that first carried out public duty. It was dissolved in the mid-1870s, which resulted in grave disappointment, as did the closing down of Lutheran Slovak secondary schools. In addition to secular associations, religious ones also played a significant role. The Slovak National Party, for example, was established under the initiative of Lutheran intellectuals, and only later, in the 1890s, did it form political ties with the Catholic People's Party of Hungary. The latter turned its attention towards the injustices suffered by the Slovak Catholics with utmost sympathy, while the intertwining of religious and national sentiments recruited the support of the Slovaks towards the party's conservative programme. The conservative programme with religious elements which was announced by the Catholic People's Party eventually led to the emergence of a radical Catholic movement which operated within an ethnic framework.

Due to the natural process of self-organisation, associations flourished in the Monarchy during the period of dualism. In addition to the nationwide and regional trade, cultural and public associations, local initiatives by people to form organisations in their respective areas of residence greatly contributed to the strengthening of the middle-class. In addition to the local branches of nationwide associations, the

Above left and right: *The Saint Stephen procession took place in 1913 on the streets of Budapest. It was here that János Csernoch appeared for the first time in his capacity of primate.*

importance of charity and recreational (sports) associations must be highlighted. The foundation of associations as well as the supervision of their lawful operation were regulated (mostly under the competence of the ministry of the interior) in both parts of the Empire. Supervision was typically carried out by the mayor's offices in towns and cities, while elsewhere it was the responsibility of the municipalities. The development of associations is well indicated by the following figures: 265 associations were registered in Budapest in 1875 and almost 1,000 in 1914, furthermore by this time the original 120 thousand membership had reached half a million. After the Compromise, the charity, burial, relief and fireguard associations established in the first half of the 19th century carried out diverse social duties in addition to their basic activities. In addition, their events greatly contributed to the development of community spaces that defined citizens' everyday lives and ways of thinking. Associations directly affiliated with a church or nationality were especially important since they played a prominent role in religious affiliations being passed on from one generation to the next, mostly in the form of bottom-up initiatives. The development of a civil society was also manifested by the State – in accordance with its middle-class character – having little or no wish to interfere with the private lives of its people; moreover, it created a legal framework in which no legal possibility was provided for certain tasks to be executed by the State administration. As Kálmán Tisza once accurately said, 'The State cannot do all; therefore, let society do something too.'

Public holidays

The public holidays of a state are a faithful reflection of both its characteristics and political and social-value system. The period of dualism was one in which both sides of the Empire began to attribute more importance to the issue of public holidays afforded prominence by the State. The public holidays favoured by those wielding power did not always correspond with the value judgement of society, but they frequently celebrated the anniversaries of historical or otherwise outstanding events regarded as important by the masses.

Major significance was attributed to one particular public holiday throughout the entire Austro-Hungarian Monarchy: the birthday of Franz Joseph, 18 August 1830. This was celebrated every year with official public holidays complemented by public festivities. In the big cities, such as in Vienna,

The Opening of the Franz Joseph Bridge

*Franz Joseph Bridge (today known as Liberty Bridge) was designed by János Feketeházy and inaugurated as part of the 1896 series of millennium celebrations. At the opening ceremony (*see pictures, left and below, to see ornamentation designs*) the very last rivet, which was made of silver and engraved with the initials E. J., was inserted by Franz Joseph himself.*

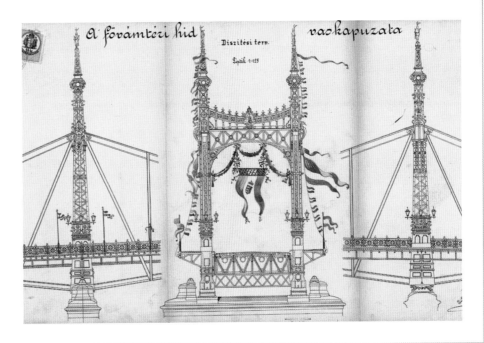

The 1,000-Year Anniversary of the Magyar Conquest

In 1896 Hungary commemorated the 1000th anniversary of the Magyar Conquest. Parliament passed a special law for the anniversary. The main attraction of the millennium celebrations was the anniversary of the coronation marked on 8th June with a splendid parade. (left) For the occasion every municipality in the country dispatched a mounted escort to the capital and the crown was taken in this escort to the vaulted hall of the new parliament building.

Separate monuments were erected at seven sites in the country that had played a significant role in the state's coming into being: Pusztaszer, Munkács, Pannonhalma, the Zobor Mountains near Nyitra, Dévény, Tampa Mountain at Brasov, and Zimony. In Budapest and the whole country important building projects were carried out and completed by the beginning of the anniversary. The plans for such projects were proposed in parliament by Prime Minister Count Gyula Andrássy. It was at this time that the monument at Heroes' Square (designed by Albert Schikedanz) at the end of Sugár Road (later Andrássy Road) was built. The statues on the semi-circle shaped edifice – which were the work of György Zala – depict the great rulers and important figures in Hungarian history. The Archangel Gabriel, standing on the central pillar, holds the Double Cross of Saint Stephen and the orb in his hands. On one side of the huge square (to the left in our picture) is the Art Gallery, which was built in the same year, and on the other side (right) is the Museum of Fine Arts, which was opened in 1906. The millennium exhibition was opened in the Városliget (City Park) behind the square and was designated to display the spiritual and material strengths of the country from both the past and the present. Models for some old and famous buildings were erected in the park, some of which have survived in a subsequently rebuilt form. Among them is Vajdahunyad Castle, which once belonged to the Turk-beater János Hunyadi.

Budapest, Prague and Zagreb, public holidays essentially had military features, including parades of various armed organisations, military bands and the shooting of cannons. The celebrations were also of a religious nature and the celebratory holy mass was regarded as an indispensable part of it. All the programmes were organised with 'the people' in mind and attracted a high level of interest from society.

The public holidays that were regarded as most important had religious roots or were linked to nationality. In fact, these two aspects often complemented each another, for example, in the case of the public holidays of national patron saints and religious holidays were used to celebrate their dignity and importance. The Catholic Churches of the Monarchy also celebrated the holy mass for the aurora (rorate), which was linked to the Advent season.

The anniversaries of events that were linked to a prominent occasion in the history of a nationality or to the life of a prominent individual from the past were not only ways of creating a nation's identity but were often an expression of national and political opposition. For example, Hungary's most important national holiday was a celebration of the nation's founder King Stephen, on 20 August, which fell embarrassingly close to Franz Joseph's birthday. The true day of celebration, however, was the anniversary on 15 March, the outbreak of the 1848 revolution in Pest. To add weight to its significance, Franz Joseph sat on the throne of Hungary and also carried personal responsibility for the military suppression of the War of Independence. In 1898, on the 50th anniversary of this holiday, the issue of some form of official recognition of the Revolution and War of Independence was raised. However, the ruler was not willing for any State celebration to take place on 15 March; therefore, the Hungarian legislation chose 11 April as a national holiday, the day on which Franz Joseph's predecessor sanctified the legislative acts on the middle-class transformation of society in 1848.

The greatest series of public celebrations in Hungary took place in 1896, on the 1,000-year anniversary of the Magyar Conquest. The grandiose commemorations were received with antipathy by the non-Hungarian nationalities since for them they represented a demonstration of the country's dominant ethnic group.

Above: *Commemorative plaque with a profile picture of Franz Joseph and Elizabeth, and a hymn by Friedrich Berndt entitled* Grosser Gott im Himmel schenke Segen unserm Kaiser-paar *(God in Heaven Bless our Imperial Couple).*

Anthems, Idols and Icons

The Austro-Hungarian Monarchy had two official State anthems: the Austrian imperial anthem, the *Gotterhalte,* and the Hungarian anthem, the *Himnusz.* The *Gotterhalte* was originally created for the 1792 enthronement of Emperor Franz I, with the music composed by Haydn. This has been the anthem of the Habsburg eternal provinces since 1826. The *Gotterhalte* aroused feelings of antipathy, especially among Hungarians. On the one hand, it anachronistically referred to Catholicism as the 'holy faith' binding the Empire together in a period when Hungarians were striving for the separation of

Church and State. On the other hand, the text referring to the 'heavenly hand' uniting the Habsburg throne with the Empire's provinces was also contrary to the historical traditions of the Kingdom of Hungary. The lyrics of the official anthem of the Hungarians was from a poem written by Ferenc Kölcsey in 1823, which was put to music by Ferenc Erkel in 1844. During the years of the Monarchy it was sung by many at both official and semi-official celebrations. The Hungarians had other official songs too, which strengthened their feelings of national solidarity: the *Szózat* (meaning appeal or proclamation) was also written before 1848 and the popular *Rákóczi March*. The issue of the anthems was a source of controversy in public life.

The majority of the anthems originated from a period of national awakening in the first half of the 19th century. For example, in Czechia the text for their anthem was originally written by Kajetán Tyl as a theatre piece in 1834 and was set to music later. The lyrics of the Slovene national anthem is from the poem 'Zdravljica' (Pledge) written by their greatest poet France Prešeren. The most important national song of the Croatians was a verse written by Antun Mihanović in 1835, *Horvatska domovina* (Croatian Homeland). It was, interestingly, set to music by Josip Runjanin, a Serb national, and was first played as the Croatian national anthem in 1891, on the eve of a trade fair in Zagreb. The Serbs living in the Monarchy were the only people whose anthem originated from a motherland beyond the borders. The anthem, composed in 1872, used the text beginning *Bože pravde* (God of Justice) written by Jovan Djordjević. It was readily accepted by the Serbs living in the Monarchy since it contained obvious references to their desire for ties with 'Serb brothers'. In general, these anthems expressed a desire to create a national identity after the tribulations that they had been forced to endure.

Above: *Franz Joseph on a bier at Schönbrunn.*

Icons and idols popular in the Monarchy were primarily linked to national consciousness. A prominent role was played in the national canons by patron saints and State founding rulers, Saint Václav; Saint Steven, the Holy Virgin and Saint Joseph, among them. Historical figures, symbolising national independence, such as Jan Hus, the founder of Husitism, and the leaders of the 1848 struggle for national independence were also very important. Among the Hungarians the heroes who had fought for independence against the Habsburgs were idols.

The celebration of national idols were sometimes controversial. For example, when Josip Jellačić's statue was erected in Zagreb's main square in 1866, it was noted that his sword pointed in the direction of Budapest. Similarly, Hungarians detested Austrian monuments that made a painful reference to the War of Independence, such as the monument erected in Buda Castle of General Heinrich Hentzi, who had bombarded Pest in 1852. The statue became a regular venue for demonstrations calling for independence and it was later removed from the square.

Right: *The funeral procession turning into the Ring.*

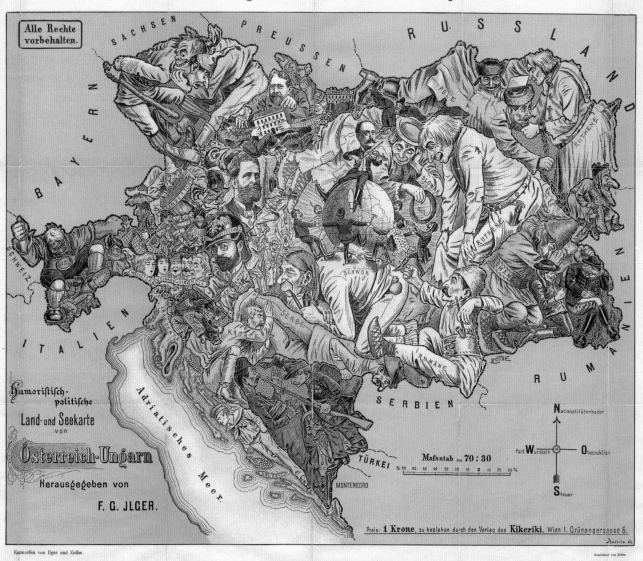

Above: *A caricature map of the Austro-Hungarian Monarchy showing the spiritual state of its peoples at the time of the parliamentary elections of 1906. Ferenc Kossuth is depicted sitting on the 'Hungarian Globe' in the middle of the map playing lively music like a Gypsy musician, although only the Hungarian gentry are stirred to dance by the sound of his violin. The nationalities appear to be preparing to fight rather than to dance. (Source: Katalin Plihál,* National Széchényi Library)

Paul Hanebrink

Sicknesses of the Empire

The years that followed the Compromise of 1867 were in many ways a 'golden age' for the Dual Monarchy. Economic growth took off in both Austria and Hungary. These were also the years of a cultural flowering in Habsburg Central Europe that has fascinated historians ever since. Beneath the glittering surface, however, there were powerful social and cultural tensions. Nationalism, the rise of working class politics and the crushing poverty in which many of the monarchy's poorest peasants lived, threatened the stability of Habsburg Central European society like no others.

The Nationalities Question

Austria

In 19th-century Habsburg Central Europe, census takers and politicians defined a nation by mother tongue. According to the 1890 census, German speakers in the Austrian half of the monarchy comprised roughly 36 per cent of the population. Czechs, the second largest group, made up 23.3 per cent. Other ethnic groups lived in Habsburg Austria, including Poles (15.8 per cent), Ruthenians (13.2 per cent), Slovenes (5 per cent), and Italians (2.9 per cent). These numbers give some sense of the polyglot variety and cultural heterogeneity that defined life in the Habsburg monarchy, but they are also misleading. Especially in the Habsburg monarchy, statistics about the size and distribution of nationalities ultimately reflected the product of bureaucrats' vain, but thoroughly modern, hope to reduce the complexities of everyday life to a simple proportion, and to put all the monarchy's subjects neatly into one or another ethnic category. In many towns throughout Austria, it was common for people to speak more than one language fluently and to switch from one to another according to the needs of the moment. Mundane as this was for so many, nationalists typically looked at multi-lingual 'side-switching' in horror. Nations were supposed to be communities of shared identity. Without clearly defined cultural traits like a common language, no nation could hope to be unified, vibrant or strong. Inevitably, this view made the interrelated issues of language use and national rights a deeply (and sometimes violently) contested matter throughout the Dualist Era.

Nowhere was this conflict greater than in Bohemia and Moravia. Here, Czech and German nationalists fought each other bitterly for political and social power. Over time, their conflict came to paralyse parliamentary life in the Austrian parliament, or Reichsrat. Rather than compromise, Austria's legislators preferred instead to throw abuse, inkwells and sometimes even fists at each other. In the long run, this gridlock compelled the emperor's prime ministers to resort ever more frequently to emergency powers to carry out the business of government. Some historians have argued that this intractable conflict doomed the monarchy to extinction. Without a doubt, the competition between German and Czech nationalists was one of the monarchy's greatest 'sicknesses'.

Census statistics say that Germans comprised 36 per cent of the Austrian population in 1890, making them the largest single ethnic group. In some areas, Germans were an overwhelming majority: in the provinces of Upper and Lower Austria and Salzburg, over 95 per cent of the population were German speakers. However, in areas where Germans and Slavic peoples mixed, they were often a

The ethnic composition of the Austrian Empire in 1900.

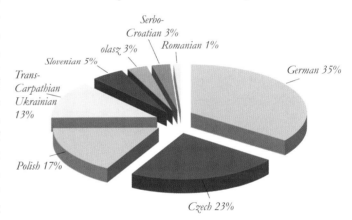

Above: *The diagram shows the distribution of peoples according to a very thorough and circumspect survey based on the census of 1900. (Source:* The Fates of Two Regions from the Austro-Hungarian Monarchy until Today *by Dr. László Gulyás)*

Above: *František Palacky roused his readership to find out about the history of the Czech people and to become conscious of belonging to the Czech nationality. Like his German rivals, he too believed staunchly that a nation and cultural development were indivisible. He believed that the Czech language, largely only used by Czech and Moravian peasants, was enough in itself to form the basis of a modern national existence like the German language.*

minority. Germans comprised perhaps 37 per cent of the population in Bohemia, where 63 per cent of people declared themselves Czechs. In Carniola and south Styria (present-day Slovenia), the ratio was even more unfavourable: 94.4 per cent of the population in Carniola counted as Slovenes; only 5.3 per cent declared themselves German. Numbers aside, many Germans nevertheless saw themselves as cultural leaders and as carriers (*Kulturträger*) of a sophisticated civilisation to the less advanced Slavic peoples of the East. Throughout much of the 19th century, German liberals had mainly understood 'Germany' as a profound ethical ideal that promised liberation through cultural and spiritual development (*Bildung*). In their minds 'Germany' and *Bildung* were inseparable. Austro-German liberals held on to these ideals, even after Bismarck's unification of Germany in 1871. Few of them demanded immediate unification with the Prussian-dominated neighbour to the north. Germans in Austria had their own calling. In a realm peopled with so many non-Germans, it was their task to lead the monarchy and raise its cultural standards.

Theirs was not the only vision of modernity. Czech nationalists had long resented the idea that modernisation in the Habsburg monarchy was tantamount to German hegemony. For some time, a small but vigorous group of intellectuals had tried to fashion a modern sense of Czech nationhood. In part, they looked back to medieval history, and to the Kingdom of Bohemia before it had become part of the Habsburg lands. František Palacký (*see left*) published the first volume of his monumental five-volume *History of the Czech Nation* in 1836. Though his Czech reading public was very small for a long time (the educated upper classes spoke and read German almost exclusively until well into the 19th century), Palacký meant to inspire his readers to learn a history of themselves and so to gain a consciousness of their own identity as Czechs. Like his German rivals, Palacký firmly believed that nationalism and cultural development, even if called by a name other than *Bildung*, were inseparable. The Czech language, used mainly by peasants in Bohemia and Moravia, could become the basis of a modern nation, every bit as capable and sophisticated as the German. His colleagues

Right: *The Czech National Museum, the largest and oldest museum in Prague, was founded in 1818. The imposing, Neo-Renaissance building that closes off Vencel Square was built between 1885 and 1890.*

in nationalist intellectual circles shared this high-minded goal. Slowly, they built a network of Czech reading societies and salons. They also created cultural institutions, like the National Museum (1818) or the *Matice česká*, an association that published scholarly and popular books in Czech. All this cultural invention was not seen as a something new, but rather as a National Revival. Nationalists believed that they were awakening a spirit that had long been dormant under the weight of German cultural hegemony.

But nationalist conflict in the Habsburg monarchy was not only an intellectual competition to assert different histories or literatures. It was also a struggle for social and political power. Throughout the Austrian half of the monarchy, even in places where German speakers were a minority, German liberals dominated the political and economic life of cities and towns. This was certainly true in the Bohemian Crownlands: Prague, Budweis (Budějovice), Pilsen (Plžeň) and Brünn (Brno) were all cities controlled for most of the 19th century by German burghers. Czech nationalists hoped to change this. They imagined Bohemia's cities as communities where a vibrant and expanding Czech middle class could dominate local economic life, run the offices of municipal government, and teach the region's children. Schools played a particularly important role in this vision. They were not only laboratories where youngsters could be brought firmly into the Czech national fold as they learned to read and write in the Czech language. Czech schools would also teach children skills they needed to compete with Germans in the marketplace and in the professions. To realise all this, Czech nationalists

Above: *Education was a fundamentally important area for every national movement.*

Left: *Brünn (Brno), the centre of Moravia, developed particularly rapidly in the second half of the 19th century. Beautiful Secessionist buildings loom in the Czech Republic's second largest city.*

demanded equality and a position for their people in constitutional law similar to that won by Hungarians in the 1867 Compromise.

What constituted equality among nationalities was precisely the explosive point. The Basic Law of 1867 declared in Article 19 that all nationalities and languages were equal in Austria. Did this mean that Czech and German would be considered equally 'official' administrative languages throughout the Bohemian Crownlands? Czech national activists insisted that this should be so. Or did it mean that Czech and German would be considered equal languages in areas where there was a clear majority of Czech speakers, but only there. German liberal nationalists favoured this view. Fears of demographic change fuelled this legal wrangling. German liberals sensed that the migration of Czech-speaking peasants to the towns and cities threatened their hold on municipal government in Bohemia. The first decennial census, conducted in 1880 to classify individuals' by their 'language of use' (*Umgangssprache*) confirmed these fears, as it painted a picture of German communities in population decline across much of the province. Allowing administrators to do business in both German and Czech could only help to solidify this trend. If Czech were an equally 'official' language of adminstration, would Germans soon be marginalised in the communities they had dominated for so long?

This sense of crisis grew stronger after 1879. In the years immediately following the 1867 Compromise, German liberals had dominated the Austrian parliament. By the end of the decade of the 1870s, however, their style of politics was discredited. Many people blamed liberals and their philosophy for the economic depression of 1873. To replace them, the emperor-king Franz Joseph I turned to an old friend, Count Eduard Taafe, to form a new government. Taafe proceeded to put together a coalition, popularly called the 'Iron Ring', that isolated German liberals by uniting conservatives, the Polish aristocracy in Galicia and the Young Czechs, a party of Czech liberals. The new arrangement clearly favoured the monarchy's Slavs. Polish nobles received substantial autonomy to govern Galicia according to their wishes (much to the chagrin of Ruthenian nationalists in the province). Czech nationalists also took advantage of the political situation to organise their efforts in Bohemia more effectively. In the years that followed, they challenged German liberals for control of towns across the Bohemian Crownlands with increasing success.

Czech nationalist leaders proved adept at organising economic competition. One tactic was to stage economic boycotts of German goods. The campaign, called 'Each to his Own' (*svůj k svému*), was orchestrated to name even the simplest purchases of clothing or food as explictly national choices.

Nationalist newspapers listed shops that were 'Czech' and 'German' and exhorted truly Czech consumers to buy only at the former. Local Czech patriots launched their own initiatives in this spirit. In Budweis (Budějovice), Czech activists worked hard to establish a Czech brewery to rival the existing Burghers' Brewery, which they saw as a German firm. In 1895, the Czech Shareholders' Brewery was created; now known as Budweiser Budvar, it continues to brew beer for domestic and international markets successfully over a century later. Whether this 'Czech' beer tasted much different from the brew produced at the Burghers' Brewery is open to question, to Czech patriots, however, it represented a clear (and perhaps also refreshing) victory in the battle against German hegemony. Other aspects of this drive towards

Above: *A Prague middle-class family.*

economic nationalism may have been less successful; after all, many people in Bohemia were slow to change their shopping habits. Even so, these efforts contributed to an increasingly nationalistic public climate.

Below: *Even nature treks served to strengthen German nationalist sentiments. Tourist clubs formed and excursions were organised to the borderlands.*

Frightened by this pressure, and haunted by visions of imminent decline, German nationalist activists mobilised. First, they had to define the problem before them. In the last decades of the 19th century, demographers did a great deal of work to describe Bohemia (and also Carniola and South Styria) as regions riddled with 'language borders' (*Sprachgrenzen*). These were areas where German and Czech (or Slovenian) speakers lived side-by-side, and where every personal or social relationship could tip the balance for or against German interests. Bilingual speakers might decide one language suited their interests better; parents might send their children to a Czech school rather than a German language school because they thought the teachers were better. Worst of all, Germans might intermarry with Czechs, sacrificing countless future generations of German children to their selfish love. All these were also prominent themes in the many maudlin 'homeland novels' (*Heimatromane*) that described the precariousness of German life on the language borders in vivid prose.

To arrest these worrying trends, German nationalist activists organised an impressive array of civic associations to defend German interests. Foremost among them were school associations, designed to create and staff truly 'German' schools where children living on the 'language borders' could develop a proper national consciousness. Nationalist activists also imagined resettlement schemes to put Germans into especially 'endangered' areas in Bohemia, Carniola or South Styria. Most imaginatively, they also saw possibilities in leisure activities, especially tourism. Nationalist tour groups organised and advertised expeditions into these cultural borderlands to see historic castles or relax in the beauty of natural attractions like the Bohemian Forest (*Böhmerwald*). This too could help to raise a more active nationalist feeling among participants.

Intense focus on the qualities that bound Germans together across space and class lines had another result. In the last two decades of the 19th century, a growing number of German nationalists came to see their nation in more exclusive racial, rather than cultural, terms. This was especially true among German nationalists in provincial small towns, who saw their social status endangered by the rising tide of Slavic nationalism. Of course, the distinction was not always so clear cut; at times, it seemed as if every nationalist had his own definition of what key terms like *Volk* (nation or people, in German) meant. And there were many nationalist politicians who refused to abandon their liberal heritage, even if it meant, as it did for the German liberal oligarchs of Prague, a slow decline towards extinction. But these years saw the rise of a new style of nationalist politics: brash, confrontational and above all anti-semitic. One icon of this shift was Georg von Schönerer (*see bottom right photograph*), who saw the entire imperial system as a tool of Slavic nationalism. He became the foremost preacher of pan-German unity. For many, increasingly illiberal, German nationalists, this went too far; most could imagine no alternative to the Habsburg state. Even so, the heated anti-Jewish rhetoric was real enough. In the Bohemian Crownlands, German anti-semitism

Above: *Georg von Schönerer (1842–1921) at his Rosenau estate, near Zwettl. Von Schönerer promoted pan-German unity.*

pushed many Jews to identify more closely with Czech nationalism. A good number, in Prague and other towns, began to speak Czech more frequently. However, many Jews in Prague, as well as those in Vienna, continued to think of themselves as German, even as the effort to maintain an identity as a German-speaking Jew in Austria became increasingly complex and psychologically demanding (though also intellectually and culturally stimulating).

Czech and German efforts to nationalise political life in Bohemia paralysed the Austrian Reichsrat. Sometimes they also produced violence. In 1897, Prime Minister Casimir Badeni tried to solve the national question and restore order to the legislative process by issuing an ordinance that guaranteed linguistic equality throughout the Crownlands. Instead, his efforts enflamed nationalist sentiment. German-speaking bureaucrats understood all too well that if both languages were equal administrative languages, then all bureaucrats would be expected to understand and speak both languages. For Czech civil servants, this was no problem; nearly all spoke and wrote German fluently. However, many German administrators knew little or no Czech at all. Some had never bothered to learn it; others had resisted learning it on principle. Now these German bureaucrats stood to lose their jobs. Badeni tried to calm these fears, by making promises about how the ordinance would be implemented. But that only incensed Czech politicians. Over the course of the year, tensions on both sides grew. In December, anti-German riots broke out in Prague, as nationalist students attacked Germans in the street and destroyed German property. The riots shocked Germans throughout Austria, who felt more than ever that German culture in Bohemia was under seige. Similar Czech-German riots – in 1904–1905 and 1908 – only deepened this feeling. Successive governments seemed powerless to contain the hostility.

Did the Habsburg state offer any alternatives to strident nationalism? The monarchy's most daring experiment only made the problem worse. Over the course of three decades, the Austrian government progressively opened the electoral process to more people, until it finally granted universal male suffrage in 1907. The emperor and his ministers reasoned that if the poorer classes could vote, they would pursue their own economic interests and demand political alternatives to middle-class nationalism. Perhaps some kind of stability could be found within that plurality of voices? But Habsburg officials underestimated the power of nationalist movements to mobilise new voters into their agendas. Each expansion of the suffrage touched off a wave of intense political activity at each level of government. The result was a public culture that only became more nationalised as it expanded.

This worrisome trend pushed Habsburg officials to think creatively about the nationality question. If the monarchy's nations continued to fight each other, then the entire Habsburg state would lose all legitimacy. To prevent this, Austria's constitutional lawyers searched for ways to introduce the principle of nationality into the monarchy's legal structures. Their efforts produced several remarkable experiments in federalism. In Moravia, a 1905 Compromise between Czechs, Germans, and Habsburg officials

Even today the writings of the Austrian Marxists Karl Renner and Otto Bauers on the state and the nation are regarded as fundamental works by politicians who are adherents of federalism.

Karl Renner (right) *joined the Austrian Social Democratic Party in 1896 and was a parliamentary representative from 1907. He was Austrian chancellor from 1918–1920 and after World War II, he became the country's first president.*

Otto Bauer (above) *was one of the leading Austro-Marxist thinkers. His analysis,* Social Democracy and the Nationalities Question, *published in 1907, was one of his most important works.*

divided that province's voters into two equal nations. (Earlier, talks for a compromise in Bohemia had broken down.) Similar arrangements were made in the Bukovina (1910) and in Galicia (1914). Municipal politicians also planned a compromise in Budweis (Budějovice), but the war came before the 1914 plan could be implemented. Technical differences aside, these plans were astonishing in that they imagined a federal system based on nations, rather than territory. Each assumed that all people in a given region would officially declare membership in one nation, and that Habsburg officials would administer lists, or cadastres, of national affiliation. In a supposedly supernational monarchy, this was a huge concession. But if keeping the monarchy's nations 'separate but equal' could produce civic peace, then many Habsburg officials were willing to pay this price. They were not the only ones. At this same time, another group theoretically committed to a supernational ideology – Austria's Marxists – also began to discuss tying nationality to individuals, rather than regions. Even today, political scientists who study federalism still refer to the theoretical works on nationality and the state written by leading Austro-Marxists like Karl Renner (*see top left painting*) and Otto Bauer (*see bottom left photograph*). Ironically, these brilliant men were not able to preserve unity within Austrian socialism. Austria's Social Democratic party split into Czech and German parties in 1900.

Despite the very real challenge that nationalism posed to the monarchy, it should be

Left: *The imperial and royal army had not seen the field of battle for decades and the officers were models of good taste and decorum for the whole of society. The officers of the imperial and royal army swore an oath of personal allegiance to Franz Joseph and the officer core consciously made the supranational spirit (esprit de corps) its own.*

emphasised that no nationalist leader (apart from a tiny minority of extremist German nationalists like Georg von Schönerer) imagined life without the monarchy. František Palacký's *bon mot* of 1848 – 'If Austria did not exist, she would have to be invented' – remained true throughout the Dualist Era. Czech nationalists did not talk seriously about national independence until 1917, after three years of war had produced a very different world. Before 1914, however, the monarchy and Habsburg institutions like the officer corps remained culturally relevant. Even if the imperial and royal army had not distinguished itself on the battlefield for decades, its officers continued to dazzle society with dashing style. Officers were stock characters in innumerable operettas and novels of the period; the outdoor concert offered by the local regimental band in summer months remained a vital social occasion when townspeople could see and be seen to the sounds of stirring polkas, waltzes, and marches. Officers in the imperial and royal army declared their loyalty to their ruler, Franz Joseph I, and consciously adopted an esprit de corps that was truly supernational. The general population shared their affection for the aged and avuncular emperor. During this Golden Age, Habsburg officials (and Franz Joseph himself) cultivated an image of the old emperor as a conscientious and absolutely fair-minded ruler who looked kindly on all the nations he ruled (including, famously, the Jews). His picture hung in every civil servant's office from the capital in Vienna to provincial backwaters like Brody in Galicia; his birthday, August 18, was celebrated as a state holiday. Nationalism posed a very real threat to the monarchy's future. But in the years before World War I, the emperor, his army, and the Habsburg state more generally remained fixed points in a world that so many believed could never change.

Hungary

Unlike the lands in the Austrian half of the monarchy, the Kingdom of Hungary had been a unitary state since the year 1000. After 1687, however, Hungary had been a part of the Habsburg lands. Memories of an earlier independence clashed with the realities of political life within the monarchy. This conflict produced a rebellion in the early 1700s and the ill-fated revolution of 1848. This background – the centuries-long struggle to regain a lost sovereignty – shaped the course of Hungarian nationalist politics after 1867, as well.

Hungary's political leaders understood all too well that the population of Hungary was divided along lines of ethnicity, faith and class, and that these divisions threatened the strength of the state. After all, Hungarian-speaking ethnic Magyars did not make up even a majority of the population; according to an 1880 census, they made up only a plurality (41.6 per cent of the population). 15.4 per cent of Hungary's citizens were ethnic Romanians; 11.9 per cent were Slovaks, and 12.5 per cent were Germans. Unifying a divided society was the first task of Hungary's liberal elite after 1867. Political events had prevented Austria's German liberals from carrying through on their plans to centralise, rationalise and unify the Austrian state. The 1867 Compromise gave Hungary's liberals a much greater freedom of action. Perhaps they would succeed where Austria's liberals had failed?

To achieve their twin goals of national and social unity, Hungary's political leaders placed their hopes in the techniques of 19th-century state-building. Erecting infrastructure was one way to turn peasants who spoke a dozen different languages into Hungarians. Railways radiating from the newly unified (in 1873) capital city of Budapest to the far-flung regions of the Kingdom might stimulate economic growth and so bind people more tightly to the metropole; by 1913, Hungary had over 22,000km of rail lines. Hungary's liberal nationalists also hoped to place personal relationships under the legal purview of the State. In particular, they believed that civil marriage could unify a divided nation. Though it took more than nearly 30 years to overcome the entrenched opposition of the Roman Catholic Church, Hungarian liberals consistently argued that civil marriage laws were an important means of securing national unity. Minister of Justice Dezső Szilágyi maintained in an 1893 speech to Parliament that civil marriage would strengthen 'the political unity of the nation' and further the 'blending together' of the 'nation's different foundational elements' by subordinating religious and ethnic

Above: *The ethnic composition of the Kingdom of Hungary in 1900. This ethnic distribution in the Kingdom of Hungary is based on the data from the census of 1900 as quoted by Dr. László Gulyás.*

Slovenian 1%
Trans-Carpathian Ukrainian 2%
other Slavs 1%
Serbian 5%
Croatian 9%
Slovakian 10%
German 11%
Romanian 15%
Hungarian 46%

identities to universal state laws. Finally, state officials looked to the schools to be engines of Magyarisation. By all these measures, Hungary's liberal political elite hoped to make good on the optimistic declaration that framers had made when they passed the first set of post-Compromise laws in 1868: 'All Hungarian citizens constitute a nation in the political sense, the one and indivisible Hungarian nation.'

At the same time, Hungary's liberal nobility harboured a deeply-felt sense of their own importance as the leading class in Hungarian society. In historic terms, they were the noble *natio*, a corporate body that had defended its traditional rights and privileges against Habsburg oppression for centuries. Belief in *libertas*, a set of historic noble freedoms, was an important element in Hungarian nationalism until well into the 19th century. Even as more modern notions of nationhood became dominant, Hungary's nobility continued to see themselves as the embodiment of national identity. After 1867, this political elite made it their task to transform Hungary into a modern nation-state. Administration of Hungary's 64 counties were already the exclusive and historic province of Hungarian-speaking ethnic Magyar gentry. As the Hungarian state expanded, nearly all significant positions in the new bureaucratic offices were also filled by ethnic Magyars drawn mainly from the lesser nobility. The transformation in the Hungarian state was rapid. As Andrew Janos puts it, 'In 1868, parliament was still made up of county gentlemen, but by 1875 it was already under the sway of a bureaucratic machine whose members refused to compromise the territorial and administrative integrity of the unity that provided them with prestige, livelihood, and identity.'

Above: *Minister of Justice Sándor Erdélyi in Hungarian ceremonial attire.*

The structure of the 1867 Dualist Compromise only further solidified ethnic Magyar supremacy. A variety of restrictions ensured that only a miniscule percentage of the population could vote; despite significant protests, Hungary's political elite never expanded suffrage in any meaningful way. (It remained highly restrictive until 1945.) Moreover, a complicated electoral system that combined aggressive gerrymandering and disproportional representation for certain communities, as well as rampant corruption and bribery, ensured that a majority in Parliament (the so-called 1867'ers) supported both the Dualist Compromise and the unassailability of Magyar hegemony in Hungary. An important minority (popularly called the 1848'ers) pushed for still greater autonomy from the Habsburg dynasty, and was even more zealous in defending ethnic Magyar supremacy throughout the country. Only a few MPs represented parties that held any other view; consequently, they were powerless and irrelevant. Decades of loud and fractious debate over the intricacies of the 1867 Compromise did not disguise the fact that this uneasy balance was basically satisfactory to nearly every Hungarian politician throughout the Dualist Era. Preserving the status quo became the alpha and omega of all Hungarian prime ministers until the last days of World War I.

Left: *Some of the Hungarian social elite attempted to ignore the present situation and its fundamental problems by escaping into the past. This 'libertas' was an important element of Hungarian nationalism until well into the 19th century.*

Despite the seeming permanence of Hungary's political system, its inherent contradictions – remaining true to liberal ideals while also defending the political supremacy of an ethnic elite – left their mark. While Hungary's politicians endlessly debated the merits of the Compromise, society outside the walls of Hungary's Parliament was changing dramatically. Transformations in the economy began to undermine the social position of Hungary's middling nobility. Even more important, other nationalist movements mobilised to challenge the near omnipotence of Hungarian elites in regions of mixed ethnicity. Hungary's political leaders typically responded to these pressures by a stubborn insistence on social unity and the historic rights of the Hungarian nation. Some Hungarian historians have described this willful blindness towards a changing society as the hallmark of an 'age of decline,' an era in which an ossified liberalism laid the seeds of later tragedy. Others have argued that, in these years, liberalism in Hungary became a 'static-defensive conservative ideology.' Concretely, Hungarian officials became increasingly intolerant of any sign of self-assertion by the country's

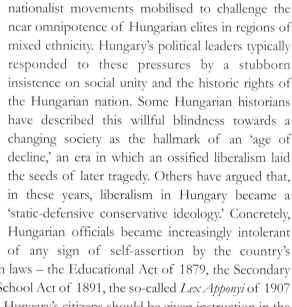

nationalities. A series of education laws – the Educational Act of 1879, the Secondary School Act of 1883, the Nursery School Act of 1891, the so-called *Lex Apponyi* of 1907 – reinforced the basic idea that all Hungary's citizens should be given instruction in the Hungarian language. The State also extended its powers of supervision to church schools, imposing minimum standards that dramatically reduced the independence of Uniate or Orthodox Christian school systems that provided instruction mainly to Romanian students. Turn-of-the-century laws also dictated that only Hungarian place-names be printed on official signs or documents in mixed ethnic regions like Transylvania.

Above: *Paragraph 19 of the widely condemned Article XXVII of 1907 decreed that children studying in minority schools, whose mother tongue was not Hungarian, should be able to express themselves orally and in writing in the latter langauge by the end of the fourth grade.*

These measures were only partly successful. Apart from Jews, whose reasons for becoming Hungarian were very different (and will be discussed later), the rates of assimilation to a Hungarian national identity were highest among Germans and Slovaks, whose proportion among the general population declined roughly 21 per cent each between 1869 and 1910. Among Romanians, Serbs and Ruthenes, where linguistic difference typically also mapped onto religious differences, the rate of assimilation was much lower. However, at no time could the Hungarian state ever create a majority of citizens who claimed Hungarian as their primary language. As sociologist Rogers Brubaker notes,

Above: *Travelling Gypsy bear-leaders.*

assimilation happened primarily in towns, and the vast majority of Hungary's ethnic minorities (especially Romanians, but also Slovaks, Ruthenes, Serbs and Croats) were peasants in rural areas. Moreover, 19th-century schools were not always as effective as their creators hoped. Despite the flurry of laws governing language of instruction, the proportion of Romanian speakers who could speak Hungarian increased only from 6 to

13 per cent between 1880 and 1910. Indeed, in 1910, 77.8 per cent of Hungary's minorities (32.2 per cent of the population) had little to no facility with Hungarian at all.

Successful or not, Hungary's nationalising policies fuelled the spread of nationalist politics among the country's minorities. In Transylvania, Romanian national activists responded to State-sponsored magyarisation by forming the National Party, in 1881, after long debate between 'passivists', who favoured abstaining from Hungarian politics, and

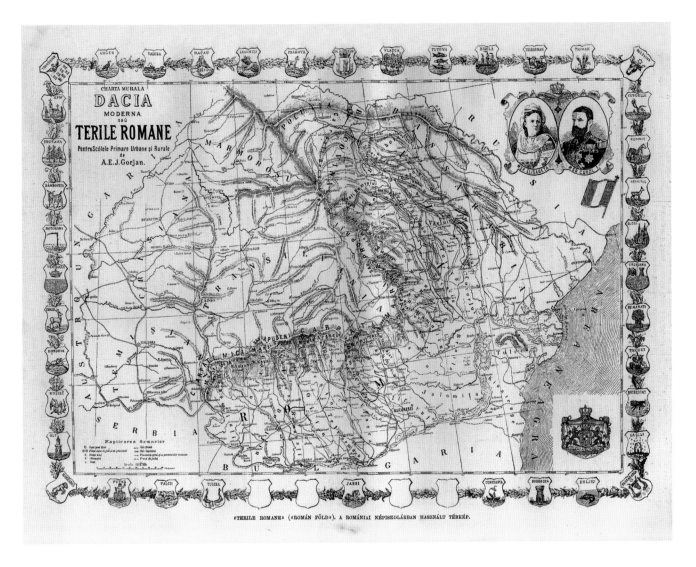

'activists', who favoured action in every available forum. Of course, Romanian nationalists could never hope to wrest power from Hungary's Magyar elites at the ballot box, as Czech nationalists had done. Nearly all Romanians were poor peasants who had no right to vote. There could be no hope of organising them politically without a substantial revision of Hungary's restrictive electoral law, which was never on the table. But nationalist activists did attempt to use their political and intellectual activities to bring the 'Romanian question' to the attention of officials in Vienna and to a wider European public. In the 1890s, for example, a young medical student in Graz named Aurel Popovici published a series of manifestos and pamphlets denouncing Hungary's magyarisation policies and advocating national autonomy and federalism as the only bases for a just solution to the nationalities question. It was a subject to which he would return again and again in the years that followed, most famously in his important book, *Die Vereinigten Staaten von Gross-Österreich*, which received wide attention when it was published in 1906.

Above: *The Romanian nationalists of Transylvania regarded the Kingdom of Romania as their spiritual homeland. In recognition of this, the Romanian state financially supported Transylvanian Romanian schools. The Romanian nationalist associations regarded the strengthening of cultural ties with their Transylvanian brothers as an important objective. Some Bucharest politicians called for the creation of a union incorporating all ethnic Romanians, but surprisingly these aggressive voices found little support in Transylvania.*

Romanian nationalist activists also focused their efforts on economic development. The small number of middle class Romanian-speakers in Transylvanian towns were themselves usually not more than one or two generations removed from village life; the rest of the Romanian ethnic population were peasants. Across the region, ethnic Magyar landlords dominated the countryside; in towns, Jews (many of whom had assimilated to a Hungarian identity), Germans, and Magyars made up most of the urban middle classes. To develop Romanian ethnic economic power, nationalist activists formed educational societies, credit co-operatives and rural self-help associations to educate Romanian peasantry, provide funds for them to acquire land, and to persuade them of the seriousness of the nationalist cause. They also formed nationalist banks and credit associations in Transylvanian towns, with the aim of financing ethnic Romanian entrepreneurs. The first and most important of these was the Albina bank, founded in 1872. The economic success of these efforts were mixed. In 1900, 'the financial transactions of Rumanian banks amounted to only 1.2 per cent of those of all banks in Hungary.' But the experience of organising and running these cooperative associations provided Romanian nationalists with important political and civic experience. As Attila Hunyadi puts it, 'the institutional system of Romanian banks and cooperatives, together with the media and the cultural organs they sustained, achieved a Romanian public sphere' in Transylvania that could challenge Magyar hegemony.

Templomszentelés vérfürdővel.
— A pánszláv izgatók áldozatai. —

Above: *In 1907, the volley of shots that was let off at Csernova took place amid confusion thus giving rise to various nationally biased explanations for the event.* Kis Újság *(Small Paper), one of the tabloids of the period, reported the incident on its front page (see page 190 for more detail).*

Romanian nationalists in Transylvania insisted on national equality. They did not, however, demand independence from Hungary. Throughout the Dualist Era, activists (who came largely from the middle-class intelligentsia) discussed how and on what basis to demand Romanian liberties. Some wanted to restore Transylvania to its historic autonomy, and let demography shift power to ethnic Romanians. Others imagined ethnic rights within Hungary, or within the wider Habsburg monarchy, that might result in greater equality. Certainly, all Romanians looked to the Kingdom of Romania as a spiritual mother country. In return, the Romanian state gave money to support Romanian schools in Transylvania. Nationalist civic organisations within Romania also tried to foster cultural ties with their ethnic brethren in Transylvania. And a few politicians in Bucharest called for Romanian unity. But the more aggressive voices in Romania found surprisingly little echo among nationalist activists in Transylvania. As the geo-political situation in south-eastern Europe became more tense in the last years before 1914, Hungarian politicians tried to capitalise on this fact by pursuing a rapprochement with Romanian nationalist leaders. Between 1910 and 1914, representatives of the Romanian National Party and of Prime Minister István Tisza's governments had a series of exchanges to discuss the possibility of more harmonious ethnic relations. Though the negotiations were sincere on both sides, the fundamental aim of the Tisza government – to strengthen the unity of the Hungarian state – was ultimately irreconcilable with National Party goals of autonomy within a federalist framework. The talks ended in February 1914. When Hungarian officials tried to renew them at the end of the war, they found their chance had passed. By that time, Transylvania's Romanian nationalists imagined their future within a Greater Romania.

As Romanian nationalists became more assertive in Transylvania, Hungarian nationalists in Transylvania and across Hungary began to fear that the region could be lost forever. This was a theme in a number of nationalist novels, such as Viktor Rákosi's *The Silenced Bells*, in which a Magyar Calvinist pastor looks on helplessly as his parishioners drift inexorably into the Romanian community. As this example shows, demographic anxieties fuelled these fears. As Hungarian scholars evaluated birth and death rates, the rate of emigration abroad, and long-term shifts in land-holding patterns, they saw trends increasingly threatening to Magyar dominance of the province. The ambitions of the Romanian bank initiatives and credit cooperative movement also worried Hungarian nationalists. These anxieties led many liberal nationalists to become obsessed with ethnic politics in the region. The personal journey of Gusztáv Beksics is exemplary. A liberal intellectual and politician, he made a name for himself as an outspoken opponent of the Roman Catholic Church and a champion of laws (like civil marriage) that would promote social unity. By the end of the century, however, his liberal ideals had been distilled into an interest in naked ethnic power. His later books deal mainly with ethnic competition that would, he feared, lead inexorably to Hungarian extinction in regions like Transylvania. Others shared these worries. In

Above: *British scholar Robert Seaton-Watson helped publicise some of the incidents between Hungarian police and Czech nationalists. This 1928 painting is by Stefan Straka, 1928.*

Far and near left: *Andrej Hlinka (1864–1938), a Slovakian Catholic priest, was one of the most significant Slovakian politicians of the period. He was one of the founders of the Slovakian People's Party (Slovenská Ludová Strana). In 1907 he was sentenced to two years imprisonment for his anti-Hungarian activities and suspended from his clerical office.*

these years, local Magyar leaders in Transylvania created civic associations to preserve their dominance by resettling Magyar peasants in strategic areas, securing Magyar smallholders, and otherwise providing government largesse to desirable ethnic families. Cultural organizations like the Hungarian Cultural Assocation of Transylvania (EMKE) also worked to promote Magyar culture in the region and to awaken their ethnic brethren everywhere to the looming disaster.

Hungarian officials also faced a nationalist movement in the northern provinces, in

Above: *Ante Starčevia (1823–1896) was a Croatian politician. His views were expressed in parliament by the Law Party, the strongest Croatian party in the 1880s.*

Above: *Fiume (Rijeka) in the 1880s.*

present-day Slovakia. There, too, Slovak-speaking intellectuals had created a nationalist movement, and were intent on spreading their vision of a national awakening to Slovak-speaking peasants using cultural means. The centre of the movement was in the provincial town of Turócszentmárton (Turčiansky Svätý Martin, now Martin), where Slovak nationalist activists formed a cultural organisation called the *Matica slovenská* in 1861 and where they began to formulate their demands for Slovak national equality. Their educational activities aroused the suspicions of Hungarian authorities, who closed the *matica* in 1875. Despite this, Slovak nationalists continued to build their movement, focusing primarily on intellectual and cultural activities.

Slovakia (or Upper Hungary, Felvidék, in Hungarian) was not as strategically sensitive as Transylvania. For one thing, there was no independent state across the border like the Romanian Kingdom that could potentially serve as a magnet for nationalist aspirations. Moreover, the Slovak nationalist movement never became as large or as powerful as that of their Romanian counterparts. Even so, Hungarian nationalists still feared the loss of Magyar influence there. In the last decades of the 19th century, they formed a variety of civic organisations to promote Magyar culture and language. Much of their activity focused on the regional capital of Pressburg (Pozsony in Hungarian, and Prešporok, later Bratislava, in Slovak). There groups like the Toldy Circle tried to wrest public cultural life from the German burghers who were the traditional urban elites. Hungarian nationalists also tried to transform Pressburg into a truly Hungarian city – Pozsony – by other means, using schools and administrative decrees to spread Hungarian language use and opposing (unsuccessfully) the construction of an electric rail line between Pressburg and Vienna that, they feared, would deepen the town's historic ties to the Austrian capital only 40 miles (60km) away. Needless to say, these political activities only fuelled animosity between Hungarian and Slovak nationalists, both of whom saw the region and its people as 'theirs'. Especially in the 1890s and the first years of the 20th century, this hostility produced a number of incidents between Hungarian police and Slovak nationalists. The most serious (and, thanks to the British scholar Robert Seton-Watson, most widely publicised) of these involved the installation of a priest in the town of Csernova/Černová in 1907 to replace Father Andrej Hlinka, a leading Slovak activist, whom the Hungarian Roman Catholic Church had suspended (and who was also in prison at the time). There was a demonstration and the Hungarian police arrived. In the confusion, they shot into the crowd, killing 15 and wounding more. Faced with such state opposition to their ambitions, a growing number of Slovak nationalist leaders began to explore the possibility of cooperation with Czech nationalists in the years immediately before the war. Many spent time in Prague and established contacts there. These explorations would prove decisive amidst the collapse of the monarchy in 1918.

Finally, the South Slav question deserves mention. As a consequence of the 1867 Compromise, Hungary's political elite accorded the historic region of Croatia–Slavonia a special constitutional status, described in an 1868 settlement called the *Nagodba*. In principle, this defined Croatia's place within the Kingdom of Hungary much as the 1867 Compromise determined Hungary's relationship to the Habsburg Crown, allowing the region a certain autonomy within the wider Hungarian state. This also allowed nationalists the possibility for cultural mobilisation. In practice, however, autonomy had clear limits. The highest official in Croatia, the ban, was officially appointed by Franz Joseph I in his capacity as King of Hungary. Throughout the Dualist Era, and especially during the 20 year reign of Count Károly Khuen-Héderváry (1883–1903), the bans constructed and managed a powerful political machine of client politicians. This precluded any effective opposition. Moreover, the Hungarian political system ensured that Croatian representatives in the Hungarian parliament were always marginal. Still, the promise of autonomy gave focus to the demands of Croat national activists. Initially, the greatest advocates of Croatian autonomy were the members of Ante Starèevia's Party of Right, a political organisation that saw enemies among the Serbs as much or more than it did amongst the Magyars. By the first decade of the 20th century, however, political circumstances changed, and a new generation of political leaders emerged who advocated the unity of all South Slavs – Croat and Serb.

The spread of Yugoslavist sentiment in Croatia was driven in part by international politics. In the years following the accession of King Petar Karadjordjević to the Serbian throne in 1903, tensions between the the Serbian Kingdom and the Habsburg monarchy mounted. South Slav nationalists of all stripes were also outraged over the annexation of Bosnia–Herzegovina in 1908. But many Croat and Serb politicians were also looking for some alternative to the stagnation that had characterised the region's political life since 1868. In this climate, Croat and Serbian nationalists met in Fiume (Rijeka) in 1905 to discuss future cooperation. Perhaps Croatian autonomy could serve the interests of both Croats and Croatian Serbs? Their conversations resulted in the Croato–Serb Coalition, an alliance that figured prominently in Croatian politics for the rest of the Dualist Era. All this fuelled fears in Budapest and Vienna that Serbs and Croats in the monarchy were potential subversives, who did the bidding of the hostile Serbian state.

The threat that Yugoslavism posed to the monarchy should not be over-estimated. Although they pushed for greater autonomy, Croatian nationalists stood no real chance of getting it, whether they espoused a Yugoslavist ideology or not. Hungary's electoral laws simply did not allow them to build any kind of mass movement. Moreover, the politicians who dreamed up the Croato–Serb Coalition represented a rather narrow

Above: *A photo of the Kolompár family taken in a studio.*

Above: *Oszkár Jászi believed that the Hungarian state would only be able to preserve its unity and integrity by securing the widest possible cultural rights for the non-Hungarian minorities. Jászi hoped that this would lead to nationalism losing its appeal to the masses and the whole of public life would become more rational. However, his vision was humane but fell far short of the reality of the situation. Despite this Jászi worked tirelessly to make his views popular and sought out ties with minority politicians, especially in the years before 1914. Following the failure of the long awaited democratic revolution, Hungary's partition and the victory of the conservative counter revolutionary regime Jászi emigrated to the United States where he became a professor at the Oberlin College of Ohio. In his remaining years, he wrote penetrating papers which analysed the forces that destroyed a monarchy with a plethora of nationalities that he had fought to save. He is seen in the photo with his brother, Viktor, in 1899.*

intellectual stratum of Croatian society. True mass suffrage would have given political power to other figures, especially to Stjepan Radić, leader of the Croat Peasant Party. Founded in 1904, the Peasant Party pursued policies that were more locally focused and were based on the ideal of ethnic Croat smallholders. Serbs were also divided in their support for the Croato–Serb Coalition. One group – the Serbian National Independent Party led by Svetozar Pribićević – was willing to pursue Serbian interests within a constitutional Croatian state. But their nascent civic nationalism was opposed by Serbian National Radicals, who had a strictly ethno-nationalist outlook and who viewed any cooperation with Croats as national treason. The possibility of a civic nationalism in Croatia was thus always tenuous, and its viability was certainly not strengthened by the historic inclination of authorities in Vienna and Budapest to treat each ethnic group as separate corporate bodies. In the end, hysteria about Croat–Serb cooperation, manifested in a series of trials, public scandals and repressive measures, only strengthened the power of ethno-nationalist politics among Serbs and Croats in Croatia. The consequences for political life in the first Yugoslav Republic were disastrous.

In Dualist Era Hungary, the goals of Hungary's political elites to unify the State, to secure Magyar hegemony, and to protect the electoral privileges of a very few were the greatest obstacle to any compromise with Hungary's national minorities. Were there, then, no attempts to reform Hungary's political system? By the turn-of-the-century, a vibrant 'counter-culture' had developed, primarily in Budapest, that brought together a wide variety of labour leaders, intelligentsia, artists and journalists. Without a mass political party like Austria's Social Democratic Party to call their own, these progressives had no public space in which to develop a common and coherent political program. Instead, reformers gathered in radical masonic lodges, academic societies like the Society for Social Science or university student associations like the Galileo Circle. The small Social Democratic Party (about which more below) was also a magnet for reformist activity as was (after 1914) an even tinier Radical Democratic Party. Still others turned to journalism or art; as the historian Péter Hanák has argued, modernist artistic circles and critical scholarly or literary reviews served as 'workshops' in which a generation of young Hungarian intellectuals tried to imagine a different society from the one in which the gentry ruled. Discussions in progressive circles covered every conceivable topic, from universal suffrage to land reform to the spread of liberal thought in society. Disagreements between associations could be intense. Still, faith in a more just and more democratic Hungarian society always shone like a polestar to inspire progressives in their struggle.

Even within the progressive movement, however, the nationalities question was always a painful 'neuralgic point'. Some of the most ardent supporters of universal suffrage believed just as strongly that Hungary should become a modern nation-state where all citizens gradually but inexorably assimilated into Hungarian national culture. But there were progressives who sought compromise. The most important of these was Oszkár Jászi (*see photograph, left*), who devoted his career to the topic of nationalist conflict in Hungary. Jászi consistently denounced Hungary's magyarisation policies, rightly seeing in them a goad that only fuelled an ever stronger nationalist backlash from Hungary's minorities. Instead, he proposed transforming Hungary into a confederation like Switzerland. Hungary, he believed, could remain a single and integral state by granting a sweeping set of cultural rights to all its non-Magyar peoples. More fundamentally, Jászi hoped to rationalise Hungarian society by stripping nationalism of its emotional appeal to primordial identities. Humane as this quixotic vision was, there was also something unrealistic about it. Still, Jászi pursued this ideal with energy, developing contacts with leaders of the minority nationalities, especially in the last years before 1914. Sadly, Oszkár Jászi was swimming against the tide of history. Before World War I, when compromise and reform with minority nationalist leaders might have been possible, Jászi was powerless to influence Hungary's government. After 1918, when Jászi became Minister of Nationalities in the short-lived democratic regime led by Count Mihály Károlyi, he found no one to talk to anymore. By then, the non-Magyar minorities had all opted for independence. In the aftermath of Hungary's partition, the failure of the democratic revolution for which he hoped for so long, and the restoration of a conservative and counter-revolutionary regime, Jászi emigrated to the United States and took a professorship at Oberlin College in Ohio. There he spent the rest of his career writing penetrating studies of the forces that destroyed the multi-national monarchy he had fought so hard to save.

The Habsburg Monarchy in a Globalising Age

In recent years, historians have come to see the three decades before World War I (roughly from the 1880s until 1914) as a period of globalisation similar in many ways to our own. New forms of transportation and communication tied markets in Europe to those in North America and to European colonies in Africa and Asia. Events in one corner of the globe, such as a glut of grain on the market, or the collapse of a respected international firm, could have powerful repercussions, even in areas seen as economically 'backward' such as East-Central Europe. Across the continent, Europeans struggled to understand the economic links that shaped their lives in such unexpected ways.

The decades of the Dual Monarchy belong to this European story. In many ways, the Monarchy benefited from the intensification of economic exchange. In the last three decades of the 19th century, the Dual Monarchy experienced an impressive rate of economic growth. But it was uneven. Certain regions of the monarchy remained economically backward, even if other places in Hungary and Austria became boom towns. In addition, certain social groups were uniquely positioned to take advantage of these changes. Others experienced these transformations very differently. In short, globalisation created winners and losers. Among the losers, responses were creative and varied, ranging from a vicious politics of resentment to utopian visions of social transformation. All had significant political repercussions. Two problems in particular dominated late 19th-

Below: *Residents protesting about rising rents in Budapest.*

Above: *An eviction in Budapest in 1908.*

century debates about these economic transformations: the 'social question' and the 'land question'.

Industrialisation and the 'Social Question'

Europe's 'social question' – the fate of workers in an industrial age – had been an explosive issue already during the 1848 revolutions. As revolutionaries in Vienna took to the streets in March 1848 demanding freedom and equality, workers called for a broader understanding of these high ideals. In meetings, and in petitions to the diet, they demanded improved working conditions, shorter hours and higher wages. As is well known, their hopes for a truly 'social' revolution were unacceptable to many liberal revolutionaries, who insisted that citizenship be tied to property ownership. This conflict played no small part in the collapse of the revolution. But the appalling social conditions that had motivated Vienna's workers to demonstrate for social

Above: *An aquarelle by Gyula Háry depicts the paper factory in Nagyszlaboda.*

rights persisted. As the tempo of industrialisation increased in the last three decades of the 19th century, the 'social question' moved once again into the political foreground.

By the 1880s, working class districts in Vienna and Budapest were teeming melting pots of impoverished journeymen and poor, mainly unskilled, migrants from the countryside who spoke all the languages of the monarchy. The workers who lived there endured hardships at work – long hours, low wages and unregulated, often dangerous, work environments – as well as horrible living conditions. Apartments were generally poorly ventilated and poorly lit. Despite this, rents in these shoddily constructed 'rent barracks' (*Mietskaserne*) were high. Many families with children of their own nonetheless rented out bed space to bed-tenants, typically migrant workingmen newly arrived from a village and alone in the city. (Single women arriving from villages generally worked as domestic help in bourgeois homes.) Others shared apartments with whole families. In 1880s Budapest, social observers considered an apartment overcrowded if 8 or more adults shared a room; about 150,000 people, 40 per cent of the city's population, lived in such conditions. High rents left little money over for other expenses. As a class, workers were poorly nourished; in 1911, there was a hunger riot in the Viennese district of Ottakring. Health care was minimal, and life expectancy was short.

Industrialisation transformed the lives of traditional artisans as well. Shoemakers, joiners, tailors – the craft workers and shopowners of the monarchy's cities – took no comfort from mechanised factories, expanding railway lines, or the explosion of new retail establishments that offered greater selection at lower prices. These innovations threatened not only their livelihoods, but indeed their very way of life. Artisans derived their social status and their sense of respectability as a burgher from their place in a clear social hierarchy. Traditionally, a master's shop embraced a network of social relations that linked the master's family to the journeymen who worked for them. But this moral and social world was incompatible with the fluid and highly mobile economies of late 19th century Central Europe. Large business owners could win huge economies of scale, and thus undercut their smaller competitors, by introducing efficient machines onto the shop floor or by distributing their products through large retailers. Faced with this pressure, the smallest artisans and handworkers were driven to extinction and into the ranks of the working poor.

Liberalism offered little to either of these groups. Orthodox liberal theory placed its faith in the 'invisible hand' of the market and promised that increasing social wealth would someday – eventually – trickle down to the benefit of even the lowest of society's subalterns. In keeping with this belief, liberals in the 1860s and 1870s pushed for laws that gave greater freedom to business entrepreneurs. In Austria, the 1859 industrial code abolished guild regulation and removed a host of other restrictions on free enterprise. Hungarian liberals pursued a similar course after the 1867 compromise. Among other things, these policies had the effect of removing the final barriers to Jewish participation in all sectors of the economy, a fact to which we will return. But unfettered capitalism also produced corruption. A series of scandals contributed to the fall of the liberal government in Austria in 1879. Similar scandals tarnished the decades of liberal government in Hungary.

There were two great alternatives to liberalism in Habsburg Central Europe. The first was socialism. Already in the 1860s, workers and journeymen in Vienna and Budapest had formed educational societies, where members discussed the ideas of socialist theoreticians like Karl Marx or Ferdinand Lasalle. In these early years, leaders of the workers' movement looked to Germany and the fledging Social Democratic Party there for inspiration and example. However, State authorities scattered many of these initial efforts to organise workers in the monarchy amidst the Europe-wide backlash to the 1871 Paris Commune. In the years that followed, activists like Leó Frankel in Hungary and formerly liberal nationalist intellectuals like Victor Adler in Austria slowly rebuilt the movement. Their efforts culminated in the founding of the Austrian Social Democratic Party at the Hainfeld Congress in 1889 and the Hungarian Social Democratic Party in 1890.

Much of socialism's appeal lay in the fact that it offered members far more than a set of powerful anti-capitalist slogans. As the new working classes fought with their masters over wages, working hours or the right to strike, they turned to socialism as a moral and social alternative to both laissez-faire liberalism and to the 'culture of paternalistic obedience and subordination' which marked the vanishing world of the artisanal workshop. Especially in Vienna, socialist leaders believed that a new order would be created not only by challenging the power of capital, but also by creating a new culture for the working class. Much like their liberal rivals, socialists believed that education, or *Bildung*, could transform the lives of workers, by raising them to class consciousness and giving them the tools and the spirit to fight for the just society of the future. Even as they organised strikes and demonstrations, socialist leaders also began to build a rich associational life that included workers' reading circles and symphony concert associations. These efforts culminated in the remarkable attempt by socialist leaders in 1920s 'Red Vienna' to create a proletarian municipal culture peopled by 'new men' and 'new women'.

Political circumstances dictated the possibilities that socialist leaders had to build a mass party. In Austria, State officials gradually gave suffrage rights to ever greater numbers of men. Certainly, this was done in ways that always weighed the votes of the

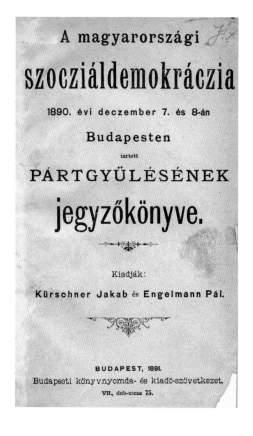

Above: *The minutes of the founding meeting of 7–8 December 1890.*

Above: *In October 1907, some 200,000 workers joined the national strike in Budapest (and in several provincial towns) to demand the right to vote.*

Right: *Franz Schumeier (1864–1913) was a well-known social-democratic politician and editor-in-chief of the Volkstribüne.*

propertied more heavily than those with less (or no) property. Even so, increasing numbers of working men could vote; after 1907, all men could, regardless of class status. This allowed socialist leaders to build a political machine from the grassroots up, and to contest elections in Vienna and across Austria vigorously. In the May 1907 elections Austria's Social Democrats won 23 per cent of the popular vote, and 83 of the 516 seats in Parliament. They were clearly a political force to be reckoned with. In Hungary, by contrast, socialist leaders had to organise in a regime that tightly restricted the right to vote throughout the Dualist Era (and even after). For this reason, the Hungarian Social Democratic Party remained much smaller, and more reliant on the trade union movement. Hungarian authorities also used police power against socialist gatherings more frequently (and more severely) than their counterparts in Austria generally did. Consequently, Hungarian socialists were always much more divided amongst themselves over fundamental questions, like whether or not to work for reforms legally and within the system. In addition, Hungary was far less industrialised than Austria, giving socialist organisers a much smaller field in which to operate. Finally, Hungary's socialists remained theoretically committed to an industrial workers' movement, and never developed much understanding for the far greater problem (in Hungary) of impoverished and exploited agricultural workers. Even so, Hungarian socialism was capable of impressive demonstrations against the liberal regime. In October 1907, for example, 200,000 workers in Budapest and several provincial cities mounted a mass strike to demand voting rights.

Despite the very different political systems in which they had to manoeuvre, neither the Austrian nor the Hungarian Social Democratic Party could translate the international promise of the working class movement into a political organisation that truly transcended nationalism. It is telling that Victor Adler, the founder of Austria's Social Democratic Party began his intellectual journey to socialism from a position firmly within the German liberal nationalist camp. Though Austria's Marxists developed arresting theories for transforming the monarchy into a federal system, they still could not imagine workers without national identities of one sort or another. In 1897, Czech separatists forced the party to divide into multiple national branches. Rifts between Austro-German and Czech socialists deepened in the years that followed. The rise of parties, like the Czech National Socialist party, that demanded socialist reforms within a strictly national context, also widened the chasm between German and Czech workers in Austria. But Hungary's socialists fared no better. There, critical socialist theoreticians like Ervin Szabó may well have been right to see class interests in the nationalist politics of both the Hungarian gentry and the middle-class leaders of Hungary's minority nationalist movements. But this insight did not bring any practical payoff. Hungary's two largest nationalities – the Romanians and Slovaks – were largely peasant, a condition for which Hungary's socialists had little feeling. Moreover, leaders of the working class movement in Hungary faced the same challenge as those in Austria. Society in each half of the monarchy was already nationalised, or rather, nationalising; political circumstances increasingly forced people to choose a national identity. How could socialists hope to swim against that current?

Above: *A young Ervin Szabó dressed as an anarchist.*

Neither the Austrian nor the mainstream of the Hungarian Social Democratic Parties were revolutionary parties. Their rhetoric was certainly heated, as they denounced the capitalist order and called for a different and more just social system. In practice, however, party leaders were much more sober. In Vienna, leaders like Otto Bauer and Karl Renner chose to contest elections, rather than launch a quixotic crusade to bring down the monarchy. In Hungary, party leaders tried to work with other reformist parties – within the legal system – to widen the franchise. Even so, their loud demands for social justice seemed menacing to many people. There had, after all, been several examples of revolutionary violence across Europe, from the Paris Commune in 1871 to the Russian Revolution of 1917. Were these not harbingers of upheavals that might break out much closer to home? Throughout the Dualist Era, police continually watched and harrassed socialist gatherings. More important, fears of socialist revolution led a variety of social groups to look for a vigorous alternative. They found it in Christian socialism, the second great challenge to liberal politics in Habsburg Central Europe.

Christian socialism originated as a movement to defend artisans. In towns throughout Central Europe, shopkeepers and artisans, traditionally the middle classes (*Mittelstand*) of society, saw their social status erode during the last half of the 19th century. This was all the more painful, since these craftsmen and store owners had a clear sense of themselves as the backbone of urban life in cities like Vienna. In their mental universe, society valued the dignity of traditional craft production. It also respected traditional social hierarchy and accorded craft masters a clear position of importance. Such a traditional vision of society had been under pressure for decades. But the economic transformations of the late 19th century accelerated its decline. Reliant on traditional craft production and sales made through personal (typically neighbourhood) connections, artisans and small shopkeepers found themselves increasingly undercut by larger companies with greater economies of scale in production or marketing. To survive, the best positioned artisans paid their employees (workers, journeymen or shophands) less. The less fortunate found themselves slipping into the ranks of the urban proletariat.

But artisans were not the only ones to fear for their occupational futures at the end of the 19th century. In many places, but especially in Vienna, Catholic parish priests also worried about their status in society. Austria's liberals had already attacked their traditional moral and cultural authority with anti-clerical reforms of the educational system. Now parish priests also were afraid that they would not be able to compete with socialism for leadership amongst the growing urban working classes. At the same time, the vision of a traditional, hierarchical and orderly society to which artisans clung so desperately was attractive to many others as well. Prominent aristocrats shared this vision. A number were willing to lend more tangible financial support to the artisan cause. Even Catholic bishops, so nervous about anything that smacked of mass politics, came to believe that the idea of a truly Christian socialism could be a useful way to defend traditional Christian values in society.

In Vienna, the talented politician Karl Lueger (see top left) began to weave these different constituencies and rhetorical elements into a mass political movement in the 1880s. Over the next two decades, his Christian Social Party became a political machine that effectively challenged Austria's liberals. In 1897, the Christian Socials won control of Vienna. In the years that followed, Lueger used all the tactics of a modern big city mayor to solidify his power. In particular, he doled out jobs and contracts to his supporters, and kept the party in the public eye by planning significant public works projects to modernise Vienna's infrastructure. Lueger's successors transformed the party into a truly imperial party (*Reichspartei*) that had grassroots organisations across Austria. Would-be imitators elsewhere were less successful. In Hungary, Catholic activists (primarily Catholic aristocrats and activist priests) could draw on the same resentments as in Vienna, but the political system did not allow them to build a mass party of any kind. Suffrage was far more restricted than in Austria. In addition social elites, like the aristocracy, were much less willing to experiment with mass politics to achieve anti-liberal goals; Catholic grandees along with the episcopate closely supervised Hungary's Christian Socialist party as well as a more aristocratic People's Party. This ultimately stunted both parties' growth and effectiveness. In Hungary, a Christian Social party never had a chance to develop into a powerful urban political machine, much less a party that could compete across the country for significant votes in Parliament. Until 1918, liberal oligarchs remained firmly entrenched in Budapest's City Hall.

As Christian Social politicians attacked liberalism so successfully in Vienna, they also attacked an important liberal belief: the

Above: *In 1897 the Christian Social Party won a majority in the Viennese city council. In order to consolidate his power Karl Lueger (pictured here) applied all the tactics at the disposal of modern municipal mayors. Municipal commissions were granted with his support, while public interest was maintained through large-scale development projects.*

Right: *A Galician Jewish couple.*

possibility (and desirability) of Jewish assimilation. In the aftermath of the economic crises of the 1870s, many artisans blamed Jews (and 'Jewish' liberalism and capitalism) for the rapid and bewildering changes around them. They were joined by members of the Roman Catholic clergy and traditional elites like the aristocracy. For all of them, the social upheavals of the age were part of a Jewish plot for power. To support these preposterous accusations, many pointed to the number of prominent Jewish business owners or financiers who had risen to the top of the monarchy's financial elite in the several decades since the revolution of 1848. That men like the Viennese Ferdinand Bloch-Bauer (whose wife, Adele, had her portrait painted by Gustav Klimt) or Baron Manfred Weiss in Hungary (awarded a title of nobility for his service to the Hungarian economy) were Jews, and that they had done extremely well for themselves was all certainly true. Emancipation had opened up opportunites for Jews who were willing to cast off traditional religious identities and seek their fortune in wider gentile society. A small number of the most successful played crucial roles in both halves of the monarchy in new industries and in the new financial institutions conceived to facilitate their work. Jews also took leading roles in other areas, such as the new media of mass market newspapers. But the vast majority of the monarchy's Jews could only dream of such success. Some were fortunate to become lower-middle class; most still lived traditional lives in the impoverished small towns of Galicia or northeastern Hungary. Despite this variety, a new anti-semitism emerged in the 1880s that focused economic and social resentments on Jews.

Christian Socialist politicians like Karl Lueger used this new anti-semitism with shrewd tactical success. Anti-Jewish rhetoric could serve as common ground and as a bond that linked together disparate constituencies into a vital coalition. Lueger admitted quite openly and cynically that anti-semitism was a political tool that could be used at some times and not at others: 'I determine who is a Jew (*Wer a Jud' is', bestimm' i'*),' he declared. But the Christian Social Party never renounced anti-semitism, nor did it ever take the view that 'the Jew' was not a social enemy. As it rose to power, the Christian Social party gave credence to the belief that Jews were responsible for economic and social dislocation. In this way, the party's leaders legitimised the political use of anti-semitism in ways that had fateful consequences decades later. Leaders in the political Catholic movement in Hungary set similar precedents. When Ottokár Prohászka, future Bishop of Székesfehérvár, declared that 'We take up not as a racial nor as a religious, but as a social, commercial reaction. This anti-semitism is the reaction of Christian moral teaching and the Christian social order' he contibuted powerfully to an inchoate but powerful idea that Hungary was a Christian nation. Before 1918, this was not a mainstream view in Hungary, as the liberal political establishment continued to condemn anti-semitism. But views expressed at the margins nonetheless had consequences. The growth of a Christian nationalist ideology revealed important dissent from the liberal mainstream. In the changed context of post-World War I Hungary, this dissent would become powerful indeed.

Below: *Ignác Darányi (1849–1927) was the minister of agriculture from 1895 to 1903 and then from 1906 to 1910. His name is associated with the suppression of the agricultural workers' strike of 1897 and the so-called servant laws of 1898 and 1907. He worked tirelessly to support the establishment of the Museum of Agriculture and participated in organising the construction of the palace for the Institute of Geology designed by Lechner.*

The Land Question

Austria and Hungary played different roles in the economy of the Dual Monarchy. As we have seen, a significant modern industrial base developed in Austria and Bohemia. Of course, agriculture was much more important in under-industrialised areas of Austria, such as Galicia. Even so, roughly one half of the active population in the

Austrian half of the monarchy worked in industry by 1910; only one-third worked on the land. In Hungary, the situation was very different. There, some two-thirds of the population worked in agriculture. For this reason, Hungary was often referred to as the 'bread basket' of the monarchy, since Austria was the leading purchaser of Hungary's agricultural exports. (During World War I, this structural peculiarity would lead to tremendous political tension between Austria and Hungary, as Austrian politicians accused Hungary of letting the people of Vienna and other industrial centres starve.) But Hungary also sold a tremendous amount of its refined agricultural produce on the world market: 25 per cent of the world's total wheat flour exports came from Hungary.

During the revolutions of 1848, serfs had been emancipated. A certain amount of land was transferred into peasant hands, creating a class of peasant landholders. However, the terms of emancipation stipulated that feudal landlords were entitled to compensation. This, combined with a good deal of legal chicanery and outright fraud in land transfer proceedings, ensured that much of the land in both halves of the monarchy remained in the possession of large estate owners. In Bohemia, for example, 33 per cent of the land was owned by 0.5 per cent of landowners. In Hungary, 1 per cent of the population owned about half the country's arable land. At the turn of the 20th century, great aristocratic families like the Schwarzenbergs in Bohemia or the Esterházys in Hungary continued to control vast estates and wield tremendous political influence. The Esterházys alone ruled over one million acres in Hungary.

Above: *The Great Plain and shepherds were favourite themes for artists of the period. This aquarelle entitled* Shepherding around Hódmezővásárhely *by Gyula Agghá zy appeared in the book* The Austro–Hungarian Monarchy in Words and Pictures (1886–1901).

All this meant that most peasants remained desperately poor. There were several types of peasants. A certain number were relatively prosperous smallholders. Most, however, owned plots too small to be viable, or simply owned no land at all. The landless became a class of wage labourers who depended on seasonal work paid in day wages for survival. Many migrated from estate to estate in search of work. Peasants with dwarfholdings shared this fate as well. Although they did own some property, they too depended on wage labour for survival. Cash-strapped landlords considered dwarfholders a kind of reserve labour force, there for employment when they were needed and invisible when they were not. Finally, in Hungary, there was a fourth class of peasant: the manorial workers. Unlike in Austria or Bohemia, estate holders had managed to win exemptions for a large amount of land during the process of emancipation. These manors, owned by powerful aristocrats or corporate bodies like the Roman Catholic Church, remained intact until well into the 20th century. Although the legal status of the peasants on these estates had changed in various technical ways, their daily lives were remarkably comparable to that of their ancestors under feudalism. 'A late-19th-century Farm Servants Act … forbade servants to leave the estates or to receive strangers in their houses and announced a penalty of 60 days imprisonment for inciting a strike. Working hours were unregulated, income was mostly paid in kind, and physical punishment was legal.'

The Hungarian writer, Gyula Illyés described what these dry statistics meant to the lives of manorial peasants in his classic account, *People of the Puszta*. In it, he describes a world apart, in which animals received far better care than did the peasants who watched and worked them. Many did not have enough to eat, especially in winter. Of those whose diets often consisted of one or two staple items, Illyés remembered a common trick: 'What of those who, for breakfast and often for dinner too, day after day, ate their boiled corn mush so salty that it burned, just so they might enjoy the drink of water afterwards?' Work was long and gruelling; herders and fieldhands rose before dawn and returned home after dusk. Overseers brutally beat workers; again, Illyés remembered the details: 'Until the age of 30–35, a peasant was slapped in the face; after that, he usually received just one blow to the back of the head or neck... Most of those over 60 already began to whimper at a raised hand. Not from fear, but on account of their degradation.' Work conditions like these left precious little time or energy for anything approaching what Illyés called 'human life'. The result was a brutalised class of people, with no hope of improving their living standards.

What responses were there to the 'land question?' The following discussion will consider each half of the monarchy separately.

Below: *An aquarelle by László Mednyánszky entitled* Debrecen's Main Square *is a fine reflection of the atmosphere in towns on the Great Plain.*

Austria

During the Dualist Era, peasants with no hope of acquiring enough land to survive, left the countryside throughout the Austrian half of the monarchy at an increasing rate. Many migrated to industrial centres in search of work, as we have seen. Still more emigrated, leaving behind everything they knew in hopes of finding a better life abroad, primarily in North America. In 1907 alone, 338,000 people from Austria–Hungary passed through U.S. immigration controls. Company agents advertised the New World in villages throughout Habsburg Central Europe as a land of unimaginable wealth. Shipping companies sold places in steerage for migrants leaving Europe. And extended family networks provided information, sometimes even financial support, and, most important, the example of those who had already dared to go. In short, a complex transatlantic network arose to entice peasants to leave the villages, to transport them across the ocean, and to settle them in communities throughout the United States and Canada, usually among brethren from the same region, who shared the same language and culture. Czechs settled in Nebraska and Texas; Slovaks toiled in the coal mines of Pennsylvania; Galician Jews settled in the Lower East Side of New York and worked in the garment industry. In the New World, life was difficult for immigrants who spoke no English and found their new surroundings harsh and utterly unfamiliar. American author Willa Cather's description of Czech farmers on the Great Plains in the novel, *My Antonia*, is one moving example. With time, though, most fashioned better lives for themselves and their families.

More prosperous peasants stayed and began to organise themselves politically. By the end of the 19th century, there were a variety of peasant associations and organisations – credit cooperatives, self-help associations, newspapers, educational societies – in many parts of Cisleithania. This social network served as the grassroots infrastructure of more formal political movements. In Bohemia, which accounted for 12 per cent of the world's sugar beet production at the end of the 19th century, small and mid-sized sugar beet farmers made common cause against large estate owners, who could dictate price through their economies of scale. From an initial coalition of several organisations and a variety of journals grew the Czech Agrarian Party. Its programme, formulated in 1903, called for the defense of rural Czech society and the protection of small and mid-sized farmers against the ravages of global capitalism. In 1904, Antonín Švehla became head of the party. In the years that followed, he built the party into a formidable national organisation. It remained a powerful political force in interwar Czechoslovakia. Another agrarian movement took shape in Galicia, where peasants (or, at least, the more prosperous ones) emerged from the protective wing of the aristocracy to create their own civic institutions and associations. They successfully challenged the nobility's paternalistic vision of rural life, which idealised peasants as the repository of national values while denying them basic civil rights. Here too, peasants built a network of self-help associations, educational organisations, and public journals into a political movement and ultimately, the Polish Peasant Party. All told, these transformations amounted to the entry of peasants into Habsburg civil society.

Above: *A rich Serb goat herd.*

Alpine Austria was, in many ways, exceptional within the Habsburg lands. There had never been large estates in the region. Instead, a free peasantry worked small plots, in communities organised around a patriarchal household economy. Land-holding peasants employed journeymen labourers or apprentices. By the end of the 19th century, however, industrialisation had also begun to transform these traditional social structures. Household labourers migrated to the new factory towns. In addition, industrial production destroyed the means by which households might supplement their income through artisanal crafts. Members of the land-holding families found themselves doing much of the household labour previously done by servants or journeymen. Needless to say, peasants felt the loss of their way of life keenly; many envisioned a future in which traditional village communities would simply die out. Novels by authors with roots in these communities, such as Peter Rosegger's *Jakob der Letzte* about the death of a traditional village community in Styria, captured these fears well. Here too peasant activists turned to civic organisation in response. In the last years of the 19th century, credit cooperatives and rural educational societies became fixtures in the Austrian countryside as well. Indeed, peasant organisers found allies among Christian Socialist politicians trying to expand their base outside Vienna. The last years of the Dualist Era saw an intense amount of organisational activity in the Austrian countryside, as credit cooperatives like the Raiffeisenbank or the Tyrolian Bauernbund became important constituencies within the Christian Social political machine.

Hungary

The economic transformation that made Hungary the 'bread basket' of the monarchy and, increasingly, a significant exporter of grain to the rest of the world did not benefit all Hungarian landholders equally. The largest landholders – those who owned the great latifundia of the Hungarian Plain – met the demand for their produce by expanding commercial wheat crops. During these decades, they borrowed money from the new financial lending institutions of Budapest (typically owned by Jews) to finance the expansion of land under cultivation or the use of mechanised farm implements. Though Hungarian agriculture remained under-developed when compared to the commercialised agriculture on the Great Plains of North America, it nonetheless made great strides in these years. Smaller landholders could not view this economic transformation so sanguinely. Increased demand may have spurred production, but these producers now had to compete in a global market. Ultimately, this drove prices down. In response, middling landholders also sought credit in the financial markets of Budapest or Vienna. Some found rates of interest prohibitively high, and so could not modernise their estates. Others borrowed money only to default. The amount of land under the control of financial institutions in Budapest increased during these years. To the gentry landlords, this seemed like nothing more than alien control over that most fundamentally national of all entities – land. As István Bernát, who would become a leading agrarian politician, put it in a pamphlet entitled 'Mortgaged Hungary', 'indebted land, stripped of its stability, also loses its entire ethical character, its political and social weight … The basis, on which our nation developed itself … vanishes into dust.'

These middling landholders attempted to organise themselves outside of the liberal political structure. Many blamed Jews for the seemingly incomprehensible destructiveness of capitalist development, and so some of them tried to form an explicitly anti-semitic party in the 1880s, much like the Anti-semitic Party in Germany, or the more anti-semitic wing of Vienna's Christian Social Party. They enjoyed short-lived success, especially in the wake of a nasty blood libel trial in Tiszaeszlár, when local prosecutors falsely accused the community's Jews of kidnapping and murdering a young Christian girl for ritual purposes. Győző Istóczy, the Anti-semitic Party's leader, helped to transform this local tragedy into a national political crisis. At its height, Hungary's Anti-semitic Party held 17 seats in the Hungarian parliament. Its star soon faded, however, since the liberal (and pro-assimilationist) political establishment kept it firmly marginalised. More successfully, the middling gentry also organised credit cooperatives. These allowed them to pool their resources and find loans at rates of interest more favourable than those on offer from the 'urban' and 'Jewish-owned' banks in Budapest or Vienna. They had a political function as well. The cooperative movement created a network in which middling landholders could focus their grievances against the liberal establishment. Of course, the political strictures of the 1867 Compromise ensured that Hungary would be ruled by a liberal, pro-business, and pro-assimilationist government. Still, cooperatives did allow landholders to develop political skills and a political voice that was heard (at least sometimes) even within the corridors of power. More fatefully, they also became incubators for an alternative conception of Hungary: a 'Christian Hungary' in which 'neo-conservative' landholders, allied with other traditional elites like the Catholic Church, might retain their authority in defiance of a rapidly changing world. After 1918, Christian nationalism would become a powerful idea in Hungarian politics.

The downward trend in prices affected Hungary's peasantry even more severely. Here also, many chose to try their luck in the United States, at least for a time. Between 1899 and 1913, there were officially 492,031 immigrants arriving in the United States from Hungary. But most were too poor to contemplate the passage; and laws kept Hungary's manorial peasants on the estate and locked in semi-feudal misery. Here, in contrast to the Austrian half of the monarchy, political circumstances were much less

Above: *Győző Istóczy (1842–1915) was a parliamentary representative. He was the first significant advocate of amti-semitism in Hungary. In 1883 he founded the National Anti-semitic Party, which however was soon dissolved. He was not elected again to parliament in 1897.*

favourable for any sort of organised peasant movement. Even so, there were signs of organised activity in the Hungarian countryside by the last decades of the 19th century.

For non-Magyar speakers, peasant politics were also nationalist politics. Romanian nationalist activists exerted a great deal of effort mobilising peasants in Transylvania. In a region where those who owned the land typically were Magyars and those who worked the land were generally Romanian speakers, the overlap of class and ethnic politics was clear. The rise of the Croat Peasant Party is an even better example. In Croatia, Stjepan Radić led a political movement that called for the dissolution of great estates and radical land redistribution, universal male suffrage and government support to promote peasant interests and improve rural standards of living. In sum, Radić dreamed of transforming Croatia into a peasant state, in which ethnic Croatian peasants would be both backbone and political leaders. Radić was tireless in spreading this message and trying to mobilise Croatian peasants to embrace it. Needless to say, local authorities were deeply suspicious of his activities. Time and again, police confiscated pamphlets and other printed matter and banned meetings and rallies. In a few instances, there were even clashes between movement organisers and police. Despite these setbacks, Radić slowly built a formidable grassroots organisation. After 1918, his political party would become the champion of Croatian interests within Yugoslavia.

Ethnic Magyar peasants faced more formidable obstacles to political activity. But even on the vast latifundia of Hungary's Great Plain, peasants acted to contest the appalling socio-economic inequities that defined rural life. In 1891 and 1892, day labourers rioted in Békés County. More riots and strikes by landless agricultural workers took place throughout the rest of the decade in this region of Hungary defined by the Tisza and Maros rivers, which earned it the nickname, Storm Corner (*Viharsarok*). Rural labour activists also made several attempts to organise agricultural workers more formally. In 1897–1898, poorly organised agrarian unions struck during harvest time, and then clashed with Hungarian authorities, as well as the strikebreakers who were found to replace them. Some peasant activists looked to the socialist movement for support; in 1891, rural labourers began Socialist Workers' Circles in several counties of the Hungarian Storm Corner. Many more saw their best chance in an independent, and truly agrarian, socialist movement. In

Above: *Ethnic Hungarians in celebratory dress.*

1897, the former farm labourer Vilmos Várkonyi called for laws to force large estate owners to lease small plots of land to poor peasants. Understanding in this a call for the forcible division of Hungary's great estates, some 15,000 peasants rallied to Várkonyi's movement. In short order, however, the Hungarian regime arrested Várkonyi, banned the publication and distribution of his newspaper, and suppressed the movement. In 1906 András Achim tried a similar tactic, founding an Independent Socialist Peasants' Party. He was elected to Parliament, and his party enjoyed a brief existence. But it too was highly supervised by the Hungarian authorities, who used violence and intimidation to ensure that no peasant organisation ever became a real challenge to the social order. Until the end of the monarchy (and even more so during the interwar years), Hungary's landless peasants endured brutal labour and crushing poverty.

Epilogue

Were these 'sicknesses' fatal for the patient? Of course, it is impossible to know how the Habsburg monarchy might have evolved (or dissolved) if East-Central Europe had enjoyed a peaceful 20th century. What is certain is that the monarchy, beset by the conflicts and contradictions described in this chapter, could not survive the enormous strains of a modern total war. In 1914, the imperial and royal army mustered troops from all corners of the monarchy and marched into battle. In the streets of Vienna and Budapest, just as in Paris, London, and Berlin, a feeling of war euphoria was

Above: *Károly Eötvös was a parliamentary representative, lawyer and writer. Many regarded him as having the combined attributes of Lajos Kossuth's enthusiasm and Ferenc Deák's common sense. He was a national authority and a parliamentary representative for decades, and his law firm was one of the best. His most famous and significant act in public life was taking on the defence and achieving the acquittal of the Jews charged in the Tiszaeszlár blood libel affair of 1883.*

palpable. For a brief period, social unity in the face of a common enemy – a kind of Habsburg *Burgfrieden* – seemed to prevail. But the war soon turned into a nightmare. The armies of the monarchy suffered 800,000 casualties in the autumn of 1914, and a further 800,000 in the first months of 1915. In the summer of 1916, a massive Russian offensive shattered the army's effectiveness. Thereafter, German forces dictated strategy in the Habsburg theatres of war. At home, the monarchy lost its most powerful unifying symbol in 1916, when the aged emperor-king Franz Joseph died. His successor, Karl, was intelligent and sensitive, but enjoyed none of the prestige and universal respect that his predecessor had. During the last two years of the war, social tensions mounted. Inadequacies in production and distribution led to widespread food shortages in Austria; starvation was a very real threat in Vienna and other cities. Divided along so many fracture lines, the Habsburg state could not rely on popular willingness to endure hardships. Across the monarchy, people had accepted the monarchy as 'part of the way things were', and as a state whose pomp and circumstance infused the substance of everyday life. But this was not the same thing as patriotism, or a willingness to make sacrifices for the good of the dynasty. Taken for granted in peacetime, the Habsburg state was widely despised in war. Amidst deprivation and hardship, the Habsburg state began to lose popular legitimacy. Industrial workers agitated more vocally for better wages and work conditions, as well as an end to war. The revolutions in the Russian Empire only made them bolder. By 1918, there were strikes throughout the Dual Monarchy. Gendarmes frequently resorted to force to suppress them. Rates of desertion from the army rose. By war's end, the threat of peasant unrest in Hungary had also become a very real concern.

At the same time, nationalist leaders began to imagine a future without the Habsburgs. Their conversion to the cause of independence was not immediate. Through the first phases of the war, many of them continued to demand cultural rights much in the way they had done before 1914. In his memoirs, Eduard Beneš, who had favoured pushing for independence from the beginning of the war, recalled a conversation he had had with Czech Social Democratic leader Bohumil Šmeral in November 1914: 'Šmeral told me that we were mad, ... the plans we had made were fantastic'. However, the instability of the Habsburg state, and widespread exasperation

Above: *Philosopher and politician Tomáš Garrigue Masaryk (1850–1937) was a parliamentary representative for the Young Czech Party between 1890 and 1893, and for the Realist Party (Czech People's Party or Progressive Party) between 1907 and 1914 in the imperial diet and the Czech national assembly. He was later one of the founders of the Republic of Czechoslovakia and its first president.*

with the exigences of mass mobilisation, allowed radical voices at home and among emigres to make bolder demands. Even more important, the Allied governments, and especially the United States, saw potential allies in the national movements, and came to endorse their calls for independence. Czech nationalist leaders, like Tomaš Garrigue Masaryk, the future president of Czechoslovakia, toured the United States, making important contacts among both emigres and U.S. officials. Indeed, it was in the U.S. city of Pittsburgh that the idea of Czechoslovakia as a dual state (Czech and Slovak) was formalised. Allied visions of independent nation-states stretching across East-Central Europe redounded to the benefit of nationalist activists in the Hungarian half of the monarchy as well. In contrast, the dynasty's efforts to seek peace proved fruitless, as did German hopes for a final victory in 1918. By the autumn of that year, the monarchy was in a state of collapse. On November 11, the emperor-king Karl stepped down. Soon thereafter, Allied forces gave their blessing as Czechoslovakia and Yugoslavia became states, and as their armies and those of Romania occupied parts of Habsburg territory. The Habsburg monarchy was no more.

Right: Increasing numbers of people emigrated to America. In 1880, 20,000 left the Monarchy and within 10 years the number of immigrants had risen to 40,000 per year. In 1903, the number of registered emigrants reached 120,000.

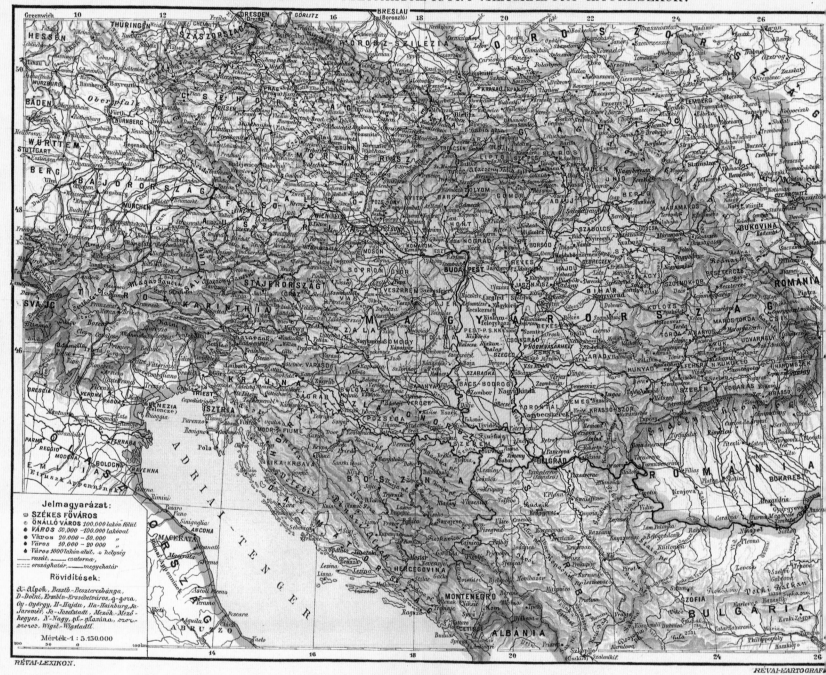

Above: *A map of the Dual Monarchy published in the* Révai Encyclopaedia *in 1915.*

GERMANY

CZECHOSLOVAKIA

POLAND

AUSTRIA

HUNGARY

ITALY

ROMANIA

KINGDOM OF SERBS,
CROATS AND SLOVENES

BULGARIA

National borders after 1918

András Gerő

The Heritage of the Empire

The era of the Austro-Hungarian Empire is just like Atlantis: a sunken world. The final form of the former Austro-Hungarian Empire affects the lives of the peoples and nations that once formed part of one state structure in different ways. In fact, for this very reason it really bears no similarity to Atlantis at all. On the contrary, it forms part of the Central European inheritance and people's everyday lives.

Despite the apparent contradiction between these two statements, they both carry an element of truth.

The Austro-Hungarian Empire ceased to exist as a territorial entity and political structure in 1918 and has not been resurrected since. The Habsburgs lost their position of power and influence after a reign of several centuries. A good many states fought over the corpse of this former state structure although several of the states that came into being at the time similarly no longer exist. The empire is dead. However, its legacy and memory have stayed and survived until this day. The legacy is a complex one, while the memory often presents differing emphases.

Above: *A postcard of József Upor's Grand Café, about 1900.*

The Memory

The most important aspect of the legacy (and the memory) is that the era of the Austro-Hungarian Empire was one of embourgoisement of the nations in the region. Significant social, economic and political changes took place over a relatively short period of time: peoples' daily lives changed and what is now referred to as modernity became a defining factor for an increasing number of people. A general educational system was devised, along with a public schooling law; hospitals were built, together with a system of medical institutions; mains water became available, which meant that people could have bathrooms; theatrical culture blossomed, accompanied by a vibrant, contemporary art scene; people enjoyed newfangled city life and freedom of the press; a railway network was constructed and women gained the right to enter further education.

The tendency was that the whole of the region – with inner discrepancies in pace and degree – became increasingly similar to a Europe that was considered to be a norm by the thinkers of the period. The era of the Austro-Hungarian Empire became one of transformation in the region.

Overall, these changes are best described as the formation of the bourgeois lifestyle and this newly adopted social behaviour having become the norm. As the bourgeois lifestyle grew to permeate all aspects of life, its presence in everyday life became obvious to all. It was just as common for a skilled labourer to go to work in a factory wearing a hat and even a watch chain as it was for a bank clerk; the poor referred to the Wiener schnitzel as 'Sunday meat' because it only found its way to their dining tables on a Sunday but that was considered to be its rightful place; everyone knew that a holiday from work was part of bourgeois life although not everyone was

Above: *The years following the Compromise were a period when important companies were founded. Foreign capital played an equal role in this to the movement of capital within the empire. In 1893, the Stock Exchange outgrew its old building and the decision was made to purchase a plot of land on Szabadság Square, which had only recently been built. The stock exchange rooms occupied the first floor of the Stock Exchange Palace, designed by Ignác Alpár, which made it possible to rent out the ground floor, so a coffeehouse opened on the Nádor Street side.*

able to enjoy their freedom in this way. However, it was still considered as the norm and everyone strove to achieve it. And, of course, an increasing number of individuals thought it fitting to take a stroll at the weekend and sit in a coffee shop to enjoy a pastry.

This breakthrough in regard to civilisation and the adoption of a bourgeois lifestyle took place in a relatively prolonged period of peace. In short, it could be said that consolidation created an atmosphere of great change. What was possible in Great Britain was considered, at the time, as miraculous in Central Europe. In general, the joint presence of peace together with change seems to transform memory into nostalgia. However, in many ways this was also an era of stagnation and unresolved, serious social dilemmas that were either responded to inappropriately or not at all.

To put it frankly, almost everybody hated everyone else within the Habsburg Empire. There was a sense of fear behind almost everything. With the enduring influence of memory, the various national movements all pleaded with equal veracity that they were somehow being suppressed by one another. They created historical heroes and these were often people who had opposed their nearest neighbours. Seen through the eyes of these heroes, the Austro-Hungarian world was a very divisive one. In many aspects and for many nations it was this memory that became the basis for their national identity.

Above: *By the second half of the 19th century city life style was already characterised by the coffeehouse and in 1908 398 coffeehouses opened in Budapest alone. The coffeehouse became an important venue of everyday life. The Petőfi (Steingasser) coffeehouse was a favourite haunt of Count Podmaniczky, a great admirer of Budapest, who would go there dressed in a chequered coat with a carnation in his buttonhole to have breakfast and read his paper.*

Europe – Central Europe

Many people have different concepts of what Central Europe is. The idea of a 'Central Europe' was first used in the first half of the 19th century, and by the 20th century the process was complete. Its history includes German expansion and general pretensions of superiority as well as the aspirations to be disassociated from the Orthodox version of Christianity. But lurking in the expression is also the sense that there is a region in Europe that is not on an equal footing with the West, but which is nevertheless not the same as Eastern Europe or the Balkans. Thus, a more modern strange expression came into being in order to clarify the concept. After 1900 the term 'Europe in-between' was frequently used, and the phrase 'the other Europe' made its appearance. Both referred to the existence of a third entity.

Aspirations for Europe to be treated as a unit with defined norms and values had begun to emerge from the 18th century. In this approach the focus was on a kind of unified Europe that reigned over differences. Three attempts have been and are being made in modern times to realise the demands for unity through power politics. In the 18th century, Napoleon wanted an anti-feudal Europe that would be built upon equality in civil rights, and under his rule. The enduring memento of his efforts is the *Code Napoleon*, a civil code which in word and spirit is inexorably built into European development. Napoleon sought to achieve his goal by force and the bayonet, and as Napoleon's foreign minister, Talleyrand, noted, a lot can be achieved with a bayonet, but one cannot sit on it.

Above: A statue of Ban Josip Jelačić stands in a square named after him in Zagreb. For the Croatians he is a national hero, while for the Hungarians he is a soldier who took up arms against the Revolution of 1848. These conflicting views illustrate that the national histories of the peoples who shared a common empire were often seen from quite different perspectives.

The next attempt to unite Europe took place more than a hundred years later. On this occasion it followed aspirations for German rather than French hegemony. Hitler's vision of a pan-European world was not based on equality in civil rights. Quite the contrary: his principle ideal was *Übermensch* and *Herrenvolk*, which he tried to enforce. Instead of the obsolete power of the bayonet he employed other weapons but it was no more possible to 'sit' on them than it was on the bayonet. All that resulted from this was destruction and death, i.e. the death of those who perished during the implementation of these pan-European aspirations based on a 'superior' race.

A new pan-European experiment began after World War II (1939–1945). This aspiration to create a common Europe was based on democratic values, an economic community and the seeking of consensus. The European Union wishes to be the institutional trustee of the ideals of a democratic, political community with the principles of legal security and equality before the law forming its foundation. The direction the process has taken can be seen, but the final outcome cannot.

The new Europe seeks to enforce common norms and in this respect it is harking back to the universalism of pre-modern Europe. At that time Christianity, by which Europe defined itself, represented a general world concept. The rulers were 'ordained by God' and the social structure was generally regarded as being the will of God. In a certain sense this universalism later also created a universal culture. In defined periods, the Romanesque, Gothic, Renaissance and Baroque styles held sway in Europe – or at least in her more important parts. The authority of the Church was relatively uniform all over, and if there were differences in church frescoes, it was rather because of the different artistic talents involved than a qualitatively different cultural approach.

Cultural regionalism was rather manifested by the quantitative representation of given areas within the pan-European style than by the emergence of art with its own content and form in individual regions.

The objective of the new Europe is to be universal and democratic yet when it comes to the Church, Europe's policy is to stay strictly secular. It is aware of differences and supports the cultures of its regions. However, Europe is also aware of the paradox: its various peoples give and can give it its unity and the guarantee of that unity. The simultaneous presence of supranationalism and nation-state aspirations – which was once one of the main problems of the Habsburg Empire – have become one of the main issues of our day throughout the whole of Europe. Today's Europe defines itself in its slogan as 'Unity in Diversity'. This diversity of course refers to the kaleidoscope that has developed throughout history and is represented by national cultures and social sub-cultures, while unity means that these nations profess unified basic principles which are similar on a political level, the key phrases of which are co-operation, tolerance, as well as respect for human rights and the basic values of democracy. On the other hand, it can be observed partly within the Union and partly outside of it that the processes in the development of nation-states that began in the 19th century are now coming to a close as they are reaching their full potential.

The various cultural emphases of different histories and the differing attitudes to a

common history lead back to what we call and can call Central Europe. The emergence of distinct histories diverging into yet further histories can be observed within the greater context of European history. Central Europe is a part of the concept of Europe understood in a general sense, but it has its own distinct history. Europe's common history creates a community and it is this shared history that distinguishes it from others.

Central Europe's own image and history is not the same as the separate histories of individual nations or the separate cultures of individual nations, but nor is it equal to the history and culture of Europe as a whole. Historically, the concept of Central Europe is rather expressed in the form of an empire which for centuries – with somewhat varying influences and changing borders – occupied that geographical region. Wedged in between the German, Russian and Ottoman empires, the Habsburg Monarchy was born, providing the framework of a common history.

The empire aspired to supranationality and the European Union professes to this very same aspiration. At the beginning of the 19th century the Monarchy faced a process which we now call nation-state aspirations. The people who lived in the Monarchy strove at varying speeds and levels of intensity to bring into being their own national territories (or even states). Lacking a better term this could be dubbed nation-state aspiration since it was actually necessarily included in these aspirations that sizable ethnic minorities lived under the dominion of given nations or ethnicities.

The two tendencies, the supranational and national, created a major area of conflict, and by the second half of the 19th century it was already causing structural tensions. Many believed that this was the chief cause of the Habsburg Empire's downfall.

Of course the aforementioned nation states only came and come into being with a major surplus of nationalistic energy, all the more so because in many cases the presence of intolerant national thinking is indispensable to

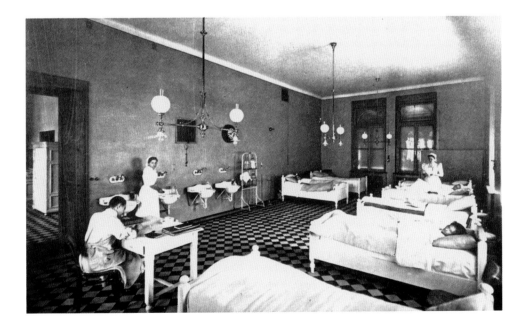

Left: *A maternity ward; healthcare infrastructure underwent significant development in the period of the Monarchy, but it was still not usual for the great majority of women to give birth in hospital or for people in general to die there. It was precisely for this reason that infant mortality figures were closer to those in Russia than to those in Western Europe.*

the creation of a nation state. A good example of this is the case of the former Yugoslavia, where nationalism assumed extreme and inhumane forms when manifesting itself. In common terms this is called a civil war, and in this case it was one that overshadowed the whole of Europe during the 1990s.

What follows from all this is that although regional co-operation, tolerance and unity in diversity would be necessary in these states, in real terms everybody tries to define themselves by contrast with what they perceive as different.

All in all, it appears that while there exists a European Union in the way of thinking and manifested in practice, there is also an historical reality which is not even remotely connected to that of the Union. There is a supranational language and mode of thinking as well as an actual historical process that realises the self-interest of individual nations.

And if anything, this is one part of the Monarchy's historical legacy that continues to live on.

Above: *The Strauss family name is synonymous with the Viennese Waltz. Johann Strauss, the Elder (1804–1849) composed 150 waltzes. However, his most famous work is the* Radetzky March. *His son, Johann Strauss, the Younger (1825–1889; seen in the picture) even became known as the 'King of Waltz'. His most famous waltz is* Blue Danube. *His operettas,* Der Flédermaus *and* The Gypsy Baron *and others, created the Viennese operetta.*

The Habsburg Monarchy

Like every medieval, early modern empire the Habsburg Monarchy was dynastic in form. However, by the time it reached the stage before its demise, it was no longer just a dynastic community but rather more typical of a manifold economic, societal and cultural system of ties. The empire was unable to outlast the process of becoming a nation, but it provided the framework for such. Before the outbreak of World War I the Monarchy had already lost its Italian provinces but still comprised of an area of 670,000 sq km, and in this regard was only exceeded on the continent by Russia. Without its 'colonies' it was still 100,000 sq km larger than Germany or France and had 300,000 sq km more than the leading power of the 19th century, Great Britain. Of course if colonies are added, the situation was different since Great Britain alone ruled over territories in excess of 30 million sq km. However, this difference lent strength to a Central European character since the territories in this region were not actual colonies and there was no colonial emigration with its attendant cultural impact. In regard to its geographical form the Habsburg Empire was somewhat reminiscent of a disproportionate haggis: from west to east, from Vorarlberg to Bukovina it spanned 1,240 km and from north to south, from Lobendara in Czechia to Sutomore in Dalmatia it was 1,046 km. Its borders thus delineated Central Europe with Liechtenstein and Switzerland to the west, the German Empire (Bavaria, Saxony and Prussian Silesia) to the north, a divided Poland to the north-west, Russia bordering on Galicia, Romania to the east, the Ottoman Empire and newly independent Serbia to the south, and the provinces of the newly united Italy – which had previously been the dominions of the Monarchy until the 1850s – to its south-west.

According to the final census, taken in 1910, the Habsburg Monarchy had a population of over 51 million with only two countries on the continent, Russia and Germany, having bigger populations. The population of Great Britain was 5 million fewer, while that of France and Italy was 12 million and 17 million fewer, respectively. However, while the aforementioned states were characterised by ethnic homogeneity or ethnic dominance, no such feature existed in the Habsburg Empire. The proportion of German speakers, comprising 25 per cent, formed the largest group. (That is not to say that they themselves necessarily were German, or even Austrian). The rest of the population were Hungarians (17 per cent), Czechs (13 per cent), Serbs and Croatians (11 per cent), Poles (9 per cent), Ukrainians (8 per cent), Romanians (7 per cent), Slovaks (4 per cent), Slovenians (3 per cent), Italians (2 per cent) and other nationalities (1 per cent).

In addition to this variety of nationalities the Monarchy was also characterised by the co-existence of various religions. In essence every religion and religious culture that existed in Europe was here. The line of division between eastern and western Christianity cut across the Empire. Every version of western Christianity was present here alongside the different faiths of the, by then, religiously divided Jewry and a significant Muslim minority represented by the Bosnians who lived within the borders of the Empire. These differences in religion often manifested themselves as national differences and in many cases particular ethnic groups also had internal sectarian divisions.

The Habsburg Monarchy was characterised by the co-existence of 11 markedly distinct nations and by a minimum of 7 religious cultures, depending on how they are counted.

Multiethnicity and Multiculturalism

The co-existence and mixture of cultures is one of the most important characteristics of Central Europe. It would be fair to say that Central Europe is multiethnic and multicultural.

Living side by side meant that everybody followed and was able to follow their own religious norms as well as cultural and national norms derived from religion. Despite the practice of the free flow of people and ideals in the Habsburg Monarchy, no internal colonisation took place in the 20th-century sense of the word, since no one ethnic group or religion was able to enforce its language or norms upon the others. This was not so much the result of the given circumstances but rather an achievement after the struggles of the Reformation and Counter Reformation of the previous centuries had been resolved. What followed was a liberal breakthrough whereby the state and the Church were separated. In fact, in numerous cases it had become clear that assimilation through force does not work.

The mingling of peoples ensued within the framework of urbanisation. By the turn of the 19th and 20th centuries, Vienna and Budapest had become true cultural melting pots with people flooding in from various territories of the Monarchy adapting to each other and in some cases switching cultural identities. Germans became Hungarians, the strictly religious became secular, and Czechs turned into Germans. The latter of which can be substantiated by a cursory glance at the Viennese telephone directory.

It must be remembered, however, that in many cases the various national, religious and cultural identities defined themselves by how they differed from others, so the elements of foreignness, hatred and condescension were inherently present.

Above: *After the premiere of* The Merry Widow, *its author, Ferenc Lehár (1870–1948), was of Hungarian origin but his career and compositions were always orientated to the Monarchy as a whole.*

The Cuisine of the Royal Court

It was public knowledge that Franz Joseph lived and ate in a puritan way. According to court confidantes all he was served for breakfast with his milk coffee was a bread bun. Franz Joseph is also remembered for the speed with which he ate and that other people were unable to keep up with him.

The emperor and king's favourite dish was called Wiener Tafelpsitz, *that is rumpsteak tenderised with vegetables and usually served with horseradish.*

The emperor was also very fond of sweet things. Tradition has it that a confectioner from Bad Ischl created a new dessert for him from pancake dough: he fried the dough in hot butter, broke it into crumbs and served it with peach jam. Since His Majesty found the result much to his liking, he allowed the dessert to be named after him and thus 'császámorzsa' (emperor's crumbs) came into being.

Queen Elizabeth

Queen Elizabeth followed a special diet that was somewhat unusual for the royal court (although today perhaps it does not sound so unusual). She had days when she ate only dairy products or only fruit, for example.

The ruler and his wife liked different kinds of Herend porcelain: Franz Joseph preferred the 'parsley' pattern, while Elizabeth favoured the 'Gödöllő' pattern, especially made for her.

Prince Rudolf

Rudolf the crown prince and heir to the throne of the Austro-Hungarian Monarchy met his future wife, Stephanie of Belgium, in 1880. The two courts announced the couple's engagement and the wedding took place the following year, in 1881. The dinner given by Jacob Palugyay on 1 September in Pozsony was most probably to celebrate the engagement. The menu card (see right) lists a series of dishes in the feast and featured a photograph of the young couple bound by a ribbon in the Hungarian national colours and decorated with the Austrian eagle. The Stephanie cake on the menu (a sponge cake filled with chocolate cream, sprinkled on the top with cocoa) has ever since then been one of the favoured delicacies of Hungarian cake shops.

The Empire was an ideal breeding ground for prejudice. Metternich, who was the Chancellor of the Habsburg Empire in the first half of the 19th century said: the Balkans begin at Karlsplatz. Thus, in his view of the world everything east of Vienna was culturally stigmatised as inferior. And this wave of condescension from west to east also permeated the national cultures. The Czechs somewhat looked down on the Slovaks, the Hungarians on the Romanians, the Croatians on the Serbs, and assimilated Jews looked down on Galician Jews. The definition of cultural identity against one another is also one of the legacies of the Monarchy and it is a trait which often persists to this day. Living side by side, mingling, and hatred built on prejudice and condescension co-existed and became integrated into the mental culture of Central Europe. Although the Hungarians were in a dominating position due to the dualistic structure that came into being, they were still dissatisfied: they served Franz Joseph but paid homage to his enemy Kossuth, the leader of the 1848–1849 war of independence, around whom they built a cult. Alternately, although the Czechs fought with the Germans they knew full well that their economic development was mainly thanks to their being bound together.

FEDÁK SÁRI. PAPP MISKA.
„JÁNOS VITÉZ"

The multi-ethnic model of Central European cultures was also manifested in dining culture, where examples of non-violent internal colonisation and heroic resistance can be found in equal measure. The 'Wiener schnitzel' of Italian origin but evocative of Vienna conquered the entire Monarchy, i.e. Central Europe. What is more, it had such a strong impact that it spread across the borders of the Monarchy and even made it to the New World. Thus, although the Monarchy did not colonise a significant part of the world, the Wiener schnitzel did. The strudel also enjoyed its own international success story after it had taken the Monarchy by storm, as did Hungarian *gulyás* (goulash), which eventually spread to almost every corner of the globe. However, the Czech *knedli* (steamed potato dumplings) demonstrated heroic resistance. It neither surrendered nor embarked upon a course of expansion, and while Czech beer – along with its Austrian counterpart – conquered the Hungarian soul and became a national beverage, pluralism reigned supreme when it came to *pálinka, schnaps, tsuika, vodka, slivovitz, borovichka* and *pesachovka*, since they majestically kept to themselves and made sure their firm positions were retained. (In fact, what can be seen in this case is something that will be referred to at a later stage in this book, i.e. nothing is what it seems, since in the last example the several ostensibly different drinks are actually one and the same.) Another important aspect of dining culture was represented by the coffee-houses, the reincarnation of which in the post-communist era played an organic part in reviving the middle-class lifestyle.

Today many people believe that sub-political elements such as lifestyle norms had a stronger integrating power than what they were attributed to in the past – perhaps they are right.

Above: In the middle of the 19th century acting was frowned upon by society and was a very poorly paid profession. Over a period of half a century the situation fundamentally changed. Fashionable actors were made into stars and their income allowed them to live a middle-class lifestyle. The whole country celebrated Sári Fedák for her performance in Pongrác Kacsóh's stage adaptation of János Vitéz (John the Valliant).

The construction of theatres throughout the Monarchy demonstrated that the cultural consumption of the middle class was conspicuously gaining ground. Some architects specialised in the construction of theatres, for example Ferdinand Fellner and Hermann Helmer. Their architect's office won commissions in other parts of Europe too. They designed 30 theatres in the Monarchy and 18 abroad.

Right: *The municipal theatre in Brünn.*

Above: *In its physical scale the National Theatre in Zagreb (modern day Croatia) was one of Fellner and Helmer's greatest theatre buildings.*

Opposite: *The Vigszínház in Budapest was also designed by their office.*

In the 19th century, the cultural standing of a big city was partly endorsed by the presence of an opera house. Unlike the theatre, the opera was always an indication that the public of the given city were culturally demanding — and well off — enough to maintain this expensive genre.

Left: The State Opera House in Prague.

Above: The Opera House in Lemberg.

Opposite: *The Neo-Baroque building of the National Theatre in Kassa (Kosice) was constructed between 1897 and 1899.*

Order and Disorder – a World of Appearances

The Austro-Hungarian Monarchy provided a stable institutional framework, more or less reliable overall conditions and a strong currency. However, people did not feel that the empire they were living in was their own. If examined more closely, what was perceived as Austrian was actually German under the surface, while if something was initially regarded as German, it soon turned out that it was actually Austrian. The empire was vast and weighed down with bureaucracy, and everybody knew that order and 'slamperei' co-existed. Therefore, it is no coincidence that Max Weber's thesis emerged in Germany and not in the Monarchy. The disorder which was at times friendly and at other times unbearable or the occasional deals going against the norm also formed part of the legacy.

It became a basic cultural norm in the Habsburg Monarchy that nothing was what it seemed. In his work *The Last Days of Mankind* Karl Kraus recorded that those that wished to emigrate had to fill in a questionnaire that included a question about their reason for wanting to emigrate. Kraus believed that the appropriate question should rather have been why people wanted to stay. Robert Musil's novel *The Man Without Qualities* reflects this phenomenon, as does the surreal world depicted in the works of Franz Kafka.

The cultural production of the region was enhanced by the feeling of 'nothing is

Right: Restaurants were key to social life in a given area.

what it seems', and the effects of this can still be perceived today. Irony was an adequate reaction to this phenomenon, since it provided a framework and meaning for what was absurd and nonsensical. As Jaroslav Hašek saw it, idiotism can only be survived with idiotism. While Hašek became famous for *The Good Soldier Švejk*, it is less well known that he was the prophet of political idiotism as early as 1906, when he founded the 'moderately progressive party within legal boundaries'. The Central European 'Wise

Fool' – Švejk – became a symbolic figure for the entire region, but naturally the Czechs feel he is really theirs. Albeit in a different way, irony appears in the works of the Hungarian writer Kálmán Mikszáth and those of the Austrian Arthur Schnitzler. Since the basic Central European tenet of 'nothing is what it seems' was not refuted by the subsequent chapters of history, the Czech film director Jiří Menzel, the Hungarian writer István Örkény, and the Polish Sławomir Mrožek actually continued a tradition.

Naturally, another cultural conclusion was drawn: if appearances rule anyway, why not make them perfect and aesthetic? Classicising, impressive buildings were designed by prominent architects to show the greatness of an empire that in reality was struggling under internal tension. Monumental buildings were constructed with their scale often in reverse proportion to the importance of the institutions they housed, which is exemplified by the building of the Hungarian Parliament. This aspiration most probably did not affect the 18th-century intimacy of Prague too much because it was not a capital. In contrast, Vienna and Budapest faithfully represent the culture of aesthecising appearances. Private construction projects – whenever it was possible – represented the peak of this trend. The facades of huge middle-class blocks were teeming with gypsum atlases. However, Secessionism and Art Nouveau were a reaction to this in that they strove to replace the aesthecising of appearances by the aesthetic representation of something else.

Creating harmony around appearances appeared in music, too, in great works by outstanding composers. Among others, Johann Strauss eternalised the cult of the lullying waltz and the genres of csárdás and polka in his oeuvre, while rendering a glossy finish to the Monarchy. And of course there was the operetta with its own world standard productions. Whenever you listen to Imre Kálmán's most famous and still successful operetta *Csárdás Queen*, you can feel that its beautiful melodies, its story transcending social differences and its happy ending give cause for nothing other than joy and optimism. The historical context is painfully clear: this operetta premiered in Vienna in 1915 and in Budapest in 1916, at a time when the battlefields of World War I were strewn with the dead bodies of soldiers in their grey uniforms.

Above: *It was not only the middle classes that began to have an increasingly marked presence in the Monarchy but also the working classes, which defined a new socio-historical trend. A relatively small proportion of the working class was organised (this came to only a few percent at the turn of the century) but their strength was far greater than their relative numbers. The photograph shows organised workers at a garden table meeting next to a beer keg on tap.*

Developed and Undeveloped

The multiethnicity of the Habsburg Monarchy was manifested in the economic arena, too. This is a region where traditional and modern or developed and undeveloped existed and continue to exist side by side up to this day.

To some extent, and on a smaller scale, the Monarchy was a precursor of the EU in regard to its economic approach. A unified currency was a reality and it was pretty impressive that the same money could be used in Lemberg, Innsbruck, Karlovy Vary and Opatija. (As a result of historical 'development' and to the 'great joy of humanity' this is no longer the case, since in the aforementioned places you can pay in euros, grivnas, crowns and kunas, so there are four currencies instead of one.) The labour market was open with the lives of employees not complicated by the system. The same applied to the internal market, with no tariffs on goods. The Hungarian company Ganz was free to transport goods as was the Czech company Skoda and the Austrian company Steyr. This meant of course that the culture of work was also allowed a free flow. German and Czech skilled workers proliferated their own culture or work and workers, and what they regarded as a norm in regard to a skilled labourer's work and lifestyle was proliferated wherever they went. Also, wherever they did not spread their influence a skilled labourer wore a cap instead of a hat. In other words, as we move east the better-off workers' movements of the Monarchy were replaced by Lenin's more modest proletarian movement.

However, the level of economic development showed significant differences within the Monarchy. Czechia retained its leading position in Central Europe all the way up to socialism, when modern-day Austria, which had always lagged behind, actually overtook it. Catching up was a general but uneven trend, and it seems to be the case that the economic hierarchy that came into being at the time has re-emerged in the 21st century, albeit with some modifications. After socialism, when an overall homogeneity was imposed on the region, the old differences that had seemingly disappeared are now resurfacing.

By the 20th century, Central Europe had become one of the most turbulent regions in the world. Out of the two world wars of the 20th century, both broke out here: the plot that served as the formal pretext for war happened in the south of the Monarchy, while World War II broke out on the German–Polish border. And to the immediate antecedents of World War II, namely the invasion of Austria and the breaking up of Czechoslovakia, originated in Central Europe. All of this demonstrates that the Central European region has the capacity to harbour and generate perilous tensions, even ones that extended beyond its own boundaries. Although similar observations may be made about other parts of the world, those events did not lead to world wars. Furthermore, the Yugoslav Civil War, which was arguably the most vicious and bloody conflict after World War II, also broke out in Central Europe.

The political culture of appearances and illusions is one of the most important as well as the

Below: *The motorcar was a new phenomenon in transport at the turn of the century. Those privileged enough to afford this luxury hurtled along at 'dizzying' speeds of 20–30 km per hour. Cars drove on the left following the British example of course. The photograph shows an Austrian Lohner-Porsche electric car exhibited at the Paris World Exhibition in 1900.*

Opposite: *One of Vienna's famous coffee houses is Rüdigerhof.*

It is not without reason that railway stations are referred to as the 'cathedrals of modernity'. Throughout the Monarchy the existence of these buildings proclaimed to the inhabitants of its cities that one of the prevailing ideas of the 19th century – progress – had arrived as a tangible reality.

Above: *The façade of the main railway station in Zagreb is historicising, just like every other railway station in the Monarchy.*

Above: *The main entrance of the railway station in Brno is decorated by the allegorical statues of movement and dynamics.*

Above: *The railway station in Lemberg.*

Left: *For the local people Prague's main railway station was known as 'Wilsonovo' after Woodrow Wilson. It was during his presidency that the USA entered World War I.*

Left: *The Secession and Art Deco appear in the style of Prague's main railway station.*

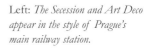

Right: *Budapest's Keleti railway station was built between 1881 and 1884 in the Eclectic style.*

On the streets of the former Monarchy the built up environment of theatres, opera houses and railway stations forms part of the heritage of the past, and so does the atmosphere of the cities created by the Eclectic buildings. It was during this period that the towns of Eastern Europe were made into cities, which were given the features they retain even today and which make them homely to anyone who knows them well – be it Budapest *(opposite left)*, Pozsony *(opposite right)*, Prague *(below left)* and Zagreb *(below right)*.

most dangerous aspect of the region's cultural legacy. The most obvious proof of its existence is that it has become common practice to think differently and more highly of ourselves than who and what we actually are. For example, the Nazis in Germany did not trust the results of the referendum that was to be held about the Anschluss and therefore marched into Austria. Then they held the referendum and won with flying colours, with even the Social Democrats in support of Austria becoming part of Germany. The truth is: nobody really understood what Austria was about or who and

Right: *The cities were growing in size at a rapid pace and this required huge numbers of workers to go to them from every corner of the Monarchy. At the same time attempts were made to create housing for all the workers streaming in – the photo shows a so-called people's hotel built for this purpose.*

how many Austrians there were at all. In the interwar period Hungary – which at that point had no sea – was led by an admiral who built his entire power politics on an illusion, which was the restoration of the Greater Hungary. Poland was governed by politicians who co-operated in the breaking up of Czechoslovakia with those that attacked them not too long afterwards. Croatians and Serbians were so busy proving their power to each other that they were eventually occupied by a third force. The rivalry that played out between the Czechs and the Slovaks did the greatest disfavour to Czechoslovakia. All in all, the distorted self-image and the culture of illusion have exacted a heavy price from the nations of the region.

The surreal period of socialism did not exactly bring any relief in this historical continuity. On the contrary, it amplified the feeling of make-believe reality while it made the cultural trends of irony and idiotism redundant. Central Europe was seemingly – another manifestation of appearances – wiped off the map by the socialist era since it became part of a Soviet, i.e. secular and Byzantine, empire. The cult imported from the Soviet empire mostly just formed a new layer on Central Europe but did not become its organic part. The truth of this statement is well demonstrated by the collapse of communism and the political disintegration of the Soviet empire, or more precisely by the cultural characteristics of the change in the political system. While the change in some parts of the Soviet Union and Romania was accompanied by bloodshed, Warsaw, Prague and Budapest put an end to Communist hegemony in a peaceful and smooth manner. Note the emergence of Central Europe – or one of her faces – one more time.

However, another face of Central Europe manifested itself almost straight away. The one marked by isolationism and confrontation as opposed to solidarity and co-operation. This period not only brought about the termination of Communism but also the revival of nationalism in its entire political and cultural verticum. Czechoslovakia fell apart and Yugoslavia burst into pieces, in the literal, bloody meaning of the word. A nationalistic rhetoric has assumed an increasingly louder voice in Hungarian politics. All these events and phenomena were and are accompanied by cults and rituals that were believed to have been long forgotten. A new kind of nationalism is seeking its own traditions and often finds them in those that earned their 'reputation' against their neighbouring nations or demonstrated their 'talents' by showing intolerance towards those that live side by side with their own people.

After the decades of Communism, Central Europe has awakened from its deep sleep. It has started to seek its own traditions and its own self. It is now part of a new Europe but is not quite the same as the so-called West and it is naturally different from all that is labelled the East. It is not like the Balkans and is certainly unlike Scandinavia, yet it represents a distinct colour on the map of Europe.

It is a hard task to describe the cultural characteristics of the Central European legacy, that is that of the Monarchy. It is difficult to say what distinguishes and what connects Central Europe to other regions. Yet, if anyone should ask how the quintessence of the Monarchy's legacy can be summed up, three names come to mind, and these three only provide a good description if taken together since in isolation they do not represent the same thing.

I would like to mention a person who once lived in the region. Born in 1889 in Branau, Austria, he left the Monarchy when he was 24. He served in the German Army and made it to the rank of corporal. He did some painting in Austria, was interested in architecture and music, and read authors who believed in the racial supremacy of the Aryans communicated through mystical symbols, such as the ancient Aryan swastika, as well as in the unification of Austria and Germany. This person embodied the racial–nationalistic version of the Central European logic of creating enemies. He came from the Monarchy but reached the peak of his career in Germany. For some unknown reason Hindenburg only called him corporal yet went on to promote him to chancellor. He committed suicide in 1945, at the end of a world war that he lost. His name was Adolf Hitler.

Left: *Adolf Hitler on the Western Front in World War I.*

I would also mention another person. Born in Hungary, in Nagyszentmiklós (now Sannicolau Mare, in Romania) in the former Torontál County in 1881, from an early age he was drawn to music and the first major influence upon him was Richard Strauss. At the age of 25, he began to collect folk music and from this point on he turned towards the ideal of 'the brotherhood of nations', which was also manifested in his work as a composer. He achieved great success as a performing artist and he was also committed to his humanist ideals in his works performed on stage. His most famous works – *Cantata Profana Concerto, Violin Concerto II* – are still played all over the world. In 1940 he left Hungary because of the aforementioned Austrian. Towards the end of his life he discovered the artistic precedent of his own work in Ferenc Liszt. He believed that the culture of the Central European nations could only be defined in terms of togetherness and mutual influence. He died in New York in 1945, surviving the Austrian who had committed suicide by only five months. His name was Béla Bartók.

Finally, there is a third person. He was born in Czechoslovakia, probably and seemingly at the same time as the other two people. He was actually ageless as he really never lived at all. He was a common soldier in World War I and never even reached the rank of corporal. He served in the army of the Monarchy and had countless adventures. Since he was ageless it is possible that this decent soldier is still alive. Either he was a fool or so clever that he was able to make everybody believe that he was a fool. He is the little man of Central Europe who knows that everything can be survived, that everything must and should be survived, regardless of whether those in power are monsters or representatives of noble ideals. He knows what he knows: narrow-mindedness is a protection and foolishness that lacks any form of reflection makes you immune to everything. His name is Švejk.

Albeit incompletely and imperfectly, I believe that these three people together – although only together – express the legacy of Central Europe and the Monarchy. They express the culture of this region which one can justifiably loathe or love, since it generated so much filth and at the same time the purest of values. And of course the little man who is able to bear and survive the presence of these extremes was also born right here.

The Empire is dead, but its legacy is here in new and renewed contexts, both beautiful and ugly. There are no real choices to be made. The most that Central Europeans can do is to decide which part of the legacy they wish to enrich.

Above: *Béla Bartók in his home in 1901.*

Above: *Jaroslav Hašek, the writer of Švejk.*

Opposite: *The Fateful Adventures of the Good Soldier Švejk. The front cover of the first edition.*

Sešit 2.

JAROSLAV HAŠEK:

2 Kč.

OSUDY DOBRÉHO
VOJÁKA ŠVEJKA
ZA SVĚTOVÉ VÁLKY.

Vydáno A. Sauerem a V. Čermákem v Žižkově,
Kollárovo nám. 22.

Index

Selected Bibliography

Albrecht, Catherine, *The Rhetoric of Economic Nationalism in the Bohemian Boycott Campaigns of the Late Habsburg Monarchy*, Austrian History Yearbook 32, 2001.

Beller, Steven, *Vienna and the Jews, 1867–1938: A Cultural History,* Cambridge, Cambridge University Press, 1989.

Beller, Steven, *Francis Joseph. Profiles in Power,* (ed. Robbins, K.), London- New York, Longman, 1996.

Boyer, John W., *Political Radicalism in Late Imperial Vienna: Origins of the Christian Social Movement, 1848–1897,* Chicago-London, 1981.

Bucur, M.,Wingfield, Nancy M., ed., *Staging the Past: The Politics of Commemoration in Habsburg Central Europe, 1848 to the Present,* Central European Studies, ed. C.W. Ingrao, 2001, Purdue University Press, West Lafayette.

Cohen, G. B., *Nationalist Politics and the Dynamics of State and Civil Society in the Habsburg Monarchy 1867–1914,* Central European History, 2007.

Nancy M. Wingfield, ed., *Creating the other ethnic conflict and nationalism in the Habsburg Central Europe,* New York-Oxford, Berghahn Books, 2003.

Deák István, *Beyond Nationalism: A Social and Political History of the Habsburg Officer Corps, 1848-1918,* New York, Oxford University Press, 1990.

Sugar, P. F., Hanák Péter, Frank Tibor, ed., *A History of Hungary,* Bloomington – Indianapolis, Indiana University Press, 1990.

Gerő András, *Emperor Francis Joseph, king of the Hungarians,* (transl. Patterson, James, Koncz Enikő) New Jersey , Centre for Hungarian Studies and Publications, 2001.

Gerő András, *Modern Hungarian Society in the Making: The Unfinished Experience,* Budapest –London –New York, Central European University Press, 1995.

Gyáni Gábor, Kövér György, Valuch Tibor, *Social History of Hungary from the Reform Era to the End of the Twentieth Century,* Boulder, Social Science Monographs, 2004.

Gyáni Gábor, *Parlor and Kitchen: Housing and Domestic Culture in Budapest, 1870–1940,* (transl. by Bodóczky Miklós), Budapest, Central European University Press, 2002.

Hanák Péter, *The Garden and the Workshop: Essays on the Cultural History of Vienna and Budapest,* Princeton, Princeton University Press, 1998.

Healy, Maureen, *Vienna and the fall of the Habsburg Empire: Total War and Everyday Life in World War I,* Cambridge, Cambridge University Press, 2004.

Höbelt, L., *Well-tempered Discontent: Austrian Domestic Politics, in The Last Years of Austria-Hungary,* (M. Cornwall, ed.) Exeter, University of Exeter Press, 1990.

Ingrao, Charles W., *The Habsburg Monarchy 1618–1815,* 2nd ed. Cambridge [etc.], Cambridge University Press, 2000.

Janos, Andrew C., *The Politics of Backwardness in Hungary, 1825–1945,* Princeton, Princeton University Press, 1982.

Jászi Oszkár, *The Dissolution of the Habsburg Monarchy,* Chicago, University of Chicago Press, 1929.

Jelavich, Barbara, *The Habsburg empire in European affairs 1814–1918,* Chicago, Rand MacNally, 1969.

Johnston, William M., *The Austrian Mind, An Intellectual and Social History, 1848–1938,* Berkeley-Los Angeles-London, 1972.

Judson, Pieter, *Guardians of the Nation: Activists on the Language Frontiers of Imperial Austria,* Cambridge, Harvard Univesity Press, 2006.

Kann, Robert A., *The Multinational Empire: Nationalism and National Reform in the Habsburg Monarchy, 1848–1918, Volume II, Empire Reform,* New York, Octagon Books, 1964.

Moravánszky Ákos, *Competing Visions: Aesthetic Invention and Social Imagination in Central European Architecture, 1867–1918,* Cambridge – London, The MIT Press, 1998.

Puskás Julianna, *Hungarian Overseas Migration: A Microanalysis. In: A Century of European Migrations, 1830-1930,* (ed. by Vecoli, Rudolph J., Sinke, Suzanne M.) Urbana, University of Illinois Press, 1991.

Rosenblit, Marsha L., *The Jews of Vienna 1867-1914: Assimilation and Identity,* Albany. N. Y, 1983.

Schorske, Carl E., *Fin-De-Siècle Vienna: Politics and culture.* New York, Vintage Books, 1981.

Sked, A., *The Decline and Fall of the Habsburg Empire, 1815–1918,* London – New York, Longman, 1989.

Somogyi Éva, *Ferenc József,* Budapest, Gondolat, 1989.

Taylor, A. J. P., *The Habsburg Monarchy 1809-1918: A history of the Austrian Empire and Austria-Hungary,* London, Penguin Books, 1981.

Unowsky, Daniel L., *The Pomp and Politics of Patriotism. Imperial Celebrations in Habsburg Austria, 1848-1916,* West Lafayette, Purdue University Press, 2005.

Picture Credits

We hereby wish to express our special thanks to the Grinnell College Art Collection, Faulconer Gallery, the Kieselbach Gallery, the Library of Congress and the Neue Galerie New York for their generous support.